DRAW Ocean Animals

by Doug DuBosque

PEEL productions, inc.

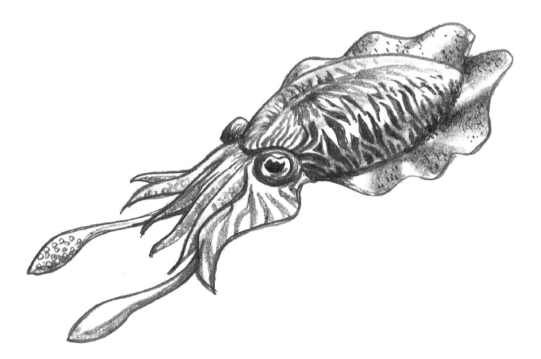

Contents

Introduction / Supplies 4

Sharks and rays 5

Great White Shark, Shortfin Mako Shark, Thresher Shark, Sand Tiger, Hammerhead Shark, Whale Shark, Basking Shark, Port Jackson Shark, Sting Ray, Atlantic Manta

Whales and other mammals 17

Sperm Whale, White (Beluga) Whale, Blue Whale, Gray Whale, Minke Whale, Humpback Whale, Bowhead Whale, Killer Whale, Atlantic Bottlenose Dolphin, Harbor Porpoise, California Sea Lion, Harbor Seal, Northern Elephant Seal, Walrus, Manatee

Coral reef animals 33

Parrotfish, Butterflyfish, Lionfish, Clown Anenome Fish, Moray Eel, Queen Triggerfish, Crown-of-thorns Starfish, Octopus

More amazing ocean animals 43

Tripodfish, Flyingfish, Anglers, Atlantic Footballfish, Gulper Eel, Squid, Cuttlefish, Porcupinefish, Swordfish, Green Turtle, California Halibut

Drawing tips 57

Index 63

Introduction

Watching ocean animals, and learning about them, creates a sense of delight and awe. Look at how they move, how they hunt and how they hide!

Wouldn't it be great to catch some of that excitement in your own drawings?

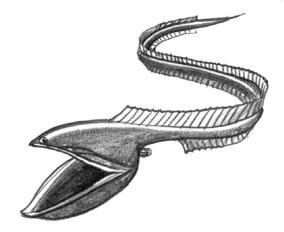

This book shows you how, with step by step instructions. You'll be surprised how easy it is to draw, without tracing, a wide range of ocean animals.

Think of drawing in three steps. The first is getting all the shapes and pieces in the right place. Always draw lightly at first! The second is finishing the drawing–adding details, textures and shading. The final step is 'cleaning up' by erasing the lines you don't need.

In these pages, I will take you through all the steps. The first step will be shown in several drawings, as we draw lightly, putting the pieces together. The final drawing of each set shows a finished drawing, with details and shading added and the 'cleaning up' completed. You can find out more about finishing techniques by looking at the last section of the book, *Drawing Tips.*

I think you'll be surprised by your own great drawings of ocean animals. Putting the pieces together, one step at a time, is much more rewarding than tracing! Have fun looking and learning!

Supplies

- **pencil** (any kind)
- **fine marker** (optional)
- **pencil sharpener**
- **eraser** (I like the kneadable type)
- **paper** (drawing paper erases best)
- **blending stump** if you want to do smooth shading (you can use your finger, too, but it's a bit messy)
- **place to draw**
- **POSITIVE ATTITUDE!**

Sharks and Rays

Always draw lightly at first!

Great White Shark

Carcharodon carcharias.
Size: 6 m (19.5 ft). Diet: fish, seals, dolphins, unlucky humans. Large and aggressive! The great white shark has protective eyelids that cover the eyes during attacks.

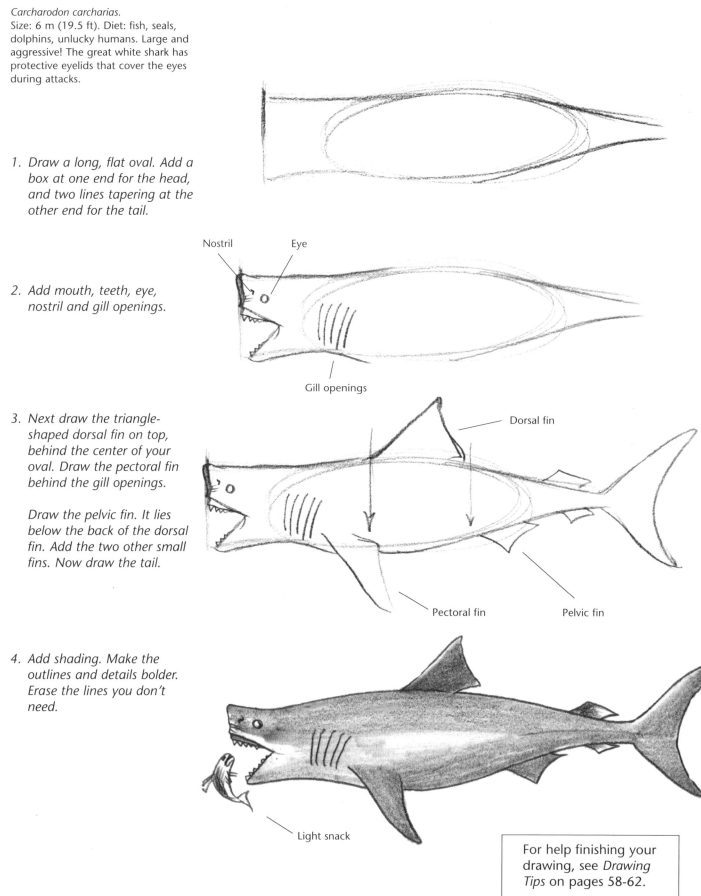

1. Draw a long, flat oval. Add a box at one end for the head, and two lines tapering at the other end for the tail.

2. Add mouth, teeth, eye, nostril and gill openings.

Nostril   Eye

Gill openings

3. Next draw the triangle-shaped dorsal fin on top, behind the center of your oval. Draw the pectoral fin behind the gill openings.

   Draw the pelvic fin. It lies below the back of the dorsal fin. Add the two other small fins. Now draw the tail.

Dorsal fin

Pectoral fin   Pelvic fin

4. Add shading. Make the outlines and details bolder. Erase the lines you don't need.

Light snack

For help finishing your drawing, see *Drawing Tips* on pages 58-62.

Shortfin Mako Shark

Isurus oxyrhincus.
Size: 3-4 m (10-13 ft). Diet: tuna, mackerel, herring, sardines, squid.

1. Start with a pointed oval. Notice the difference between the top and bottom. Draw two triangles for the tail. Which is bigger?

Dorsal fin

2. Next, draw the dorsal fin, above the middle of the oval.

   The back of the pectoral fin lines up with the front of the dorsal fin. Draw it.

Pectoral fin

3. Add gill openings, eye, nostril, mouth and other fins.

Eye

Mouth

Gill openings

4. Add shading. Sharpen details (did you catch the notch in the tail?). Clean up with your eraser.

Thresher Shark

Alopias vulpinus.
Size: 6 m (19.5 ft). Diet: fish. Long tail is used to herd schooling fish, making them easier to catch.

1. Draw an oval with pointed ends. Add the tail. Make it as long as the body.

2. Add the dorsal fin above the middle of the body.

   Carefully look at the top and bottom part of the tail. Now draw them, lightly at first.

3. Add the other fins and details. Pay close attention to the spatial relationships (in other words, put things in the right places)!

5. Add shading. Sharpen lines and details. Clean up any smudges with your eraser.

   Cool looking shark!

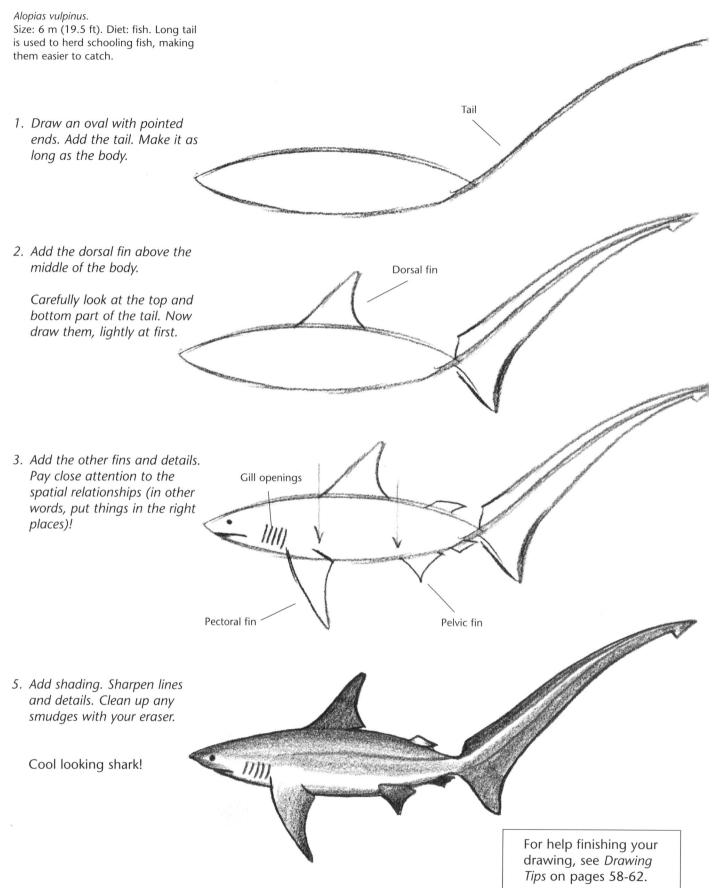

Tail

Dorsal fin

Gill openings

Pectoral fin

Pelvic fin

For help finishing your drawing, see *Drawing Tips* on pages 58-62.

8 **Draw Ocean Animals**

Always draw lightly at first!

Sand Tiger

Odontaspis taurus.
Size: 3.2 m (10.5 ft) Diet: fish. Lives at the bottom of shallow waters.

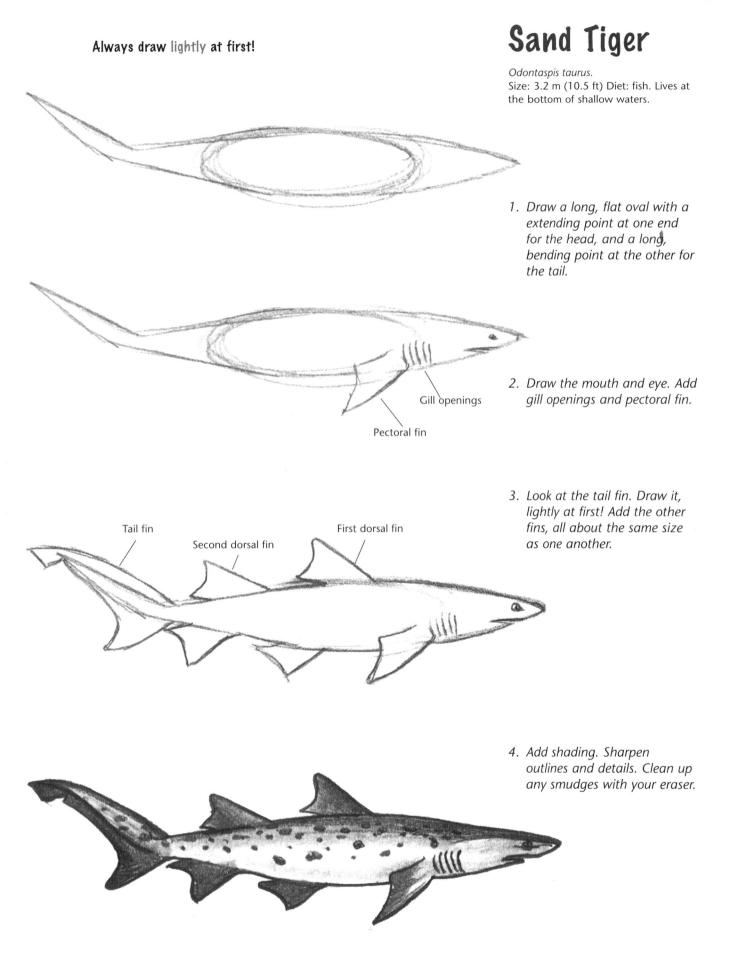

1. Draw a long, flat oval with a extending point at one end for the head, and a long, bending point at the other for the tail.

2. Draw the mouth and eye. Add gill openings and pectoral fin.

Gill openings

Pectoral fin

3. Look at the tail fin. Draw it, lightly at first! Add the other fins, all about the same size as one another.

Tail fin

Second dorsal fin

First dorsal fin

4. Add shading. Sharpen outlines and details. Clean up any smudges with your eraser.

Hammerhead Shark

Sphyrna mokarran (Great hammerhead). Size: 6m (19.5 ft) Diet: fish, especially rays. With eyes facing out to the side, hammerheads have to turn from side to side as they swim.

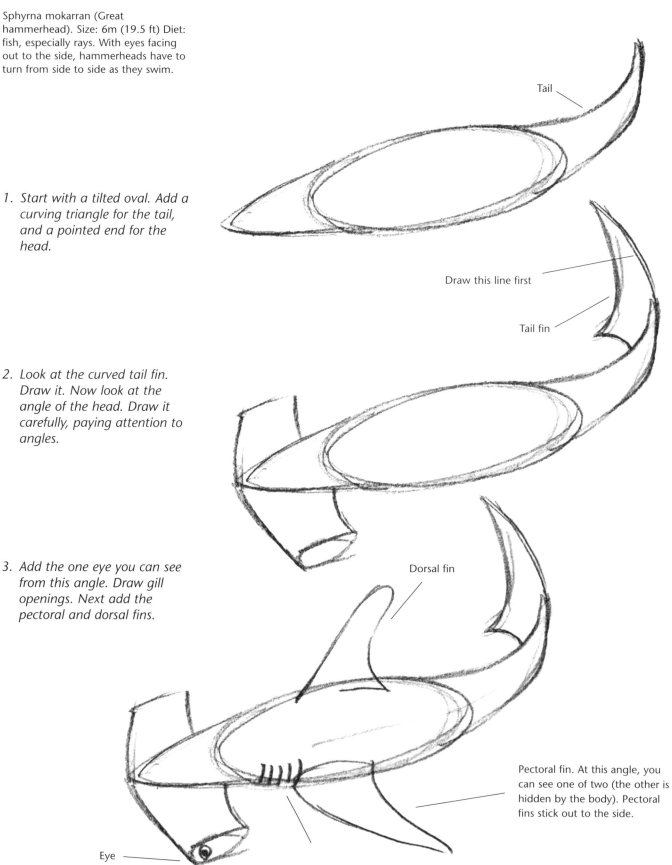

Tail

Draw this line first

Tail fin

Dorsal fin

Pectoral fin. At this angle, you can see one of two (the other is hidden by the body). Pectoral fins stick out to the side.

Eye

Gill openings

1. Start with a tilted oval. Add a curving triangle for the tail, and a pointed end for the head.

2. Look at the curved tail fin. Draw it. Now look at the angle of the head. Draw it carefully, paying attention to angles.

3. Add the one eye you can see from this angle. Draw gill openings. Next add the pectoral and dorsal fins.

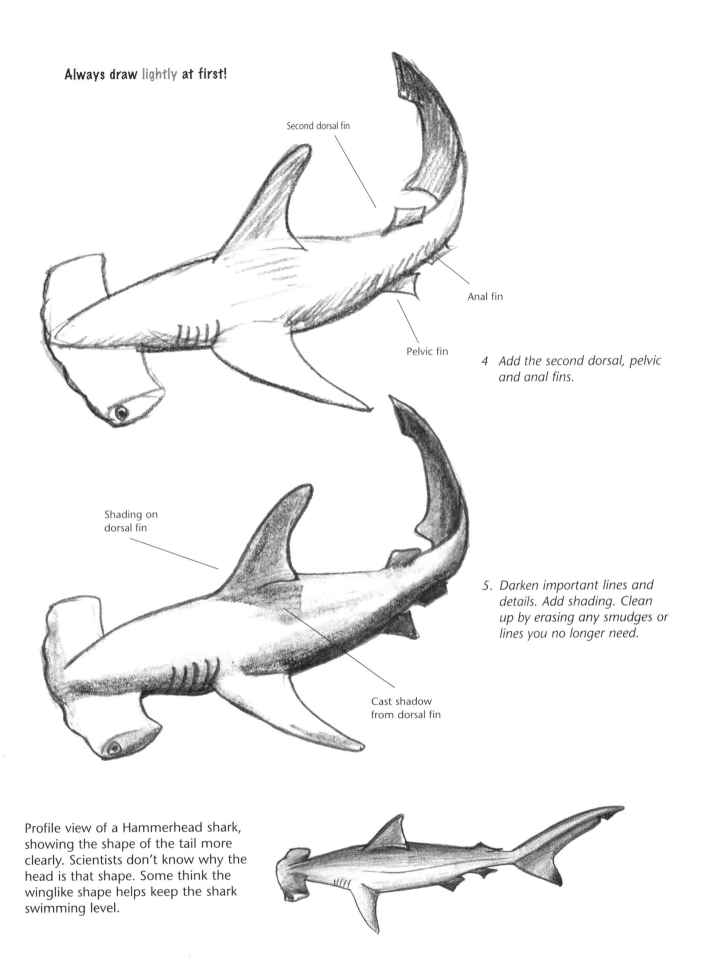

Always draw lightly at first!

Second dorsal fin

Anal fin

Pelvic fin

4 Add the second dorsal, pelvic and anal fins.

Shading on dorsal fin

5. Darken important lines and details. Add shading. Clean up by erasing any smudges or lines you no longer need.

Cast shadow from dorsal fin

Profile view of a Hammerhead shark, showing the shape of the tail more clearly. Scientists don't know why the head is that shape. Some think the winglike shape helps keep the shark swimming level.

Whale Shark

Rhincodon typus.
Size: 15.2 m (50 ft). Diet: small fish, plankton. Filter feeder (notice the very large gill openings). The projections on the front of its mouth are not teeth. It's huge, but a very gentle shark.

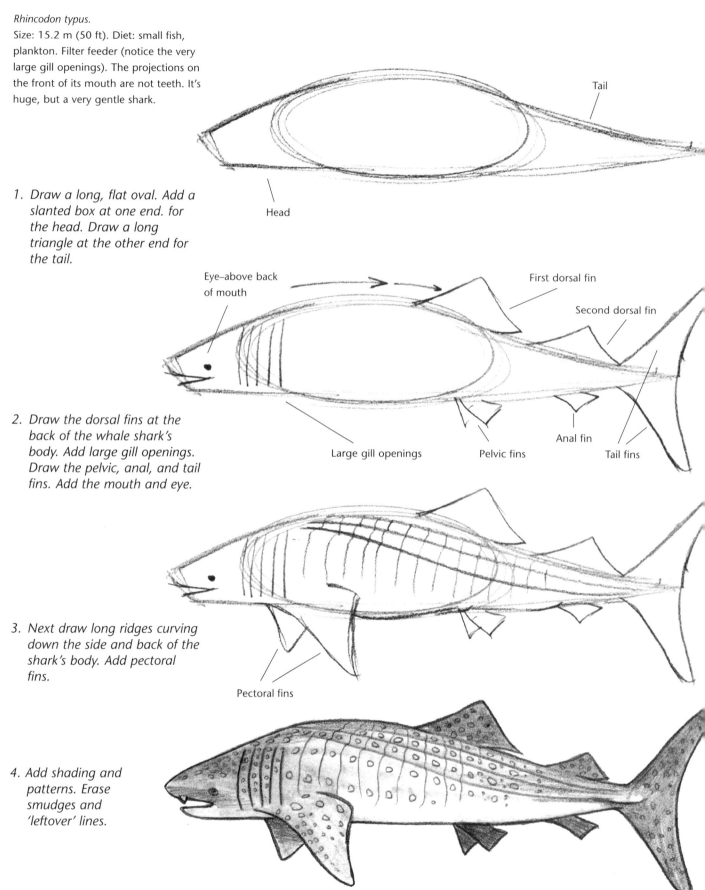

Tail

Head

1. Draw a long, flat oval. Add a slanted box at one end. for the head. Draw a long triangle at the other end for the tail.

Eye–above back of mouth

First dorsal fin

Second dorsal fin

Large gill openings

Pelvic fins

Anal fin

Tail fins

2. Draw the dorsal fins at the back of the whale shark's body. Add large gill openings. Draw the pelvic, anal, and tail fins. Add the mouth and eye.

3. Next draw long ridges curving down the side and back of the shark's body. Add pectoral fins.

Pectoral fins

4. Add shading and patterns. Erase smudges and 'leftover' lines.

Always draw lightly at first!

Basking Shark

Cetorhinus maximus.
Size: 10.4 m (34 ft). Diet: plankton.
Filter feeder. Swims along with its
mouth wide open to catch plankton.

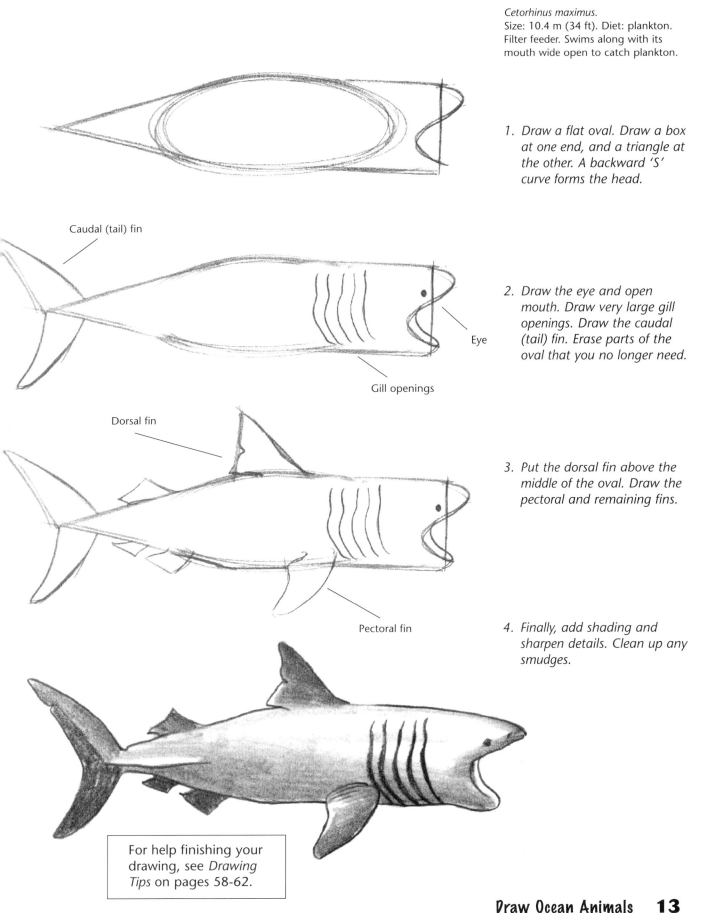

Caudal (tail) fin

Eye

Gill openings

Dorsal fin

Pectoral fin

1. Draw a flat oval. Draw a box at one end, and a triangle at the other. A backward 'S' curve forms the head.

2. Draw the eye and open mouth. Draw very large gill openings. Draw the caudal (tail) fin. Erase parts of the oval that you no longer need.

3. Put the dorsal fin above the middle of the oval. Draw the pectoral and remaining fins.

4. Finally, add shading and sharpen details. Clean up any smudges.

For help finishing your drawing, see *Drawing Tips* on pages 58-62.

Port Jackson Shark

Always draw lightly at first!

Heterodontus portusjacksoni.
Size: up to 1.5 m (5 ft). Diet: probably mollusks, sea urchins and mollusks; feeds at night. Has stout spines in front of each dorsal fin.

1. Draw a long, flat oval with a rat-like tail. Add a slanting box shape for the head.

2. At the front of the oval, draw gill openings and the pectoral fin. Add the dorsal fin, with its pointed spine in the front.

3. Draw the eye high in the head. Draw the mouth, quite unlike other sharks'. Carefully add the caudal (tail) fin, and the lateral line.

4. Draw the second dorsal fin, and the fins on the bottom.

5. Add shading. Sharpen outlines and details. Clean up with your eraser.

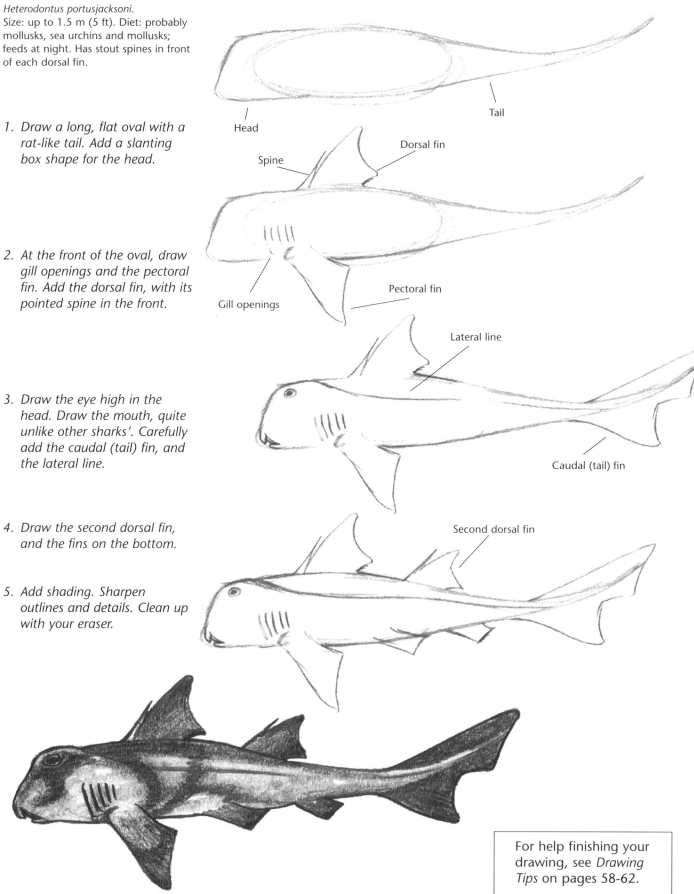

Head
Tail
Spine
Dorsal fin
Gill openings
Pectoral fin
Lateral line
Caudal (tail) fin
Second dorsal fin

For help finishing your drawing, see *Drawing Tips* on pages 58-62.

Always draw lightly at first!

Sting Ray

Family *dasayatidae*. Size: 1.5 m (5 ft). Diet: Mollusks and crustaceans on the seabed. Graceful swimmers who live on sandy and muddy bottoms. The sharp spine can be used as a weapon. There are about a hundred species.

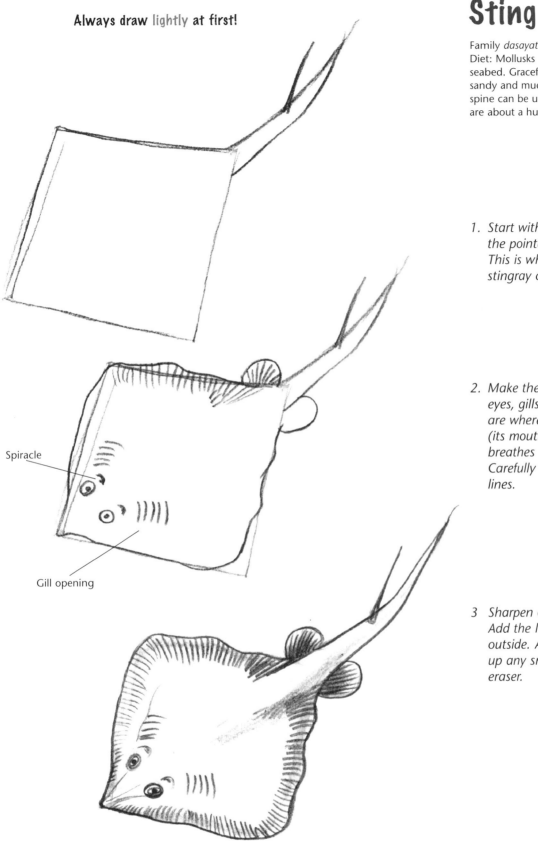

Spiracle

Gill opening

1. Start with a box shape. Add the pointed tail with its spine. This is where the 'sting' in stingray comes from.

2. Make the outline wiggly. Add eyes, gills and spiracles, which are where the ray breathes in (its mouth is on the bottom; it breathes out through its gills). Carefully erase your straight lines.

3 Sharpen outlines and details. Add the little lines around the outside. Add shading. Clean up any smudges with your eraser.

Atlantic Manta

Manta birostris.
Size: up to 6.7m (27ft) wide. Diet: plankton, fish and crustaceans. The 'hands' on either side of the mouth can be extended, or used as scoops to direct food into the mouth.

1. Draw a big, swooping curve.

2. Add a bump in the middle.

3. Next draw an arching curve to make one 'wing.'

4. Lightly draw in a 'C' shape for the projections at either side of the mouth.

5. Add a line for the bottom of the closer wing. Draw the eye. Look carefully at my example to see how to finish the mouth.

6. Add the tail. Sharpen outlines, add shading, and clean up any smudges with your eraser.

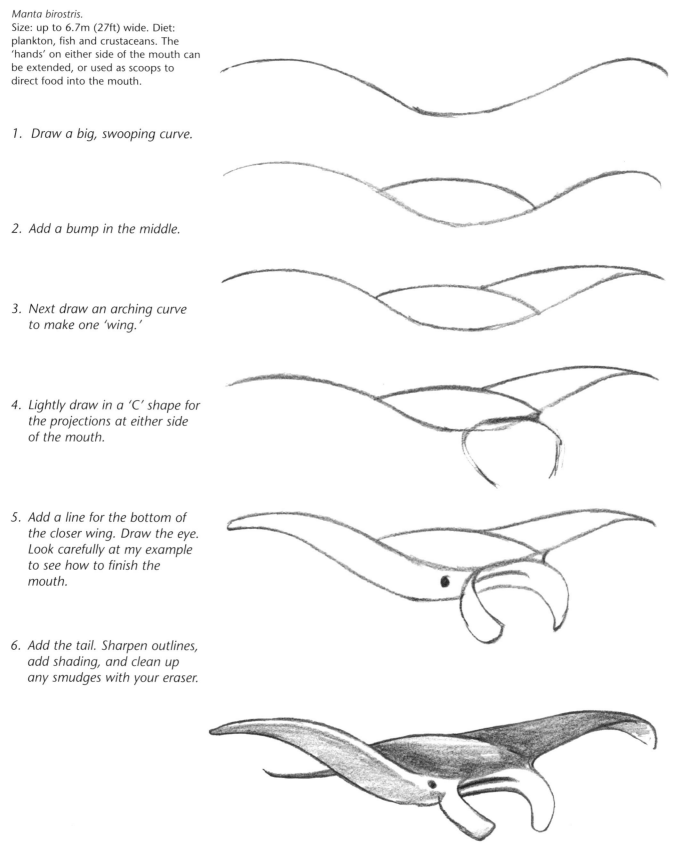

Whales & Other Mammals

Always draw lightly at first!

Sperm Whale

Physeter catodon.
Size: 11-20 m (36-66 ft). Diet: mainly
large, deepwater squid.

1. Draw a long rectangle.

*2. Add one big triangle and two
small triangles for the tail
flukes.*

Tail fluke

Tail fluke

*3. Draw a bump for the nose,
and a long line for the mouth.
Add the eye, and small flipper.*

Eye

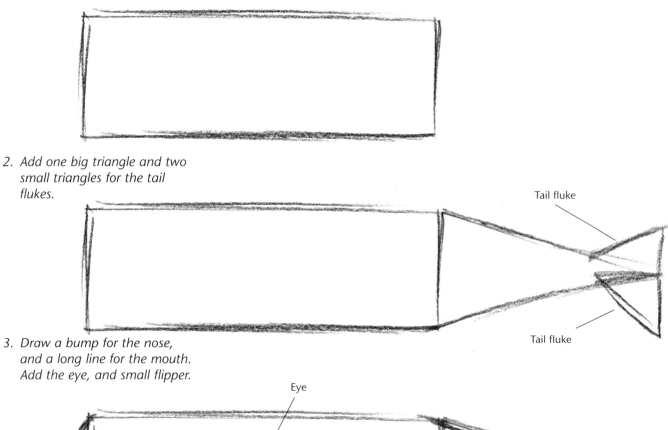

*4. Erase lines you no longer
need, add shading, and clean
up any smudges.*

Flipper

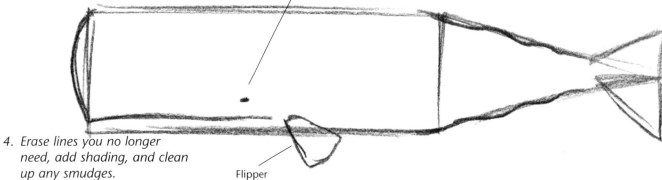

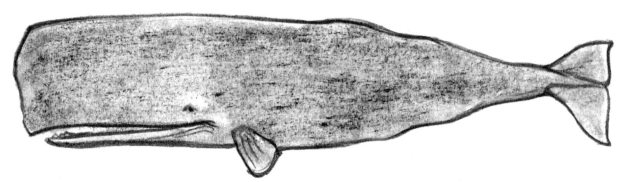

Always draw lightly at first!

White (Beluga) Whale

Delphinapterus leucas.
Size: 4-6 m (13-20 ft). Diet: fish and crustaceans from the sea bottom. White whales sing a variety of songs. Nineteenth century whalers called them sea canaries.

Tail

1. *Draw a large, flat oval with another oval overlapping it. Add a triangular projection at the other end for the tail.*

Tail flukes

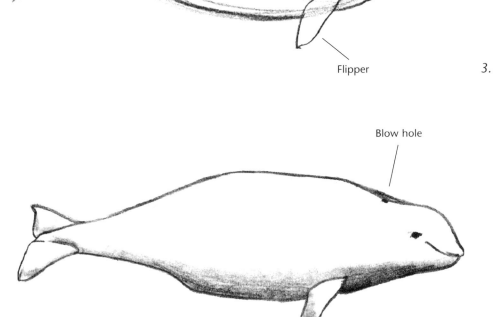

Flipper

2. *Add two small triangles for the tail flukes. Draw the flipper on the lower front of the big oval. Draw the mouth upward like a smile. Add the eye.*

3. *Erase what's left of the ovals. Go over outlines. This whale is very light in color, so there's not much shading to do. Clean up any smudges with your eraser.*

Blow hole

Easy, eh?

For help finishing your drawing, see *Drawing Tips* on pages 58-62.

Blue Whale

Balaenoptera musculus.
Size: 25-32 m (82-105 ft). Diet: plankton. Strains food through the baleen plates attached to upper jaw. The largest mammal that has ever existed. Feeds in polar waters during summer months, eating four tons of tiny shrimp each day. Migrates to warmer waters to breed. Endangered.

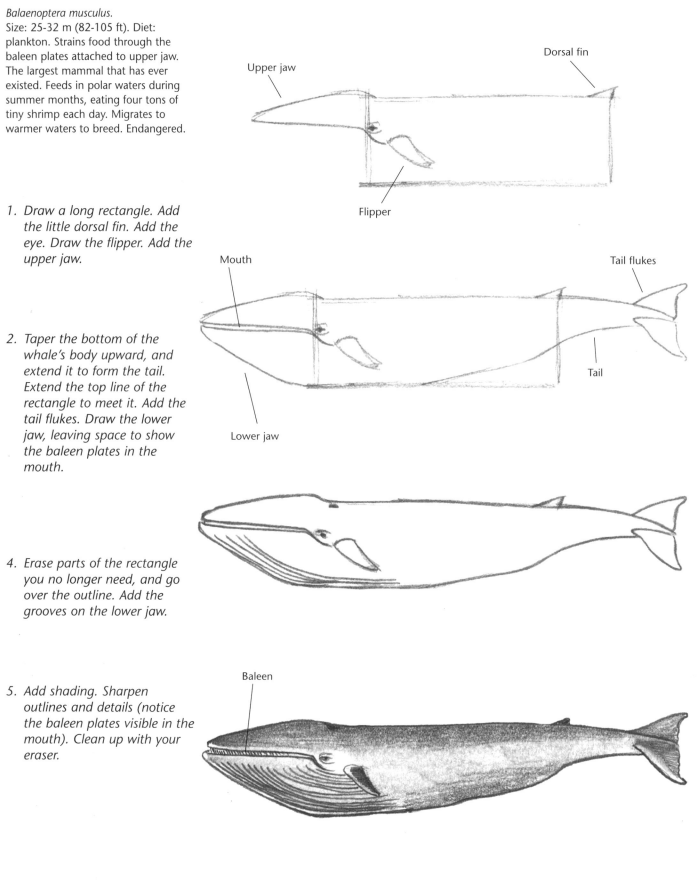

1. Draw a long rectangle. Add the little dorsal fin. Add the eye. Draw the flipper. Add the upper jaw.

2. Taper the bottom of the whale's body upward, and extend it to form the tail. Extend the top line of the rectangle to meet it. Add the tail flukes. Draw the lower jaw, leaving space to show the baleen plates in the mouth.

4. Erase parts of the rectangle you no longer need, and go over the outline. Add the grooves on the lower jaw.

5. Add shading. Sharpen outlines and details (notice the baleen plates visible in the mouth). Clean up with your eraser.

Upper jaw   Dorsal fin   Flipper   Mouth   Tail flukes   Tail   Lower jaw   Baleen

Always draw lightly at first!

Gray Whale

Eschrichtius robustus.
Size: 12-15 m (40-50 ft). Diet: planktonic shrimp, which it stirs up from the bottom, unlike other whales. Strains food through the baleen plates attached to upper jaw.

Eye

Flipper

1. Draw this oval carefully, with a slight point at the top and a sloping bottom. Add a dot where the eye will be. Draw the flipper.

Tail

Tail flukes

2. Draw the tail, with bumps. Add tail flukes.

Mouth

3. Add the head, with a bump on the top. Draw a line for the mouth.

4. Add shading. Sharpen outlines and details. Clean up any smudges with your eraser.

For help finishing your drawing, see *Drawing Tips* on pages 58-62.

Minke Whale

Balaenoptera acutorostrata.
Size: 8-10 m (26-33 ft). Diet: plankton, fish, squid. Strains food through the baleen plates attached to upper jaw.

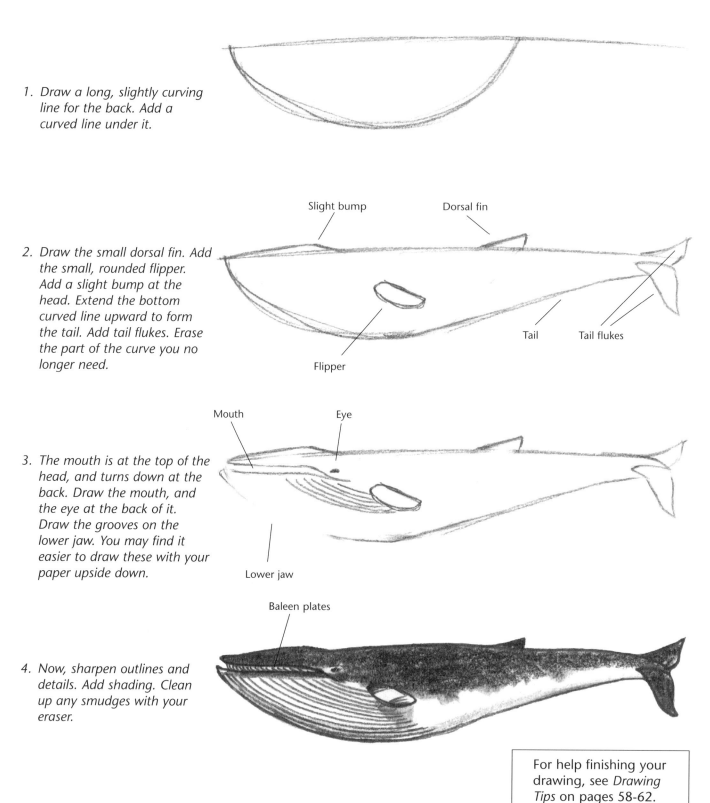

1. Draw a long, slightly curving line for the back. Add a curved line under it.

2. Draw the small dorsal fin. Add the small, rounded flipper. Add a slight bump at the head. Extend the bottom curved line upward to form the tail. Add tail flukes. Erase the part of the curve you no longer need.

Slight bump   Dorsal fin

Tail   Tail flukes

Flipper

3. The mouth is at the top of the head, and turns down at the back. Draw the mouth, and the eye at the back of it. Draw the grooves on the lower jaw. You may find it easier to draw these with your paper upside down.

Mouth   Eye

Lower jaw

Baleen plates

4. Now, sharpen outlines and details. Add shading. Clean up any smudges with your eraser.

For help finishing your drawing, see *Drawing Tips* on pages 58-62.

Always draw lightly at first!

Humpback Whale

Megaptera novaeangliae.
Size: 14.6-19m (48-62 ft). Diet: plankton and fish. Strains food through the baleen plates attached to upper jaw. Many knobs and barnacles on body and very long flippers. Feeds in polar waters in the summer, and migrates to tropical waters for the winter. Endangered.

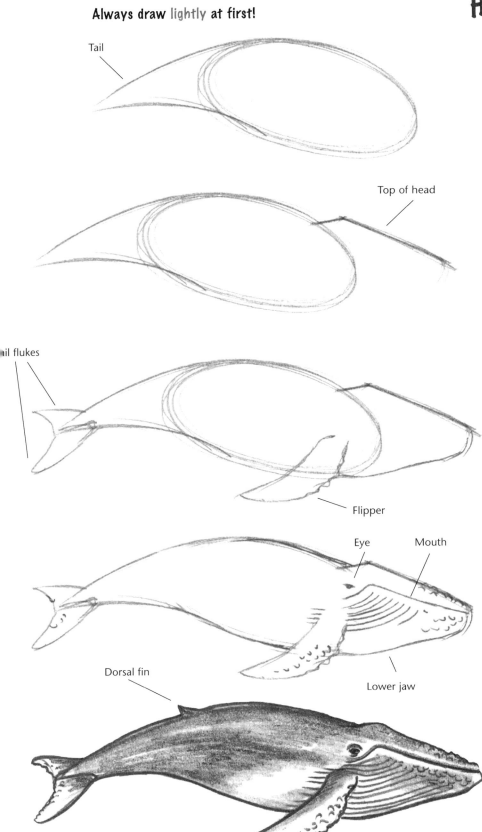

Tail

Top of head

il flukes

Flipper

Eye   Mouth

Dorsal fin

Lower jaw

1. Draw a tilted oval. At the high end, make a curving-down triangle for the tail.

2 Draw the top of the head.

3. Add the bottom of the head. Add a long, slightly curving flipper with one bumpy side. Draw two triangle shapes for the tail flukes.

4. Add a line for the mouth. Draw the eye. Add curved lines on the lower jaw. Add bumps and barnacles on the head and flipper.

5. Draw the dorsal fin. Add shading. Sharpen outlines and details. Clean up any smudges with your eraser.

Great whale!

Listen to a recording of humpback whales singing sometime....

Bowhead Whale

Balaena mysticetus.
Size: 15-20 m (49-66 ft). Diet: plankton. The large vertical lines in the mouth are baleen, with which the whale strains plankton out of the water as it swims. *Endangered.*

1. Draw a box. Add three curving triangle shapes for the tail and tail flukes.

2. Draw the upper jaw. Notice where the line for the mouth and the box intersect. Add the eye.

3. Draw the flipper, then the bottom of the mouth, lower jaw, and baleen plates. Draw lightly and take your time! Add the flipper. Add the bump on top.

4. Add shading. Sharpen outlines and details. Clean up any smudges with your eraser.

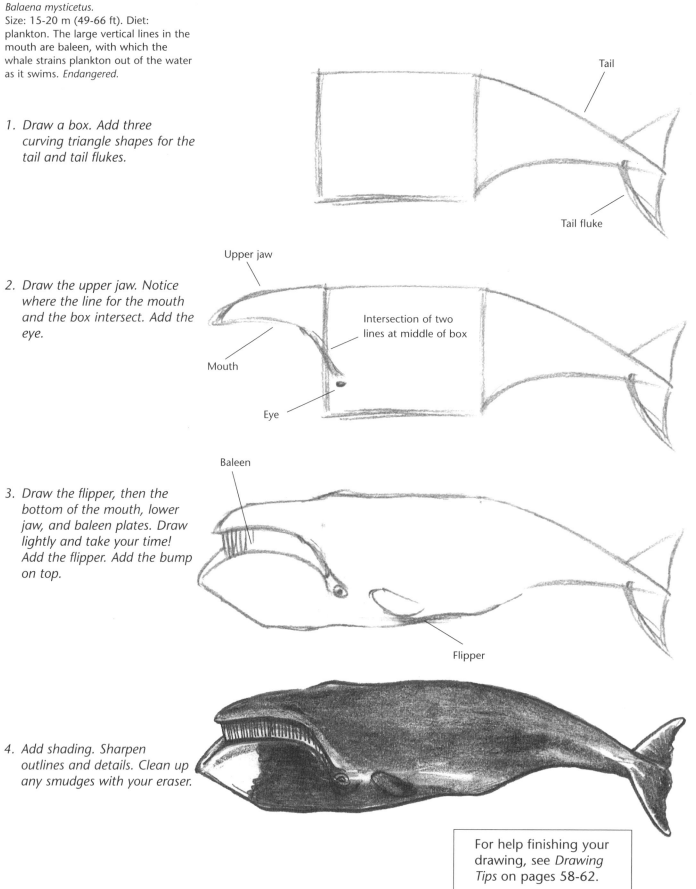

Tail

Tail fluke

Upper jaw

Intersection of two lines at middle of box

Mouth

Eye

Baleen

Flipper

For help finishing your drawing, see *Drawing Tips* on pages 58-62.

Killer Whale (male)

Orcinus orca.
Size: 7-9.7 m (23-32 ft). Diet: fish, squid, sea lions, birds. Males have the distinctive dorsal fin (smaller and curved on females and juveniles). Killer whales are black on top, and white on the bottom. Each has a unique pattern.

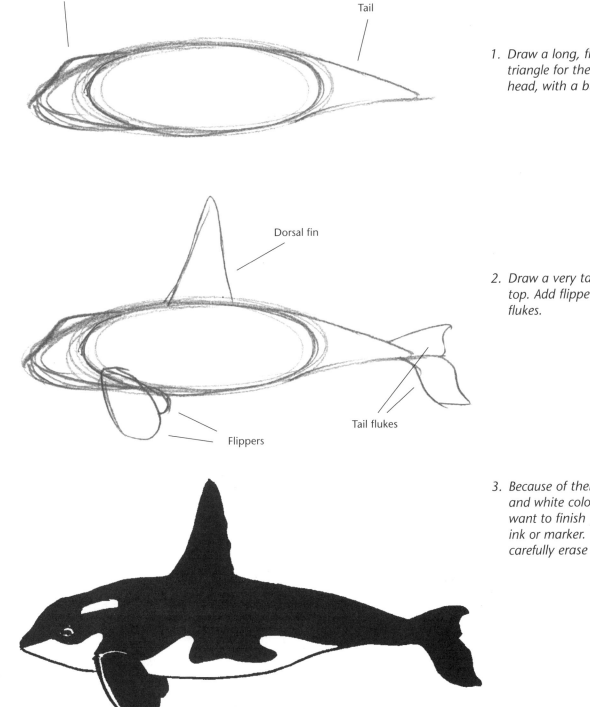

Head

Tail

1. Draw a long, flat oval. Add a triangle for the tail. Draw the head, with a bump on top.

Dorsal fin

Flippers

Tail flukes

2. Draw a very tall dorsal fin on top. Add flippers and tail flukes.

3. Because of their strong black and white coloring, you may want to finish your drawing in ink or marker. Then you can carefully erase pencil lines.

Atlantic Bottlenose Dolphin

Tursiops truncatus.
Size: 4 m (12 ft). Diet: fish. Highly intelligent animals who live in groups. These are the dolphins you usually see in movies or on TV.

1. Draw a crescent shape.

2. Add a pointed nose, and two triangles for the tail flukes. Add the curved line on the side, and the eye.

3. Draw the flippers (you only see part of the far one, which I've shaded) and the dorsal fin.

4. Make your dolphin jumping out of the water if you like. Add shading. Sharpen outlines and details. Clean up any smudges with your eraser.

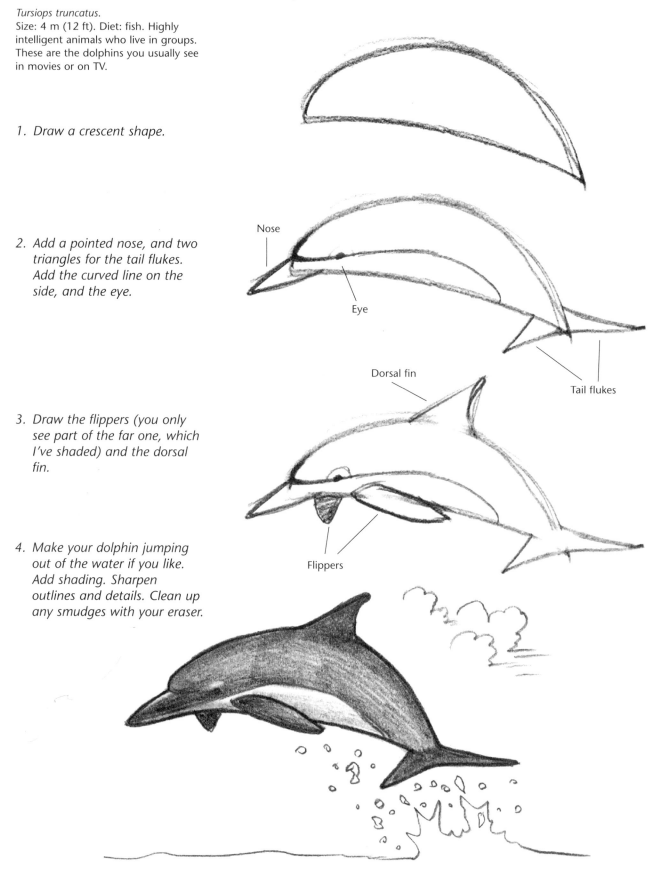

Always draw lightly at first!

Harbor Porpoise

Phocoena phocoena.
Size: 1.5-1.8 m (5-6 ft). Diet: fish.
Harbor porpoises live in groups and
'talk' a lot. They can dive for up to six
minutes, using clicking sounds and
echolocation to find their prey.

Dorsal fin

Flipper

1. *Start with an oval. Add the flipper at one end, and the dorsal fin at the other.*

Eye

Mouth

2. *Extend the oval to form the head. Draw the mouth and eye.*

Tail flukes

Tail

3. *Add the tail and tail flukes. Erase unneeded lines .*

4. *Add shading. Sharpen outlines and details. Clean up with your eraser.*

For help finishing your drawing, see *Drawing Tips* on pages 58-62.

California Sea Lion

Zalophus californianus.
Size: 6 ft (1.8 m). Diet: fish, octopus, and squid. Unlike seals, sea lions can turn their rear flippers forward, which helps them move on land. Sea lions have ear flaps; seals don't.

1. Draw three tilted ovals. Look carefully at how, and where they connect. Also look at how they tilt.

2. Draw the forward-facing rear flippers and the front flipper. Connect the two largest ovals.

3. Draw the head, and lines to connect it to the middle oval. Add the ear, nostril, eye and whiskers.

4. Now add shading. Notice how I use short strokes of the pencil to suggest fur. Sharpen outlines and details. Clean up any smudges with your eraser.

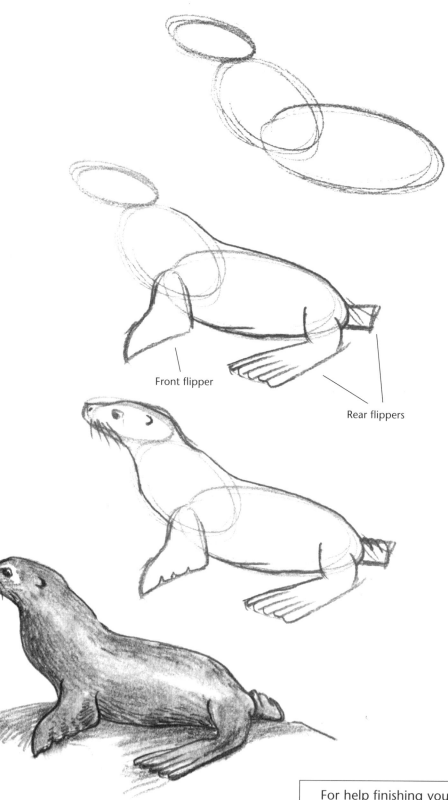

Front flipper

Rear flippers

For help finishing your drawing, see *Drawing Tips* on pages 58-62.

Harbor Seal

Phoca vitulina.
Size: 5 ft (1.5 m). Diet: fish, squid, and crustaceans caught on 4-5 minute dives. Colors vary from light gray to dark brown or black. They come out of the water to spend much of their time on rocks. Unlike sea lions, seals' rear flippers do not turn forward. Seals have no ear flaps.

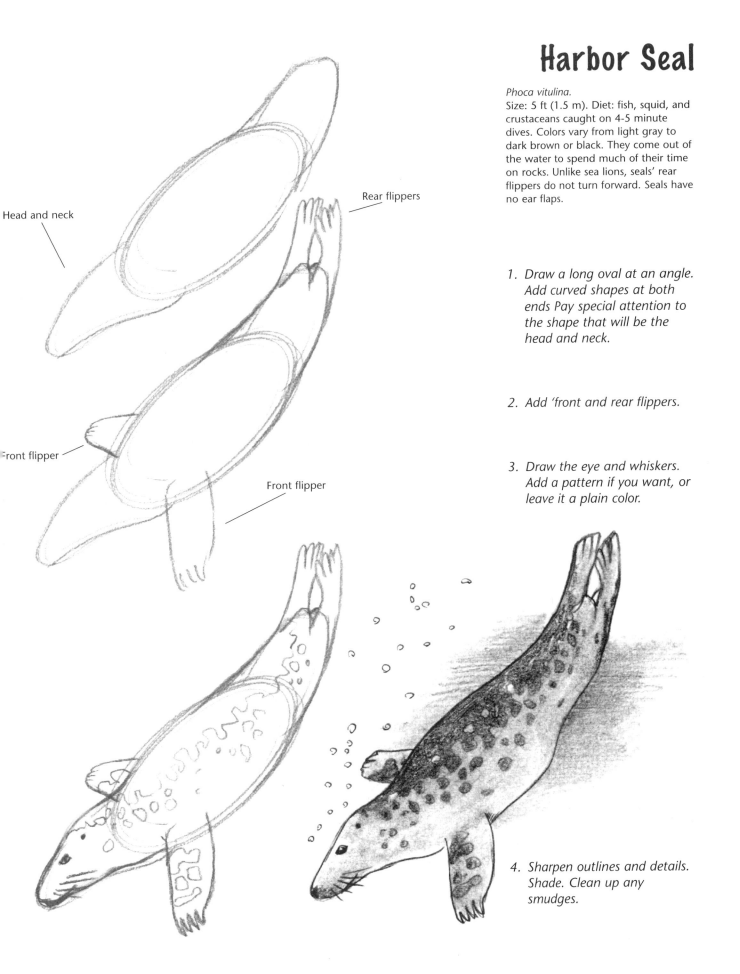

Head and neck

Rear flippers

Front flipper

Front flipper

1. Draw a long oval at an angle. Add curved shapes at both ends Pay special attention to the shape that will be the head and neck.

2. Add 'front and rear flippers.

3. Draw the eye and whiskers. Add a pattern if you want, or leave it a plain color.

4. Sharpen outlines and details. Shade. Clean up any smudges.

Northern Elephant Seal

Mirounga angustirostris.
Size: males up to 6m (20 ft), females up to 3m (10 ft). Diet: fish and squid, caught on long, deep dives. Breed on offshore islands; were hunted almost to extinction but have recovered. Unlike sea lions, seals' rear flippers do not turn forward. Seals have no ear flaps.

1. Draw two ovals for the body. Extend both ends with partial ovals.

2. Connect the shapes to make the outline of the seal, with wrinkles. Draw flippers, front and back.

3. Carefully draw the head with its distinctive bulge, mouth and eye (sideways in this posture).

4. Add shading. Sharpen outlines and details. Clean up any smudges with your eraser.

Mouth

Eye

Front flipper

Rear flippers on a seal cannot turn forward.

For help finishing your drawing, see *Drawing Tips* on pages 58-62.

Always draw lightly at first!

Walrus

Odobenus rosmarus.
Size: males 2.7-3.5 m (9-11.5 ft); females a bit smaller. Diet: mollusks, crustaceans, starfish, fish. They dive to feed, and use their tusks to help pick up food from the sea bottom.

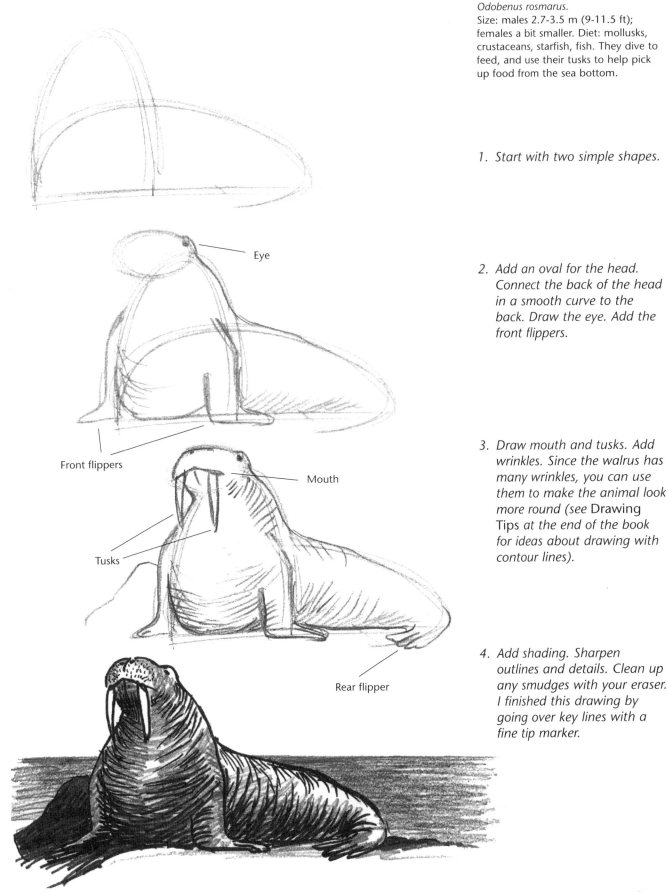

Eye

Front flippers

Mouth

Tusks

Rear flipper

1. Start with two simple shapes.

2. Add an oval for the head. Connect the back of the head in a smooth curve to the back. Draw the eye. Add the front flippers.

3. Draw mouth and tusks. Add wrinkles. Since the walrus has many wrinkles, you can use them to make the animal look more round (see Drawing Tips at the end of the book for ideas about drawing with contour lines).

4. Add shading. Sharpen outlines and details. Clean up any smudges with your eraser. I finished this drawing by going over key lines with a fine tip marker.

Manatee

Trichecus manatus (American manatee).
Size: up to 3m (10ft). Diet: mainly
vegetation, found at night by touch
and smell. Manatees sleep in shallow
waters, coming to the surface every
few minutes to breathe–without even
waking up!

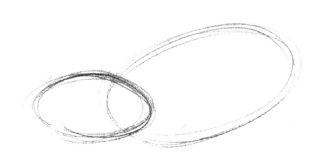

1. Draw two overlapping ovals.

2. Add lines for wrinkles at the
   neck, and lines for the tail.

Tail

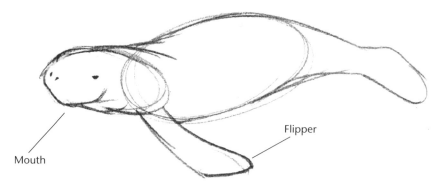

3. Draw the mouth and face.
   Add the rest of the tail and
   flipper.

Mouth

Flipper

4. Add shading. Sharpen
   outlines and details. Clean up
   any smudges with your eraser.

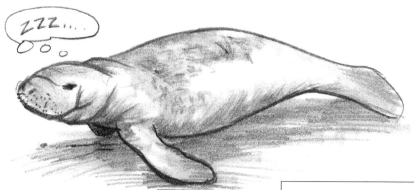

ZZZ......

For help finishing your
drawing, see *Drawing
Tips* on pages 58-62.

Coral Reef Animals

Always draw lightly at first!

Parrotfish

Scarus guacamaia (Rainbow Parrotfish). Size: 1.2 m (4 ft). Diet: Algae and coral, which it scrapes off reefs with a parrot-like beak. Like some other parrotfish species, this one can create a mucus 'sleeping bag' around itself at night to protect it from predators.

1. Start with a long oval. Add a point at one end and a rounded shape for a tail at the other.

2. Add the dorsal fin. Next draw the pectoral fin. Add the pelvic, anal and tail fins.

3. Draw the mouth, eye, and gill openings. Add scales, spines in the fins, and shading. Sharpen outlines and details. Clean up any smudges with your eraser.

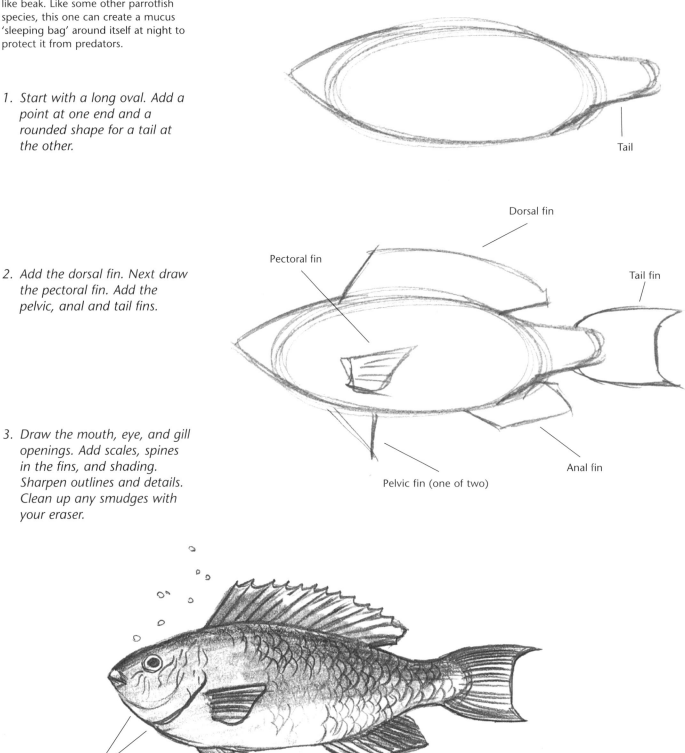

Tail

Dorsal fin

Pectoral fin

Tail fin

Pelvic fin (one of two)

Anal fin

Gill openings

Butterflyfish

Always draw lightly at first!

Snout

Tail

Dorsal fin (front part jaggy; back part smooth)

Tail (caudal) fin

Pectoral fin

Anal fin

Pelvic fin (one of two)

Chelmon rostratus (copperband or beaked butterflyfish). Size: 20 cm (7.5 in). Diet: small plants and animals that it pulls out of crevices in coral. The big spot on the tail is probably to fool predators into thinking it's the eye. the eye itself is partially camouflaged by the stripe running through it.

1. *Start with a light circle. At one end, in the middle, add the tail. At the other end, draw the long beaklike snout. Add a line for the mouth. Draw the eye.*

2. *Your next challenge is to draw all the fins with spines. Five fins are visible in this drawing. Draw them all!*

3. *Next, add the camouflage pattern, including the second 'eye' to fool attackers.*

4. *Darken the patterns. The eye and band on the tail are black. The stripes are copper-colored. Sharpen outlines and details. Clean up with your eraser.*

For help finishing your drawing, see *Drawing Tips* on pages 58-62.

Draw Ocean Animals 35

Lionfish

Pterois volitans.
Size: 38 cm (15 in). Lives in the Pacific and Indian Oceans. This is a "look but don't touch!" fish. Colorful fins conceal poisonous spines that will kill other fish and even people. Bright orange and reddish colors make this a very pretty fish. Just don't touch!

1. Start with a simple oval shape. Add a rounded part for the tail at one end, and a point at the other. Draw the eye. Notice where it lies on the oval.

2. Add a line for the mouth, barbels on the chin, and the 'eyebrow' above the eye. Lightly draw radiating curved lines for the spines of the pectoral fin.

3. Complete the pectoral fin. Add the caudal (tail) fin and anal fin. Erase any body lines you no longer need.

4. Add the large dorsal fin, which is in many parts. At the front of each is a spine.

5. To sharpen the lines, you can go over outlines and important details with a fine marker. Clean up with your eraser.

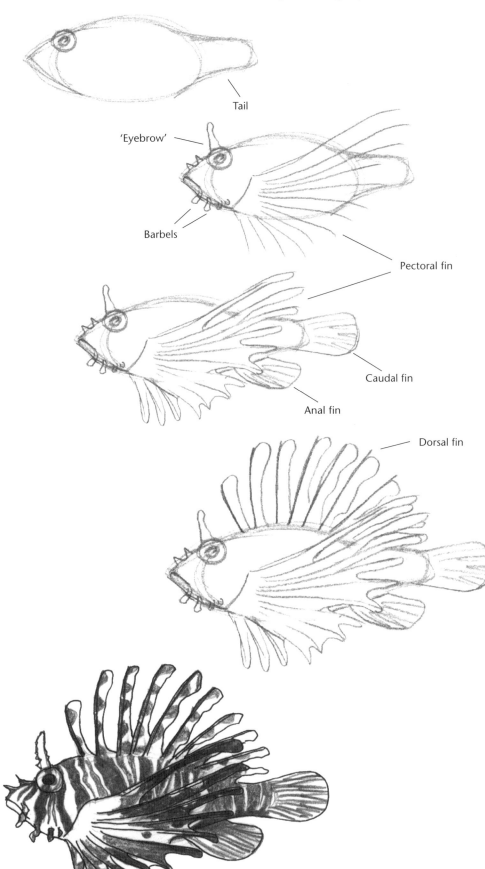

Tail

'Eyebrow'

Barbels

Pectoral fin

Caudal fin

Anal fin

Dorsal fin

Clown Anenome Fish

Amphiprion percula.
Size: 6 cm (2.25 in). Diet: tiny
crustaceans and other organisms. Lives
in safety amidst the tentacles of sea
anenomes, which kill other fish.

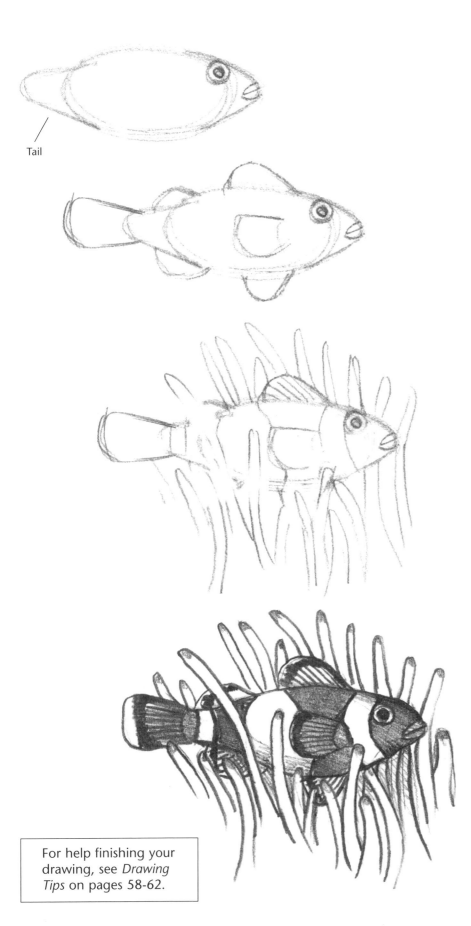

Tail

1. *Start with an oval. Add a
   rounded part at one end for
   the head. Draw a large eye
   and the mouth. Notice that
   the eye touches the outside of
   the oval. Add the tail.*

2. *Draw top and bottom fins in
   line with each other.*

3. *Add tentacles of the sea
   anenome, with some in front
   of the fish. Lightly erase lines
   they cross at the bottom of
   the fish.*

4. *Draw the bold pattern
   (orange, black and white if
   you're drawing in color). Add
   shading. Sharpen outlines and
   details. Clean up any
   smudges with your eraser.*

For help finishing your
drawing, see *Drawing
Tips* on pages 58-62.

Moray Eel

Mureana helena.
Size:90 cm (35.5 in)
Diet: fish, squid, cuttlefish
Hides in rock or coral crevices, waiting
to lunge at prey swimming by.

This drawing involves depth, and it's a bit more complicated. For that reason, I've broken it down to one line at a time.

1. *Start with a curvy line.*

2. *Add straight vertical lines at the ends and the curves. Hold your pencil flat on the paper if you have trouble seeing how to draw the vertical lines. Add more curved lines beneath the first ones, connecting to the vertical lines. See how you can turn it into a ribbon?*

3. *You may need a couple of tries to figure out the next few steps, so draw lightly at first! Pay special attention to the arrows.*

   From the left side of the ribbon, draw a sausage shape, with your line ending at the arrow.

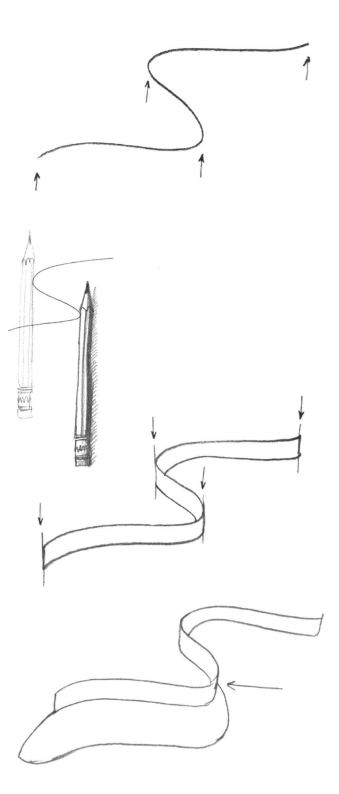

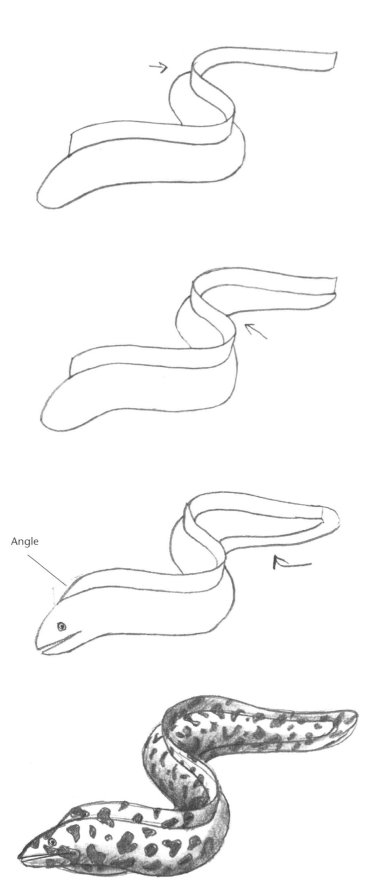

4. Draw a small line to make the second part of the body...

5. Add a third line. Now you've drawn the entire body of the eel. Take a moment to look at your drawing. Does it look like it's swimming toward you?

Cool!

Angle

5. Next add the ribbon-like fin along the bottom of the eel. Draw the mouth and eye. Add an angle to the front of the dorsal fin.

6. Add shading and spots. See Drawing Tips at the end of the book for help with the pattern. Clean up any smudges with your eraser.

For help finishing your drawing, see *Drawing Tips* on pages 58-62.

Queen Triggerfish

Balistes vetula.
Size: 33 cm (13 in). Diet: various invertebrates, primarily sea urchins. 'Trigger' in its name refers to the second dorsal spine, which can be locked against the first dorsal spine. The Triggerfish does this when alarmed, wedging itself in a crevice so that it's almost impossible to get out. When the 'trigger' spine is lowered, the fish swims out again.

1. *Draw a tilted oval. Add the jaws and mouth. Extend the bottom jaw to make the body slightly pointed at the bottom. Draw a small shape for the base of the tail.*

2. *Draw the eye–notice how far back it is from the mouth. Add the pectoral fin. Draw the first dorsal fin with spines. Behind it, draw the long pointed second dorsal fin.*

3. *Draw the tail (caudal) fin and the anal fin. Erase parts of the oval you no longer need.*

4. *Add stripes, patterns on fins, scales and other details. Clean up any smudges with your eraser.*

The Queen triggerfish has tipped over a sea urchin by blowing a jet of water at it. Now it can attack the soft underside. Its eyes are protected by their distance from the mouth.

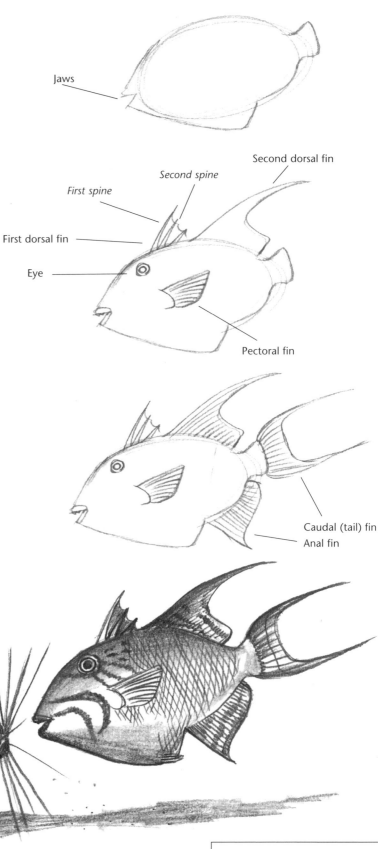

Jaws

Second dorsal fin

Second spine

First spine

First dorsal fin

Eye

Pectoral fin

Caudal (tail) fin

Anal fin

For help finishing your drawing, see *Drawing Tips* on pages 58-62.

Always draw lightly at first!

Snail

Oval

Arms

Soft body

Feelers

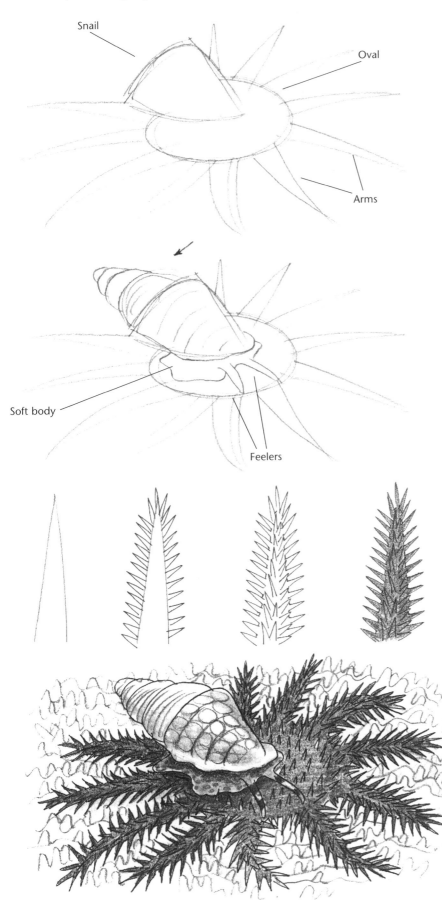

Acanthaster planci (Crown-of-thorns starfish). Size: up to 40 cm (16 in) across. Diet: coral. In the mid-1960's, population of this starfish started growing, and large areas of some of the world's coral reefs have been destroyed. Was it because collectors killed too many Triton snails for their shells? Scientists don't know.

Charonia (Triton snail). This snail, whose shell is prized by collectors, feeds on the Crown of Thorns by spearing it with poison, then eating it.

This starfish is making its way slowly across a coral reef, killing coral. But a triton snail has found it, and is killing the starfish. Unlike other animals, the snail isn't bothered by the sharp spines of the starfish.

1. Draw the starfish as an oval, with pointed arms. Draw a triangular shape for the main part of the snail.

2. Add the back parts of the snail shell, and the soft body with feelers.

3. Complete the starfish arms by adding thorns on the outside and inside of each arm (I used a fine marker). Shade the arm gray, so the black thorns still show.

4. Draw light squiggly lines for the coral.

   Add shading and details to the snail. Clean up any smudges with your eraser.

   Snail eating starfish eating coral–chow time!

Octopus

Class *Cephalopoda*, genus *Octopus*. Mollusk with eight tentacles, or arms, with suction cups. Related to squid, cuttlefish, and nautilus, an octopus has no bones. It moves by squirting water out of the siphon, an opening under its head. Has three hearts, can change colors, and shoots clouds of black 'ink' in self defense. Size: varies among 50 varieties, from 8 cm (3 in) to 8.5 m (28 ft). Diet: clams, crabs, lobsters, mussels and other shellfish. Octopuses live along coasts; not just in coral reefs.

1. *Draw an oval for the body. Next draw a cylinder shape for the head, with an eye at the end. Add the opening for the siphon.*

2. *Because the octopus has no bones, the tentacles can go just about any direction. often they're curled. Draw the siphon.*

   Suggestion: put tentacles curling every which way. Make a fun design!

3. *Draw suction cups on the bottom of each tentacle. When you like the design, you can go over your final lines with a fine-tip marker. Erase the pencil lines, add shading, and clean up with an eraser.*

Siphon opening

Siphon

Tentacles

42 Draw Ocean Animals

For help finishing your drawing, see *Drawing Tips* on pages 58-62.

More Amazing Ocean Animals

Always draw lightly at first!

Tripod Fish

Bathypterois bigelowi.
Lives at depths of 3000 m (9,800 ft).
Stands on the bottom, on extended
pelvic fins and its tail, waiting for prey.

1. Start with a long, sausage-like
   body. Draw two 'legs' and the
   tail fin.

Tail fin

2. Turn the 'legs' into pelvic fins,
   which they actually are. (Fish
   don't have legs!) Add the anal
   fin.

Anal fin

Pelvic fins

3. Draw long, curving pectoral
   fins above the body. Add
   mouth and eye.

Pectoral fins

4. Add shading. Sharpen
   outlines and details. Clean up
   any smudges with your eraser.

For help finishing your
drawing, see *Drawing
Tips* on pages 58-62.

Flyingfish

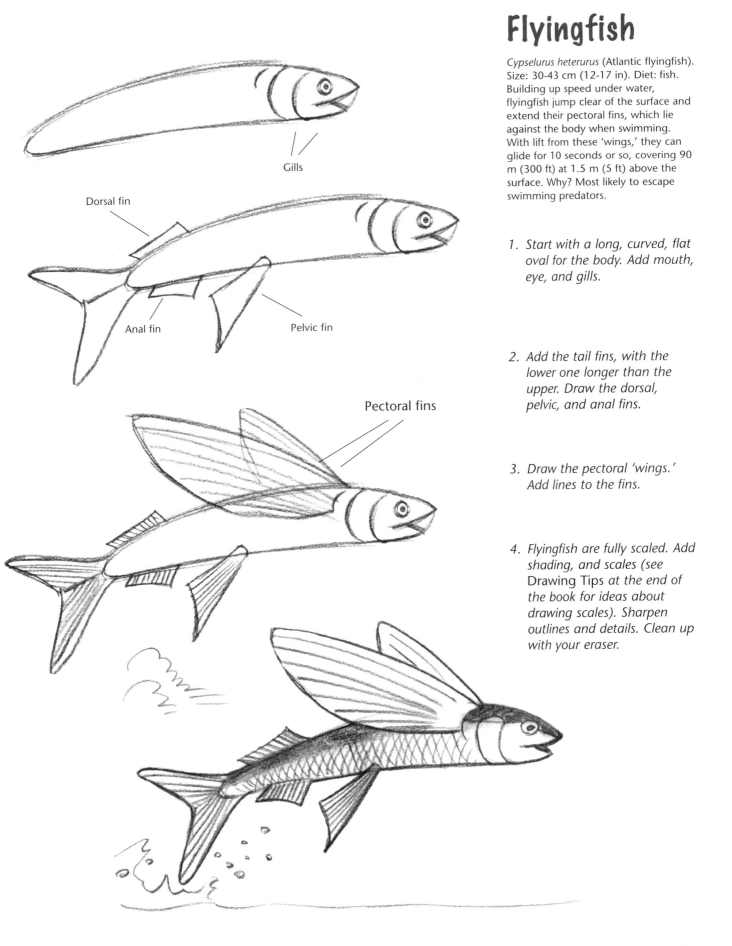

Cypselurus heterurus (Atlantic flyingfish).
Size: 30-43 cm (12-17 in). Diet: fish.
Building up speed under water,
flyingfish jump clear of the surface and
extend their pectoral fins, which lie
against the body when swimming.
With lift from these 'wings,' they can
glide for 10 seconds or so, covering 90
m (300 ft) at 1.5 m (5 ft) above the
surface. Why? Most likely to escape
swimming predators.

1. *Start with a long, curved, flat oval for the body. Add mouth, eye, and gills.*

2. *Add the tail fins, with the lower one longer than the upper. Draw the dorsal, pelvic, and anal fins.*

3. *Draw the pectoral 'wings.' Add lines to the fins.*

4. *Flyingfish are fully scaled. Add shading, and scales (see* Drawing Tips *at the end of the book for ideas about drawing scales). Sharpen outlines and details. Clean up with your eraser.*

Gills

Dorsal fin

Anal fin

Pelvic fin

Pectoral fins

Angler 1

Lophius piscatorius.
Size: 1-2 m (3-6 ft). Diet: fish. Unusual flat coastal fish lies on the bottom, waiting for prey. The fringes at the edge of the body help conceal its outline. When it opens its huge mouth, its prey is sucked in with a large quantity of water. The water gets back out. The unfortunate prey stays in.

1. Draw a flat oval, with an arc across the top of it for the center line of the fish's body. Draw the rough outline of the tail–lightly!

2. Along the centerline (start far enough back to leave room for the mouth!) draw the 'fishing rod' and other dorsal spines. Add the pectoral fins and tail details.

3. Draw the mouth with teeth. Add eyes. Draw lightly at first! Now comes the part requiring patience–slowly draw the frills around the outside edge. Do a little bit at a time, erasing part of the oval as you draw.

4. Add shading. Sharpen outlines and details. Clean up any smudges with your eraser.

Always draw lightly at first!

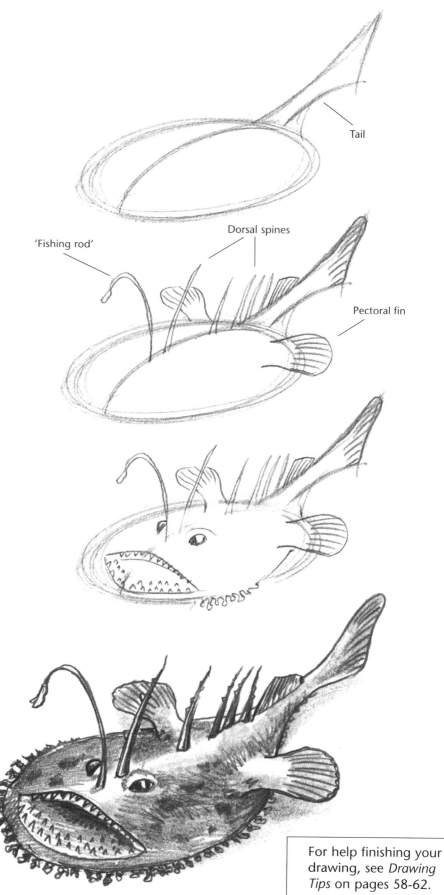

Tail

Dorsal spines

'Fishing rod'

Pectoral fin

For help finishing your drawing, see *Drawing Tips* on pages 58-62.

Always draw lightly at first!

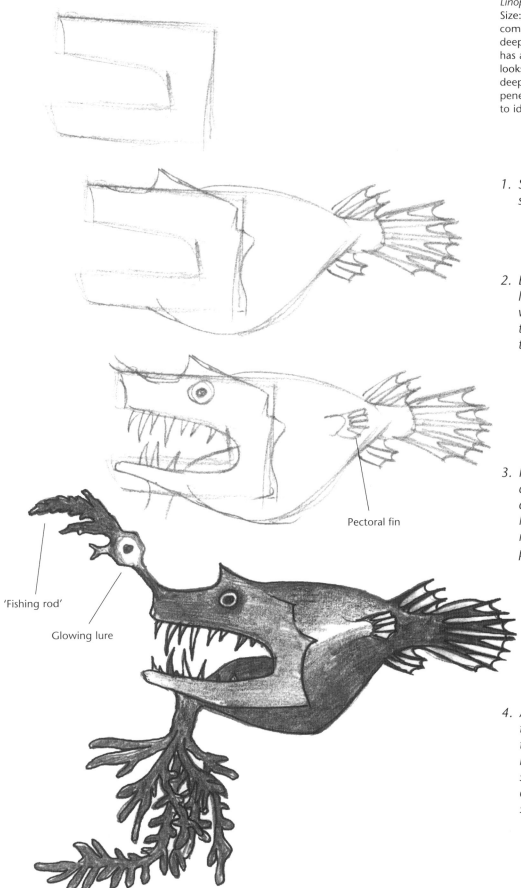

'Fishing rod'

Glowing lure

Pectoral fin

Angler 2

Linophryne arborifera.
Size: 7 cm (3 in). This small (tiny compared to Angler 1) fish lives in the deep sea. The 'fishing rod' on its snout has a luminous lure. The chin barbel looks like a piece of seaweed. In the deep sea, where no sunlight penetrates, many animals have lights, to identify species and lure prey.

1. *Start out with a sideways U shape.*

2. *Extend the body back almost like a triangle. Add the tail, with its forked spines, plus the top and bottom fins. Draw the peak above the mouth.*

3. *Round out the mouth and add teeth (you may want to do some careful erasing first). Narrow the lower jaw as you make it rounder. Add the pectoral fin.*

4. *Add the distinctive chin barbel that looks like seaweed, and the 'fishing rod' on top with its glowing decoration. Add shading. Sharpen outlines and details. Clean up any smudges with your eraser.*

Draw Ocean Animals 47

Atlantic Footballfish

Himantolophus groenlandicus.
Size: 61 cm (24 in). Diet: fish attracted
by the light in its forehead 'fishing rod.'
This deep sea angler lives 100-300 m
(330-980 ft) below the surface.

Always draw lightly at first!

1. Start with an almost circular
   oval. Lightly divide it into four
   parts to help you place mouth
   and fins.

2. Draw the mouth. Notice that
   the front of the bottom jaw
   lines up with the centerline.
   Add teeth. Draw the eye and
   'fishing rod.'

3. Draw the remaining fins.

4. Draw the forked spines in all
   the fins, and bony plates on
   the side of the fish. Add
   shading. Sharpen outlines and
   details. Clean up any
   smudges with your eraser.

*Congratulations! You have
drawn one magnificently ugly
fish.*

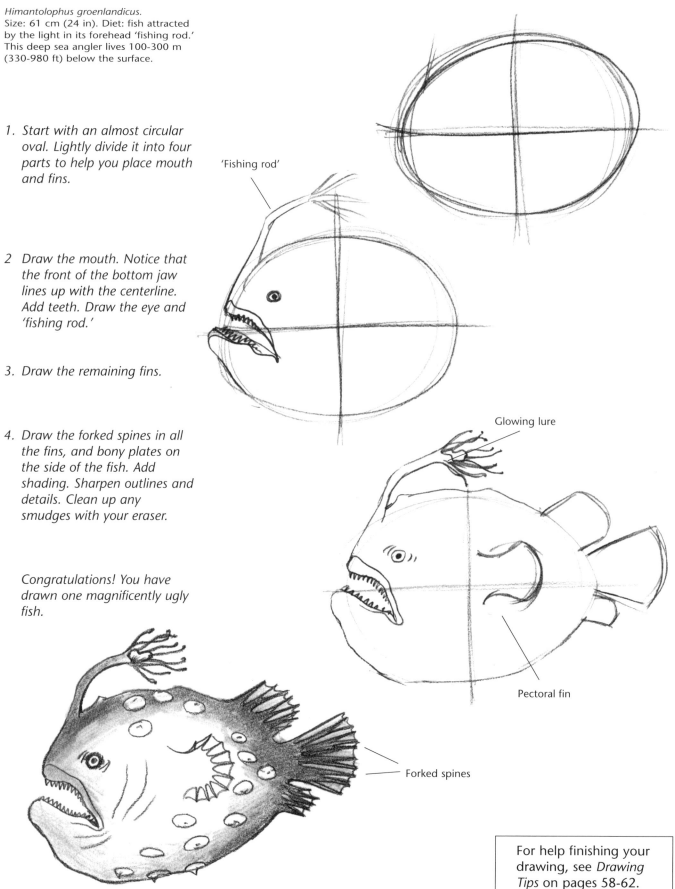

'Fishing rod'

Glowing lure

Pectoral fin

Forked spines

For help finishing your
drawing, see *Drawing
Tips* on pages 58-62.

Always draw lightly at first!

Gulper Eel

Eurypharynx pelecanoides.
Size: 61 cm (24 in). Diet: fish, crustaceans. Another deep sea fish. Lives at 1,400 m (4,500 ft) and below. Can feed on quite large fish even though it's not much of a swimmer. Thought to swim slowly with its mouth open catching whatever it can.

1. Start with a curvy ribbon (see moray eel on pages 38-39 if you're not sure how to do this). Extend the bottom line and add the eye.

2. Next draw the mouth, a sideways 'V.' Curve the lower jaw up behind the mouth. Continue that line below the curve of the tail.

3. Add the inside section of the mouth. Drawing the remaining sections of the tail and fin can be confusing. I've tinted the part that is already drawn. The areas that aren't tinted are the parts you need to add now. Draw them.

4. Add lines on the fins, and shading. Sharpen outlines and details. Clean up any smudges with your eraser.

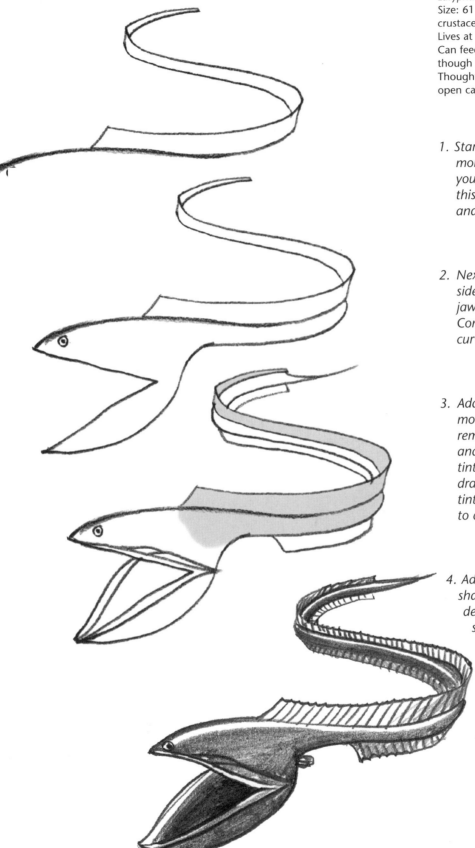

Squid

Loliginidae family. A mollusk related to octopus, cuttlefish, nautilus. Size: Many varieties, ranging from less than 30 cm (1 ft) to 12 m (40 ft). Diet: fish, caught with suction cups on its ten arms. Two arms are longer, and used for drawing caught prey to the mouth. Squid move by jet propulsion, filling their body with water then shooting it out. They create clouds of 'ink' to confuse predators and escape.

1. Start with a rectangle and a slightly larger triangle.

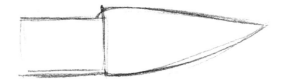

Fin

2. Draw the eye looking toward you, and the little bit you can see of the other eye. Add the fins.

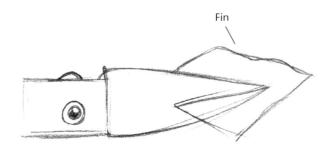

Tentacles

3. Add the tentacles. Two of them are longer, with little 'paddles' on the end.

4. Add pattern and shading. Sharpen outlines and details. Clean up any smudges with your eraser.

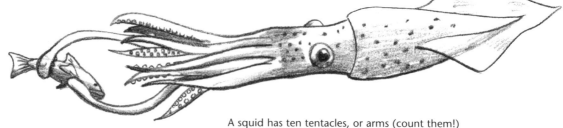

A squid has ten tentacles, or arms (count them!)

Cuttlefish

Sepia officinalis (common cuttlefish).
A mollusk related to octopus and squid.
Can change color at will. Grab their
prey with suction cups at the end of
two long tentacles. They draw it into
their beak, then inject it with poison.

1. *Start with an oval,
   surrounded by the 'wings' the
   cuttlefish uses to swim.*

2. *Draw one eye looking straight
   toward you. Draw the other
   eye, noticing that you only
   see the side of it. To help you
   draw the shorter tentacles the
   same length, you can draw a
   light arc.*

3. *Add eight short tentacles and
   two longer ones.*

4. *Add patterns and shading.
   Sharpen outlines and details.
   Clean up any smudges with
   your eraser.*

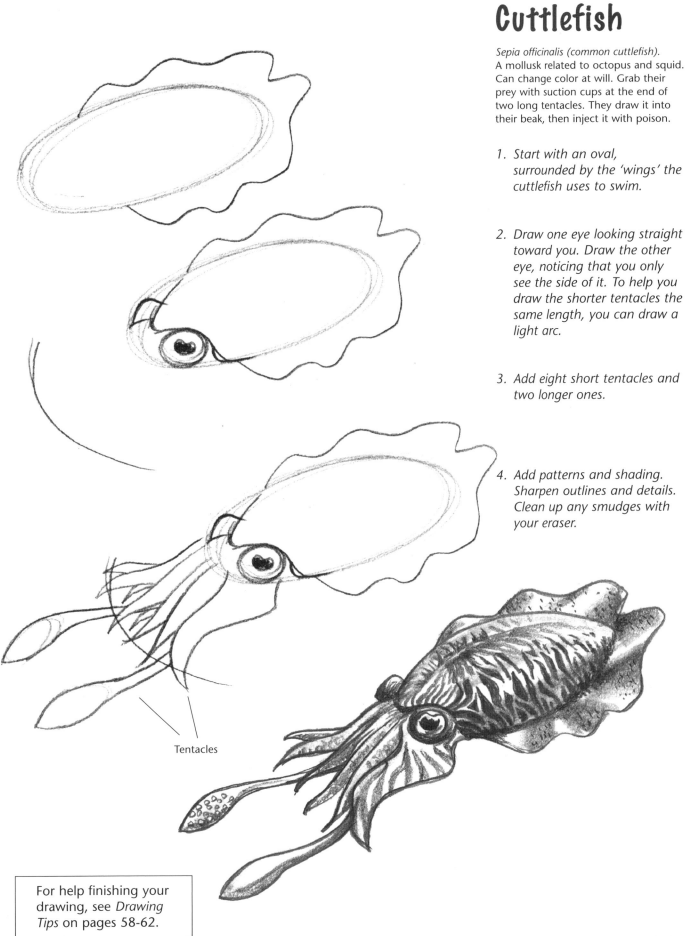

Tentacles

For help finishing your
drawing, see *Drawing
Tips* on pages 58-62.

Draw Ocean Animals **51**

Porcupinefish

Diodon hystrix.
Size: 90 cm (35 in). Diet: crabs, mollusks, sea urchins. This fish has a most unusual defense—when threatened, it puffs itself up into an almost round ball, with spines sticking out all over!

1. Draw a flat oval. Add the mouth, which sticks out. Draw the eye. Add the two parts for the tail.

2. Add fins, with lines in them.

3. Draw spikes. They all point backwards when the porcupinefish is deflated.

4. If you want to draw the fish expanded, do the same drawing, only this time starting with a circle.

5. When expanded, the spines stick out from the center. I've drawn a few. You'll want to keep going until you've drawn them all.

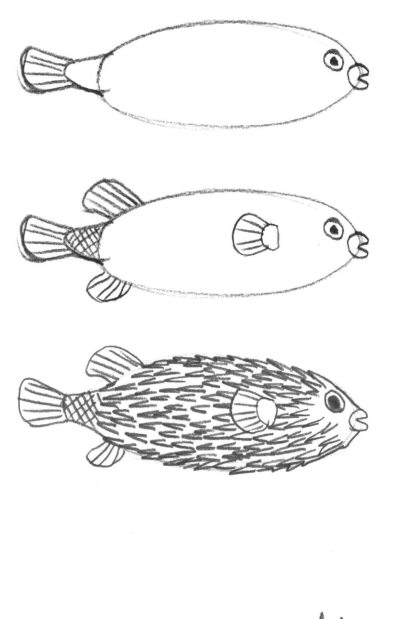

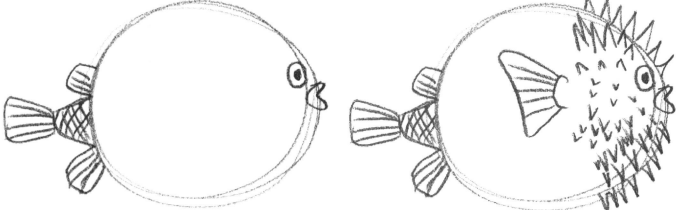

Swordfish

Xiphias gladius.
Size: 2-5 m (6.5-16 ft). Diet: small fish, squid. Function of the 'sword' isn't clear; it may be for striking at schooling fish or just to help the swordfish swim faster. This is a very fast fish!

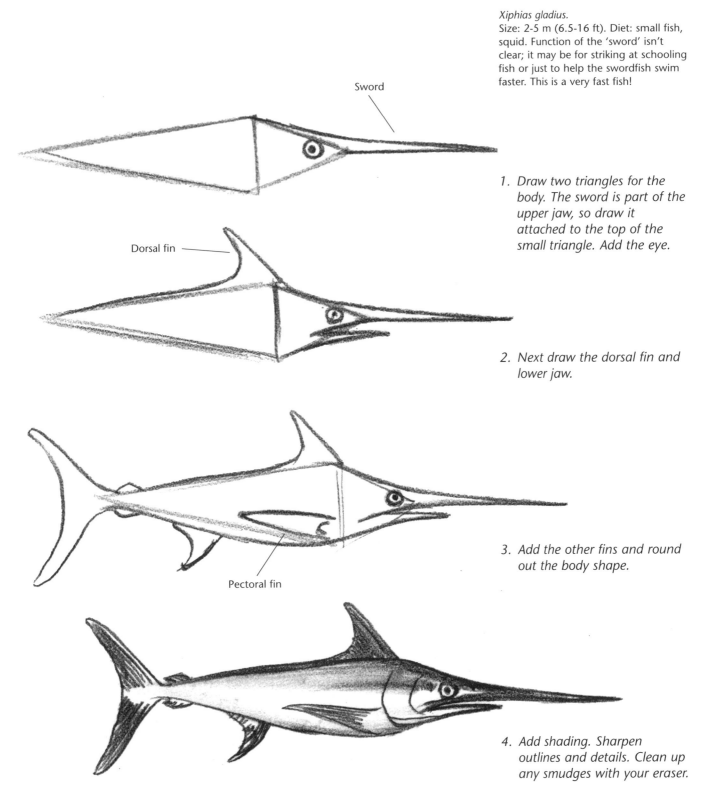

Sword

Dorsal fin

Pectoral fin

1. *Draw two triangles for the body. The sword is part of the upper jaw, so draw it attached to the top of the small triangle. Add the eye.*

2. *Next draw the dorsal fin and lower jaw.*

3. *Add the other fins and round out the body shape.*

4. *Add shading. Sharpen outlines and details. Clean up any smudges with your eraser.*

For help finishing your drawing, see *Drawing Tips* on pages 58-62.

Draw Ocean Animals 53

Green Turtle

Chelonia mydas. Size: 1-1.5 m (3-4 ft).
Diet: sea grasses and seaweed, some
jellyfish and crustaceans. Endangered.

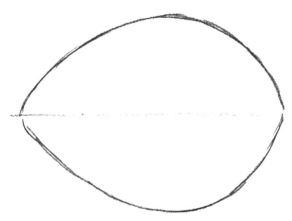

1. Draw the outside of the shell, with center line.

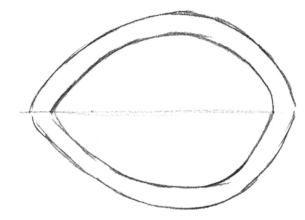

2. Draw the same shape inside the shell.

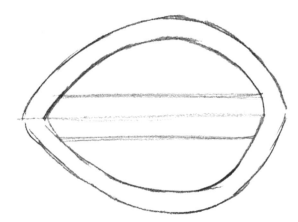

3. Draw a line either side of the center line.

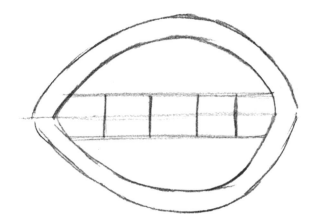

4. Divide the center into five spaces.

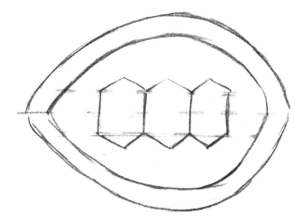

5. Turn the middle three spaces into hexagons.

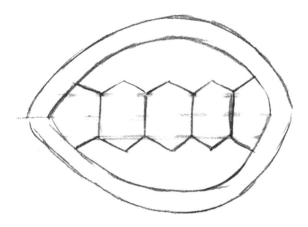

6. Draw lines for the front and back segments.

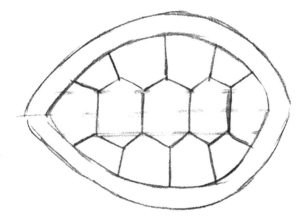

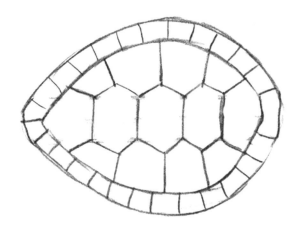

7. Draw radiating lines from the hexagon points.

8. Make lots of little segments on the outside rim. Now the hard part is done!

9. Add flippers and head. The front flippers have two parts. Notice which direction each part goes.

10. Draw the tail. Add shading and patterns of scales on the flippers and head. Sharpen outlines and details. Clean up any smudges with your eraser.

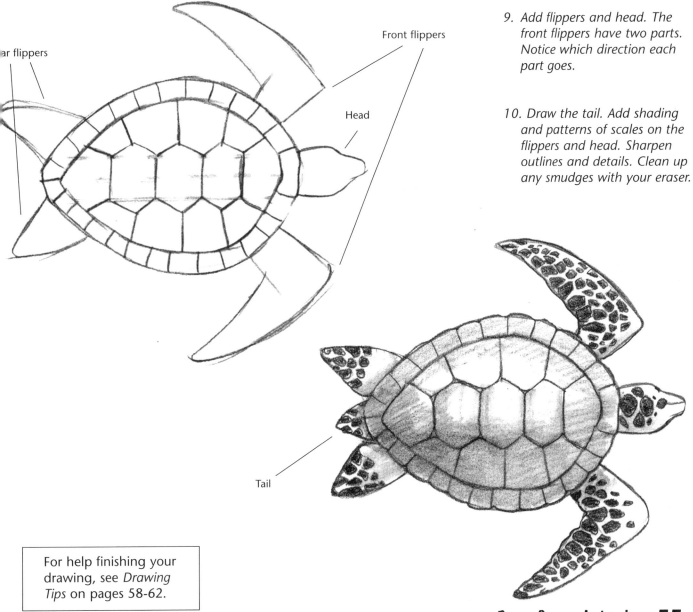

ar flippers

Front flippers

Head

Tail

For help finishing your drawing, see *Drawing Tips* on pages 58-62.

Draw Ocean Animals **55**

California Halibut

Always draw lightly at first!

Paralichthys californicus.
Size: 1.5 m (5 ft). Diet: fish, particularly anchovies. Is in turn eaten by rays, sea lions, porpoises and people. Like the 500 or so other species of flatfishes, young halibut swim like normal fish, with an eye on either side of their head. As they develop, one eye moves to the other side of the head. From then on, the fish swims on its side, with its eyes facing up. Flatfishes are bottom feeders.

1. Draw an oval, with one end pointed. Draw the mouth. Add the tail.

2. Draw the dorsal fin with spines. Draw the lateral line, pectoral fin and gill openings.

3. Add the two separate fins on the bottom. Draw the eyes and spines in tail. Lightly erase lines you don't need.

4. Add shading and spots. Sharpen outlines and details. Clean up any smudges with your eraser.

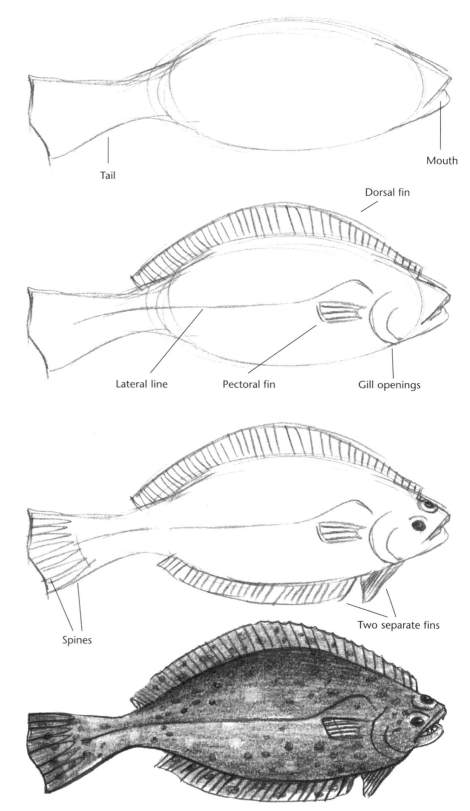

Tail

Mouth

Dorsal fin

Lateral line

Pectoral fin

Gill openings

Spines

Two separate fins

For help finishing your drawing, see *Drawing Tips* on pages 58-62.

56 **Draw Ocean Animals**

Drawing Tips
Always draw lightly at first!

Drawing Tips

Scales and fins

1   Start with your basic outline.

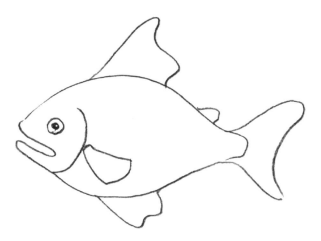

2   Add lines in the fins.

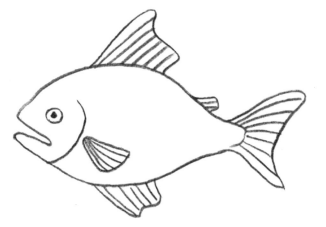

3   Make a 'checkerboard' with diagonal lines.

4   Round edges of diamond shapes to make scales.

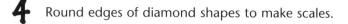

Always draw **lightly** at first!

Drawing Tips

Contour scales

It's not easy drawing scales evenly, but with a little practice, this technique might work well for you.

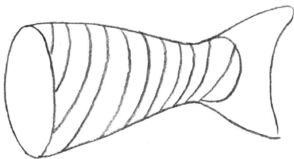

Angled contour lines

1. *Draw angled contour lines around the fish (not vertical contour lines).*

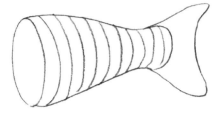

Vertical contour lines—not what you want

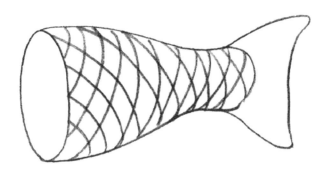

Angled contour lines going the other way

2. *Draw angled contour lines in the other direction, as evenly spaced as possible.*

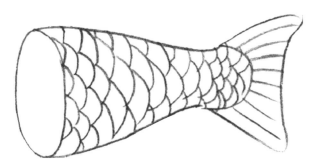

Scales!

3. *Carefully turn each small diamond shape into a scale shape. This will take some practice, but the results can be very impressive!*

Draw Ocean Animals 59

Drawing Tips

Contours

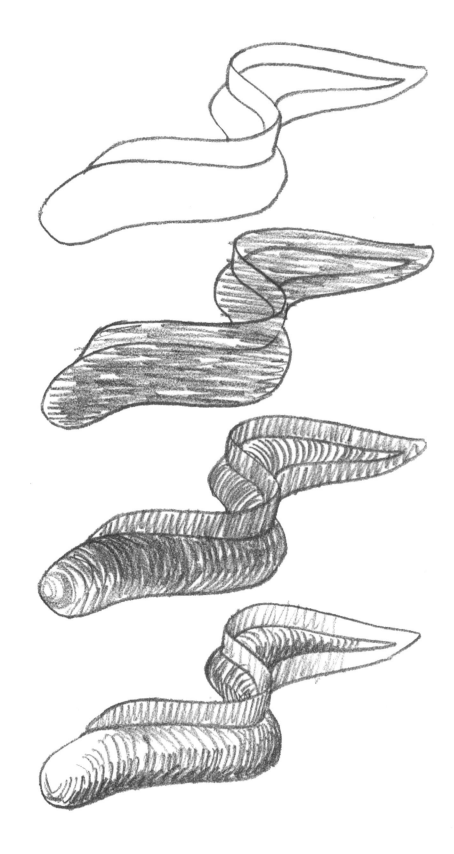

1. Here's the outline of the moray eel from page 39. Because of the way it's drawn, the eel appears to be swimming toward you.

   Now let's shade it.

2. Just 'coloring' it with a pencil works, but you can do better. Here I've shaded the lazy way, using just back-and-forth lines.

3. A more effective approach: imagine the contours of the form—how the sides curve—and try to draw your shading lines so they follow the contours.

4. One step better is to think about light as you follow the contours. Make the top of the form a little lighter than the bottom. Can you see the difference, with the light and dark areas?

Drawing Tips

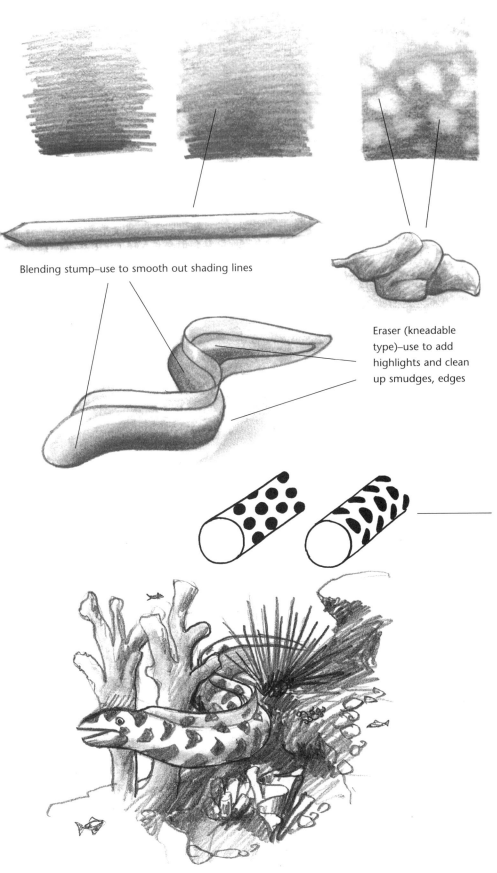

Blending stump–use to smooth out shading lines

Eraser (kneadable type)–use to add highlights and clean up smudges, edges

Shading

Sometimes the effect you want is a very smooth surface, with no contour lines showing on it. When that's the case, try using a blending stump.

First, carefully shade, trying not to make any obvious lines.

Next, blend the pencil marks with a blending stump (or a piece of paper or paper towel, or even your finger–that's kind of messy, though…).

Finally, use your eraser to add highlights and clean up any smudges. This technique may take some practice, but it's worth it!

Contour patterns

Look at these two cylinders with spots on them. Which looks rounder? Why?

Notice that I've carefully drawn the pattern so that it appears to wrap around the right cylinder. When you add patterns to your drawings of ocean animals, look for ways to make the patterns 'bend' around the animal to show its form.

It takes practice, but it can make a big difference in your drawing!

Drawing Tips

Basic Approach

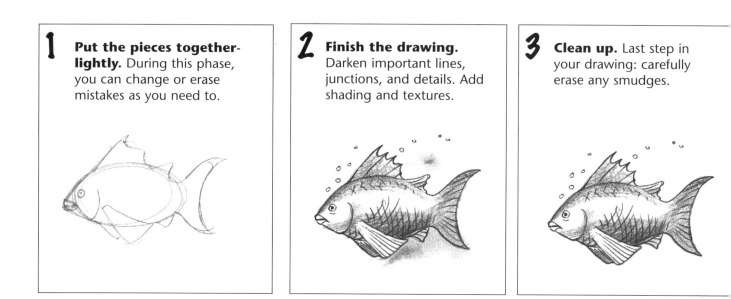

**1 Put the pieces together-
lightly.** During this phase,
you can change or erase
mistakes as you need to.

2 Finish the drawing.
Darken important lines,
junctions, and details. Add
shading and textures.

3 Clean up. Last step in
your drawing: carefully
erase any smudges.

Save your work!

Whenever you do a drawing–or
even a sketch–put your initials
(or autograph!) and date on it.
And save it. You don't have to
save it until it turns yellow and
crumbles to dust, but do keep
your drawings, at least for
several months. Sometimes,
hiding in your portfolio, they
will mysteriously improve! I've
seen it happen often with my
own drawings, especially the
ones I knew were no good at
all, but kept anyway....

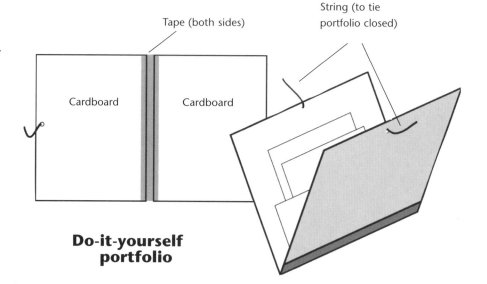

Tape (both sides)

String (to tie
portfolio closed)

Cardboard   Cardboard

**Do-it-yourself
portfolio**

Index

Angler..46, 47
Atlantic Footballfish 48
Basking Shark...13
Beluga Whale...19
Blue Whale...20
Bowhead Whale..24
Butterflyfish..35
California Halibut 56
California Sea Lion 28
Clown Anenome Fish...................................37
Crown-Of-Thorns Starfish 41
Cuttlefish...51
Dolphin 26
Eel, Gulper..49
Eel, Moray 38, 39
Flyingfish...45
Footballfish...48
Gray Whale...21
Great White Shark.....................................6
Green Turtle.......................................54, 55
Gulper Eel...49
Hammerhead Shark...................................10, 11
Harbor Porpoise......................................27
Harbor Seal..29
Humpback Whale 23
Killer Whale...25
Lionfish...36
Manatee 32
Manta..16
Minke Whale..22
Moray Eel 38, 39
Northern Elephant Seal...............................30
Octopus..42
Parrotfish...34
Porcupinefish..52
Porpoise...27
Port Jackson Shark 14
Queen Triggerfish 40

Sand Tiger 9
Sea Lion...28
Seal, Harbor...29
Seal, Northern Elephant 30
Sharks
    Basking..13
    Great White.......................................6
    Hammerhead 10, 11
    Port Jackson.....................................14
    Sand Tiger..9
    Shortfin Mako.....................................7
    Thresher 8
    Whale..12
Shortfin Mako Shark 7
Snail, Triton..41
Sperm Whale..18
Squid..50
Starfish, Crown-Of-Thorns 41
Sting Ray..15
Swordfish..53
Thresher Shark..8
Triggerfish..40
Tripod Fish..44
Triton Snail...41
Turtle, Green......................................54, 55
Walrus...31
Whale Shark..12
Whales
    Beluga...19
    Blue...20
    Bowhead..24
    Gray...21
    Humpback...23
    Killer...25
    Minke..22
    Sperm..18
    White..19
White Whale..19

Learn about other books in
this series online at
www.drawbooks.com!

by Doug DuBosque

For my brother Rick, who encouraged
my car enthusiasm at an early age.

*(Without revealing how to work the
clutch on his Triumph TR-4)*

Contents

Supplies 4

What you need to get the wheels spinning

Part One: Draw a car from the side 5

Step by step, a close look at drawing a car in profile

Part Two: More cars in profile 13

From Lamborghini to Uncle Bill's ratty ol' pickup…

Part Three: Draw a car from an angle 35

Add dimension to your drawings

Part Four: More cars from angles 41

Some are easy. Some aren't…

The Gallery 60

A wild collection of automotive drawing ideas

Tips and Tricks 62

Use reference material, turn your paper…

Supplies...

Find a **comfortable place to draw** – with decent light, so you can see what you're doing.

As you start to learn about car designs, shapes and proportions, don't worry too much about materials.

Use a **pencil that's longer than your finger.**

Sharpen your pencil when it gets dull!

Get a **separate eraser.** My favorite is a *kneaded* type, available in art supply and craft stores (the eraser on your pencil will disappear quickly).

For smooth shading with a soft pencil, consider a **tortillon, or blending tool.**

For practice drawings, use **recycled paper** – for example, draw on the back of old photocopies or computer printouts.

Always **draw lightly at first**, so you can erase problems as you need to.

Save your drawings and learn from them.

Enjoy drawing *great* cars!

Positive attitude!
Persistence!
Practice!

Part One

Draw a car from the side

In the next *few pages, you'll look closely at the basic body parts and lines that shape a car. You'll learn how to get proportions and details just right. Pay close attention!*

Do this chapter first!

(Really!)

Dodge Stratus

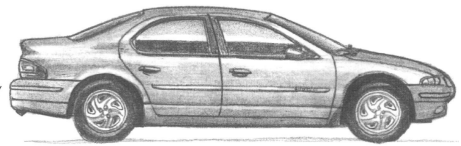

Before you start, look carefully at your **reference material**.

For this drawing, your reference material will be this finished drawing (my reference material for this drawing was a magazine advertisement.)

Start with a light horizontal line for the ground.

The Ground.

Carefully draw a circle for the wheel.

Always ask yourself: how many wheels (or wheel *diameters)* would fit between the front and back wheel?

A Wheel. Don't worry if it isn't perfectly round at first.

You won't see many cars where the answer is two.

Nor will you see many cars where the answer is seven!

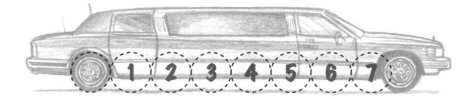

On the Stratus, the front and rear wheel are separated by about 3½ diameters, which is typical of many cars.

Always start out *lightly!*

Carefully measure the distance between the wheels, then draw a light circle for the second wheel.

Look again at your *reference material.* Lightly draw the line at the bottom of the windows. Observe its height above the wheels, and notice how it slopes slightly down to the front.

Look again at your *reference material.* Find the top of the roof. Lightly draw this line.

*These three lines—the ground, bottom of window, and roof—are **basic lines** you'll need to draw **any** car.*

The details can be a little complicated at the front and rear end of the car. For now, just make a light vertical line to mark the front of the car, with another line cutting back to the wheel.

Look again at your *reference material* to see where to end the car. Make a light vertical line there, then another cutting forward to the wheel.

windshield
(windscreen)

Look at the windshield. How far forward does it extend, compared to the back of the front wheel? *(This varies from car to car.)* Lightly sketch the windshield line.

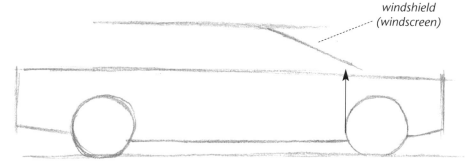

hood
(bonnet)

Add the line, joining the bottom of the windshield and carrying forward, with a slight curve.

trunk
(boot)

Notice how the rear window and trunk are higher than the hood. Draw them. Now take another look at your *reference material*, and add the curves of the bumper and tail light.

tail light

bumper

Always start out *lightly!*

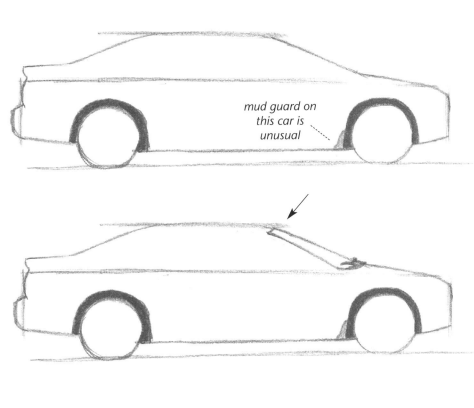

mud guard on
this car is
unusual

Extremely

important...draw the dark cut-out portion of the body that surrounds the wheels. These dark *wheel wells* are key to making your car drawing look real!

Add the side and top windshield lines (notice the angle at the top of the windshield). Draw windshield wipers.

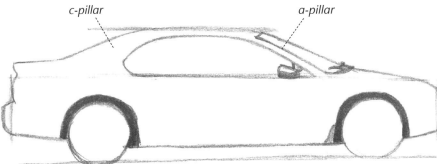

c-pillar

a-pillar

The outline of the side windows contributes much to the car's style. Draw the outline of the side windows. By drawing this shape, you've also drawn the A- and C-pillars. Add the mirror.

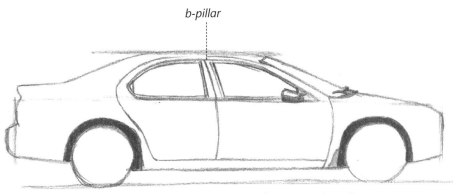

b-pillar

Look carefully at the size of the doors. Typically, on a four-door *sedan,* the front doors are bigger (a *coupe* has two doors). Outline the doors, windows and b-pillar (draw the door seam through the middle of it).

Why do chicken coops have two doors?

(Because if they had four doors, they'd be chicken sedans.)

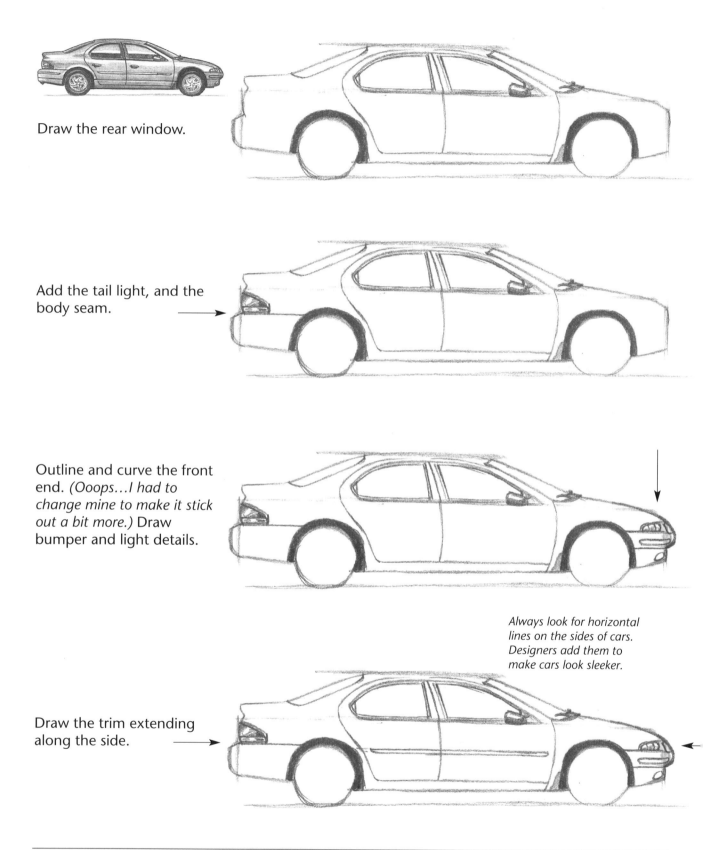

Draw the rear window.

Add the tail light, and the body seam.

Outline and curve the front end. *(Ooops...I had to change mine to make it stick out a bit more.)* Draw bumper and light details.

Always look for horizontal lines on the sides of cars. Designers add them to make cars look sleeker.

Draw the trim extending along the side.

Always start out *lightly!*

Add another horizontal line, above the bottom of the doors, and extending to the rear end of the car.

Draw door handles. Erase guidelines you no longer need.

highlights

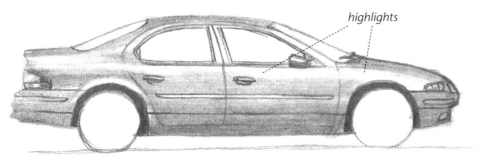

Look carefully at the *reference material,* and add shading to your drawing. You might smooth it, as I did, with a *tortillon* or blending tool (see page 4). Then you can use your eraser to add highlights. Spend as much time as you need at this stage.

Turn your drawing as you draw to avoid smudging it with your hand.

Now sharpen your pencil and go over details and lines, making them as crisp as you can.

All done!

...just kidding!

Notice those *round things* the car sits on. They have two parts: the *wheel* and the *tire.* Draw a smaller circle in each tire for the real wheel.

Having trouble drawing circles? See page 61 to learn how to draw them perfectly!

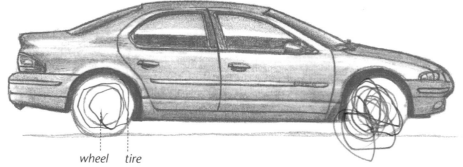

wheel   tire

Darken the tires. For best effect, leave a little highlight at the top of the top, and the top of the bottom.

Draw the pattern of the wheels.

Add details to the wheels, and shading.

All done!

(Really!)

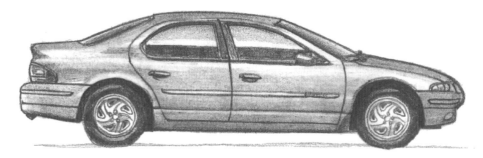

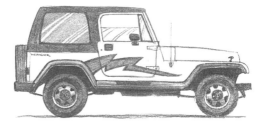

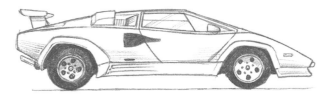

Part Two

More cars in profile

In the next few pages you will use the final drawing as your reference material. Look carefully at the finished drawing, then follow a few easy steps to add the lines, shapes and details you see.

Outrageous!

None of the cars pictured here have step by step instructions in this book. But, with these drawings as reference material, and your positive attitude, persistence and practice…

…you'll be drawing outrageous cars in no time!

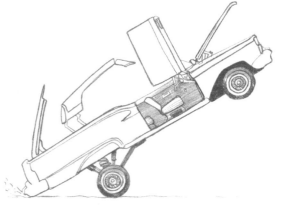

Audi Avus

*Before you start, look carefully at your **reference material** (for now, my finished drawing).*

Draw the ground line. Using the wheel diagram above, draw the wheels the correct distance apart. Draw the basic body lines.

Complete the overall shape of the car.

Add:
- front and rear bumpers
- windows
- wheel wells
- lights
- rear view mirror
- tires and wheels

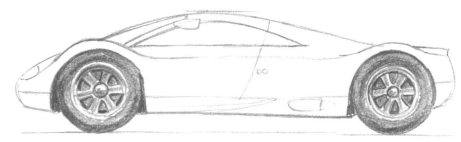

Draw other details you see (or want—hey, it's your drawing!). Add shading.

Remember:
- *Start out lightly!*
- *Turn your drawing as you work. Use a piece of scrap paper to keep your hand off finished parts.*
- *While your pencil is sharp, go over fine details and make lines cleaner. As it gets duller, add shading.*
- *Clean up any smudges with your eraser. Make sure all final lines are crisp and sharp.*

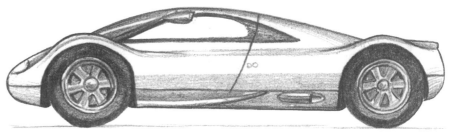

Always start out *lightly!*

*Before you start, look carefully at your **reference material** (for now, my finished drawing).*

Draw the ground line. Using the wheel diagram above, draw the wheels the correct distance apart. Draw the basic body lines.

Complete the overall shape of the car.

Add:
- windows
- air scoops
- wheel wells
- lights
- rear view mirror
- fuel cap
- tires and wheels

Draw other details you see (or want—hey, it's your drawing!). Add shading.

Remember:
- *Start out lightly!*
- *Turn your drawing as you work. Use a piece of scrap paper to keep your hand off finished parts.*
- *While your pencil is sharp, go over fine details and make lines cleaner. As it gets duller, add shading.*
- *Clean up any smudges with your eraser. Make sure all final lines are crisp and sharp.*

Ferrari F50

*Before you start, look carefully at your **reference material** (for now, my finished drawing).*

Draw the ground line. Using the wheel diagram above, draw the wheels the correct distance apart. Draw the bottom body line, the distinctive slanting center line, and the front and rear bumper lines.

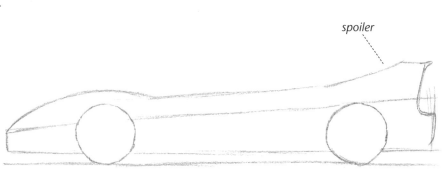

spoiler

Add the line for fenders and spoiler, which curves down to the bumper. Draw the windshield and engine cover. Reshape the rear bumper.

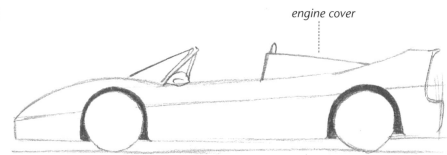

engine cover

Add:
- wheel wells
- tail lights
- side air scoop
- rear view mirror

Draw other details you see (or want—hey, it's your drawing!). Add shading.

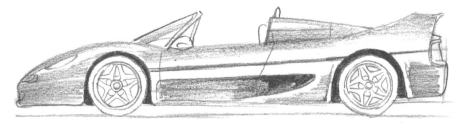

Remember:
- *Start out lightly!*
- *Turn your drawing as you work. Use a piece of scrap paper to keep your hand off finished parts.*
- *While your pencil is sharp, go over fine details and make lines cleaner. As it gets duller, add shading.*
- *Clean up any smudges with your eraser. Make sure all final lines are crisp and sharp.*

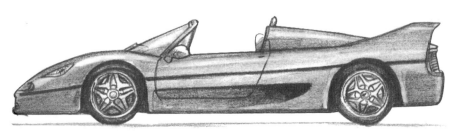

Always start out *lightly!*

Before you start, look carefully at your reference material (for now, my finished drawing).

Draw the ground line. Using the wheel diagram above, draw the wheels the correct distance apart. Draw the basic body lines.

Complete the overall shape of the car.

Add:
- windows
- pillars A and B
- wheel wells
- side body seams
- radical side vent
- lights
- rear view mirror
- fuel cap

Draw other details you see (or want—hey, it's your drawing!). Add shading.

Remember:
- *Start out lightly!*
- *Turn your drawing as you work. Use a piece of scrap paper to keep your hand off finished parts.*
- *While your pencil is sharp, go over fine details and make lines cleaner. As it gets duller, add shading.*
- *Clean up any smudges with your eraser. Make sure all final lines are crisp and sharp.*

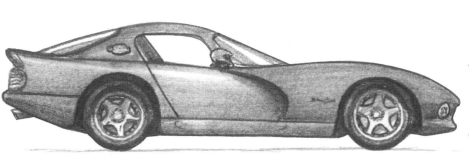

Shelby Cobra

*Before you start, look carefully at your **reference material** (for now, my finished drawing).*

Draw the ground line. Using the wheel diagram above, draw the wheels the correct distance apart. Draw the basic body lines.

Complete the overall shape of the car.

Add:
- windshield
- roll bar
- wheel wells
- side exhaust, vents
- lights
- rear view mirror

Draw other details you see (or want—hey, it's *your* drawing!). Add shading.

Remember:
- *Start out lightly!*
- *Turn your drawing as you work. Use a piece of scrap paper to keep your hand off finished parts.*
- *While your pencil is sharp, go over fine details and make lines cleaner. As it gets duller, add shading.*
- *Clean up any smudges with your eraser. Make sure all final lines are crisp and sharp.*

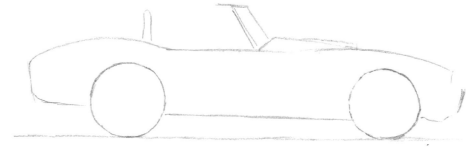

Corvette

*Before you start, look carefully at your **reference material** (for now, my finished drawing).*

Draw the ground line. Using the wheel diagram above, draw the wheels the correct distance apart. Draw the basic body lines.

Complete the overall shape of the car.

Add:
- windows
- pillars A and B
- wheel wells
- side vent
- side lights
- rear view mirror
- fuel cap

Draw other details you see (or want—hey, it's *your* drawing!). Erase guide lines. Add shading.

Remember:
- *Start out lightly!*
- *Turn your drawing as you work. Use a piece of scrap paper to keep your hand off finished parts.*
- *While your pencil is sharp, go over fine details and make lines cleaner. As it gets duller, add shading.*
- *Clean up any smudges with your eraser. Make sure all final lines are crisp and sharp.*

BMW 318

*Before you start, look carefully at your **reference material** (for now, my finished drawing).*

Draw the ground line. Using the wheel diagram above, draw the wheels the correct distance apart. Draw the basic body lines.

Complete the overall shape of the car.

Add:
- windows
- split rear window
- pillars A, B, and C
- wheel wells
- side trim
- lights
- rear view mirror
- steering wheel

Draw other details you see (or want—hey, it's *your* drawing!). Add shading.

Remember:
- *Start out lightly!*
- *Turn your drawing as you work. Use a piece of scrap paper to keep your hand off finished parts.*
- *While your pencil is sharp, go over fine details and make lines cleaner. As it gets duller, add shading.*
- *Clean up any smudges with your eraser. Make sure all final lines are crisp and sharp.*

Always start out *lightly!*

Subaru Outback

*Before you start, look carefully at your **reference material** (for now, my finished drawing).*

Draw the ground line. Using the wheel diagram above, draw the wheels the correct distance apart. Draw the basic body lines.

Complete the overall shape of the car.

Add:
- windows
- four window pillars
- wheel wells
- side trim
- lights
- rear view mirror
- fuel cap
- luggage rack

Draw other details you see (or want—hey, it's *your* drawing!). Add shading.

Remember:
- *Start out lightly!*
- *Turn your drawing as you work. Use a piece of scrap paper to keep your hand off finished parts.*
- *While your pencil is sharp, go over fine details and make lines cleaner. As it gets duller, add shading.*
- *Clean up any smudges with your eraser. Make sure all final lines are crisp and sharp.*

Lamborghini Diablo Roadster

*Before you start, look carefully at your **reference material** (for now, my finished drawing).*

Draw the ground line. Using the wheel diagram above, draw the wheels the correct distance apart. Draw the basic body lines. Look carefully—they're unusual!

Complete the overall shape of the car.

Add:
- wheel wells
- side scoops
- running lights
- rear view mirror

Draw other details you see (or want—hey, it's *your* drawing!). Add shading.

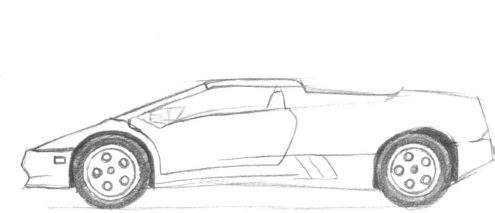

Remember:
- *Start out lightly!*
- *Turn your drawing as you work. Use a piece of scrap paper to keep your hand off finished parts.*

This little number costs more than many people's houses—a lot more. There's not much cargo room (!), so if you did own one of these, you'd probably drive it a lot. For example, grocery shopping: you'd need one trip for milk, another for bread, another for vegetables....

Always start out *lightly!*

b-pillar

*Before you start, look carefully at your **reference material** (for now, my finished drawing).*

Draw the ground line. Using the wheel diagram above, draw the wheels the correct distance apart. Draw the basic body lines.

Complete the overall shape of the car, starting with the distinctive window shape.

Add:
- wheel wells
- blacked-out b-pillar
- door handle
- lights
- rear view mirror

Draw other details you see (or want—hey, it's *your* drawing!). Add shading.

Remember:
- *Start out lightly!*
- *Turn your drawing as you work. Use a piece of scrap paper to keep your hand off finished parts.*
- *While your pencil is sharp, go over fine details and make lines cleaner. As it gets duller, add shading.*

The one millionth VW beetle was built 'way back in 1955 (see page 58). Unlike the old beetle, this new design has the engine in front.

1906 Franklin

*Before you start, look carefully at your **reference material** (for now, my finished drawing).*

Draw the ground line. Using the wheel diagram above, draw the wheels the correct distance apart. Draw the basic body lines.

Complete the overall shape of the car.

Add:
- windows
- pillars A, B, and C
- fenders
- side trim
- wheel spokes
- head light, side lantern
- rear view mirror*

Draw other details you see (or want—hey, it's *your* drawing!). Add shading.

Remember:
- *Start out lightly!*
- *Turn your drawing as you work. Use a piece of scrap paper to keep your hand off finished parts.*
- *While your pencil is sharp, go over fine details and make lines cleaner. As it gets duller, add shading.*
- *Clean up any smudges with your eraser. Make sure all final lines are crisp and sharp.*

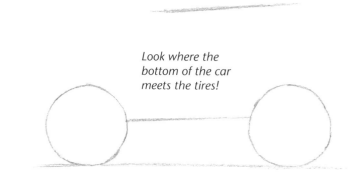

Look where the bottom of the car meets the tires!

Look where the front and rear meet the tires!

I-don't-think-soooo…

Always start out *lightly!*

rumble seat

*Before you start, look carefully at your **reference material** (for now, my finished drawing).*

Draw the ground line. Using the wheel diagram above, draw the wheels the correct distance apart. Notice where the bottom of the car meets the tires! Draw the basic body lines.

Complete the overall shape of the car. Notice where the front and rear meet the tires!

Add:
- windows
- pillars A, B, and C
- fenders
- side vents
- lights
- rumble seat
- bumpers
- spare tire

Draw other details you see (or want—hey, it's *your* drawing!). Add shading.

Remember:
- *Start out lightly!*
- *Turn your drawing as you work. Use a piece of scrap paper to keep your hand off finished parts.*
- *While your pencil is sharp, go over fine details and make lines cleaner. As it gets duller, add shading.*
- *Clean up any smudges with your eraser. Make sure all final lines are crisp and sharp.*

1946 Chrysler Town and Country

*Before you start, look carefully at your **reference material** (for now, my finished drawing).*

Draw the ground line. Using the wheel diagram above, draw the wheels the correct distance apart. Draw the basic body lines.

Complete the overall shape of the car.

Add:
- windows
- pillars A, B, and C
- wheel wells, fenders
- side paneling
- lights
- rear view mirror
- luggage rack
- hood ornament

Draw other details you see (or want—hey, it's *your* drawing!). Add shading.

Look how big the roof is!

Remember:
- *Start out lightly!*
- *Turn your drawing as you work. Use a piece of scrap paper to keep your hand off finished parts.*
- *While your pencil is sharp, go over fine details and make lines cleaner. As it gets duller, add shading.*

1961 Corvette

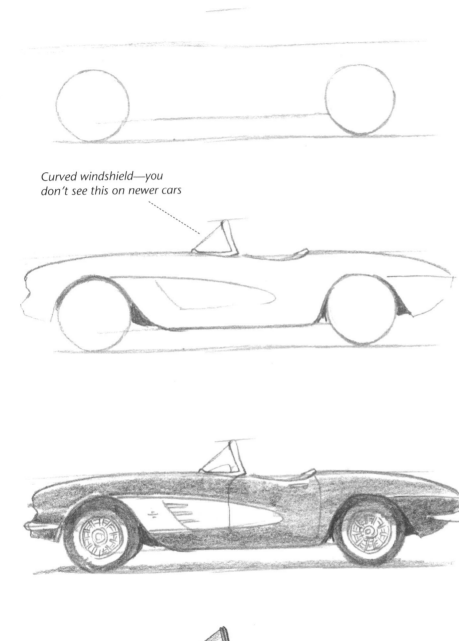

Curved windshield—you don't see this on newer cars

*Before you start, look carefully at your **reference material** (for now, my finished drawing).*

Draw the ground line. Using the wheel diagram above, draw the wheels the correct distance apart. Draw the basic body lines.

Complete the overall shape of the car.

Add:
- wheel wells
- side trim
- (useless) bumpers
- door handles

Draw other details you see (or want—hey, it's *your* drawing!). Add shading.

Remember:
- *Start out lightly!*
- *Turn your drawing as you work. Use a piece of scrap paper to keep your hand off finished parts.*
- *While your pencil is sharp, go over fine details and make lines cleaner. As it gets duller, add shading.*
- *Clean up any smudges with your eraser. Make sure all final lines are crisp and sharp.*

1956 Chevy

*Before you start, look carefully at your **reference material** (for now, my finished drawing).*

Draw the ground line. Using the wheel diagram above, draw the wheels the correct distance apart. Draw the basic body lines.

Complete the overall shape of the car.

Add:
- windows
- pillars A, B, and C
- wheel wells
- side trim
- rear view mirror
- hood ornament

Draw other details you see (or want—hey, it's your drawing!). Add shading.

Note the angle

Remember:
- *Start out lightly!*
- *Turn your drawing as you work. Use a piece of scrap paper to keep your hand off finished parts.*
- *While your pencil is sharp, go over fine details and make lines cleaner. As it gets duller, add shading.*
- *Clean up any smudges with your eraser. Make sure all final lines are crisp and sharp.*

Always start out *lightly!*

1959 Cadillac

*Before you start, look carefully at your **reference material** (for now, my finished drawing).*

Draw the ground line. Using the wheel diagram above, draw the wheels the correct distance apart. Draw the basic body lines.

Complete the overall shape of the car.

Add:
- windows
- pillars A, B, and C
- wheel wells
- side trim
- fin with tail light
- rear view mirror
- windshield wipers
- door handle

Draw other details you see (or want—hey, it's *your* drawing!). Add shading.

(Invent a character to drive this gas-guzzling monster!)

Remember:
- *Start out lightly!*
- *Turn your drawing as you work. Use a piece of scrap paper to keep your hand off finished parts.*
- *While your pencil is sharp, go over fine details and make lines cleaner. As it gets duller, add shading.*
- *Clean up any smudges with your eraser. Make sure all final lines are crisp and sharp.*

Land Rover

*Before you start, look carefully at your **reference material** (for now, my finished drawing).*

Draw the ground line. Using the wheel diagram above, draw the wheels the correct distance apart. Draw the basic body lines.

Complete the overall shape of the car. Notice where the bottom of the car meets the tires.

Add:
- windows
- pillars A, B, and C
- wheel wells
- side trim
- lights
- spare tire, mud flaps
- luggage rack

Draw other details you see (or want—hey, it's *your* drawing!). Add shading.

Remember:
- *Start out lightly!*
- *Turn your drawing as you work. Use a piece of scrap paper to keep your hand off finished parts.*
- *While your pencil is sharp, go over fine details and make lines cleaner. As it gets duller, add shading.*
- *Clean up any smudges with your eraser. Make sure all final lines are crisp and sharp.*

Hummer

*Before you start, look carefully at your **reference material** (for now, my finished drawing).*

Draw the ground line. Using the wheel diagram above, draw the wheels the correct distance apart.

Draw the basic body lines. Notice where the bottom of the car meets the tires!

Complete the overall shape of the car.

Add:
- windows
- pillars A, B, and C
- wheel wells
- side details
- lights
- fuel caps

Draw other details you see (or want—hey, it's *your* drawing!). Add shading.

Remember:
- *Start out lightly!*
- *Turn your drawing as you work. Use a piece of scrap paper to keep your hand off finished parts.*
- *While your pencil is sharp, go over fine details and make lines cleaner. As it gets duller, add shading.*
- *Clean up any smudges with your eraser. Make sure all final lines are crisp and sharp.*
- *When you see it coming, this vehicle has the right of way.*

Uncle Bill's Ratty Old Pickup

*Before you start, look carefully at your **reference material** (for now, my finished drawing).*

Draw the ground line. Using the wheel diagram above, draw the wheels the correct distance apart. Draw the basic body lines.

Complete the overall shape of the wreck.

Add:
- windows
- wheel wells
- side trim
- door handle
- exhaust system

Draw other details you see (or want—hey, it's *your* drawing!). Add shading.

Remember:
- *Start out lightly!*
- *Turn your drawing as you work. Use a piece of scrap paper to keep your hand off finished parts. Uncle Bill will be grateful.*
- *While your pencil is sharp, go over fine details and make lines cleaner. As it gets duller, add shading.*

Uncle Bill thinks of this ratty, clunky, smoking old pickup truck as family. Which it is, sort of. Unfortunately.

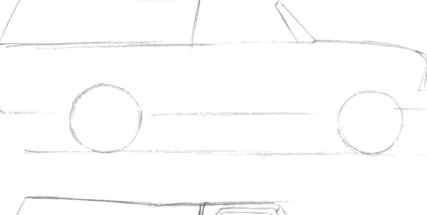

Always start out *lightly!*

But think of the possibilities!

If…Uncle Bill takes it into the garage, gets out his welding torch, chops and channels it, adds some aircraft hydraulics… suddenly it's a screaming lowrider street rod!

Or maybe he installs a few dozen extra shock absorbers, raises the whole thing so high you need a stepladder to get in, then drops in an engine like something from Cape Canaveral.

Then again, maybe Uncle Bill's going to light up a quarter mile drag strip with a nitro-burning funny car so powerful it needs extra wheels behind to keep it from flipping over backward!

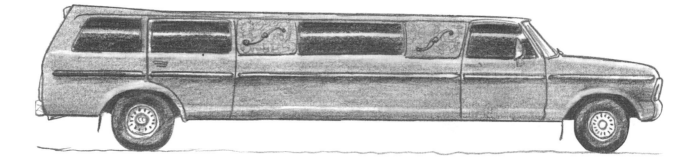

It may turn out that Uncle Bill is a very practical sort, saving to turn his ratty ol' pickup into a classy limo…

…then again, perhaps he lives a secret life as a undercover defender of democracy. He just wants you to think it's a ratty ol' pickup, when in fact it's a high-tech Scud-buster!

Perhaps you don't have an Uncle Bill.

(Do you have a bus driver?)

Part Three

Draw a car from an angle

In the *next few pages, you'll look closely at a car from an angle. You'll learn how to draw the basic body parts and lines that shape the car—step by step.*

Dodge Stratus (again!)

Drawing a car from an angle is more complicated than drawing it from the side. Always use *reference material.*

For this drawing, your reference material will be this finished drawing (my reference material for this drawing was a magazine advertisement.)

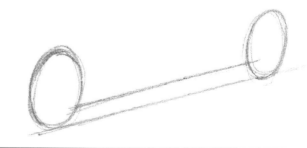

When you draw a car from an angle, the ground line will usually be at an angle. Draw the ground line.

Notice how perspective makes the rear wheel smaller than the front.

Draw ovals (ellipses) for the wheels. Take care to space them properly.

Add the line of the bottom of the car.

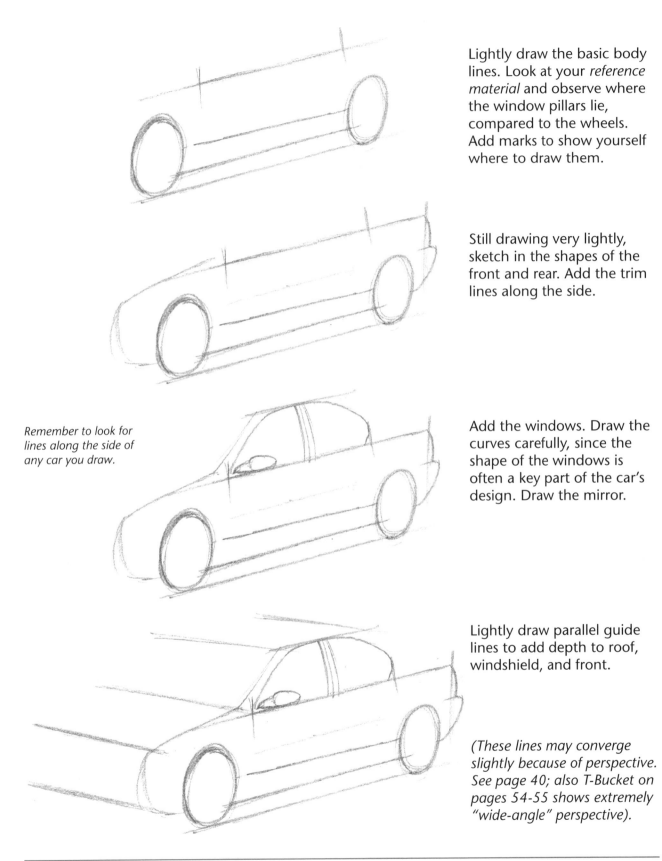

Lightly draw the basic body lines. Look at your *reference material* and observe where the window pillars lie, compared to the wheels. Add marks to show yourself where to draw them.

Still drawing very lightly, sketch in the shapes of the front and rear. Add the trim lines along the side.

Remember to look for lines along the side of any car you draw.

Add the windows. Draw the curves carefully, since the shape of the windows is often a key part of the car's design. Draw the mirror.

Lightly draw parallel guide lines to add depth to roof, windshield, and front.

(These lines may converge slightly because of perspective. See page 40; also T-Bucket on pages 54-55 shows extremely "wide-angle" perspective).

Draw a curved line to form the contour of the roof and the windshield.

Look carefully at your *reference material,* and draw guide lines to form the front.

You may be able to draw the front without first drawing guide lines. I find, though, that it's easy to get it wrong without the guide—especially when the front curves, as it does here.

Add the rear deck and C-pillar.

C-pillar

Draw headlights and other details. Erase guide lines you no longer need.

Always start out *lightly!*

Look for light and dark areas in your *reference material*. (Generally, the wheel wells are the darkest part.)

Using a soft pencil, add shading.

If you have a tortillon (see page 4) for blending, you can use it (you can also use a small wad of paper or even your finger to make the shading smoother).

With a sharp pencil (HB is better than 2B or 3B), carefully draw the details of the wheels. Turn your paper to make it easier. Put scrap paper between your hand and the drawing to avoid smudging it.

To finish, go over all lines with a sharp pencil (preferably HB), and add any remaining details: door seams, handles, windshield wipers, headlight details….

Don't forget the cast shadow!

All done!
Super Stratus!

About Perspective

Perspective comes into play every time you draw a car from an angle.

Sometimes—as in the case of this 1959 Cadillac—the effects are very noticeable. If you draw the basic body lines, you'll see they extend back to a single *vanishing point.**

The wide-angle lens on the camera makes this photograph more dynamic.

Here you can see a Mercedes-Benz sport utility vehicle with a similar "wide-angle" view. This customized vehicle appeared in a certain dinosaur movie. Because of the dramatic wide-angle view, it looks as though it's ready to leap into action, perhaps chasing a *Pachycephalosaurus.***

The basic lines converge (get closer together) as they go toward the background.

With a telephoto lens, this advertising photo gives a different impression: the vehicle looks much less wild.

(Which is probably just as well; most people don't buy cars to chase dinosaurs.)

* for more on perspective, see *Learn To Draw 3-D*

** for more on Pachycephalosaurus, see *Draw Dinosaurs*

Part Four

Draw more cars from an angle

In the next few pages, you'll look at different cars from different angles. Following the basic approach laid out in Part Three, explore their similarities and differences, in design and form, and in the viewpoints from which you see them.

Surprise!

The cars pictured here don't appear in Part Four! Use them as reference material, and you can draw them using what you learned in Part Three.

BMW Z3

*Before you start, look carefully at your **reference material** (for now, my finished drawing).*

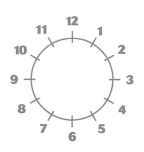

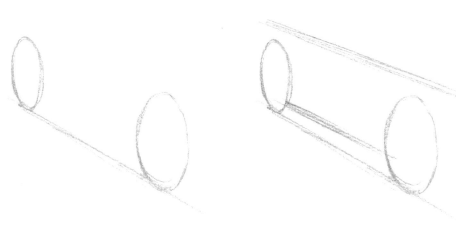

What are the angles formed by the wheels, on the side, and—if you could see them—the two front wheels? Compare these basic angles with the clock face if you need to. Pay special attention to perspective: how much do the lines converge toward the background? How much smaller is the rear wheel?

Draw the side ground line and the wheels. Add the basic body lines.

Draw lines to show depth, on the rear deck, front, and windshield. Look at the clock face if you find the angles confusing. Add the distinctive curves of the hood.

With all these lines in place, add more details.

Always start out *lightly!*

Finishing the drawing takes the most effort, so make sure you're happy with your drawing so far.

Look at it in a mirror, or hold it up to the light and look at it through the back of the paper. Does everything look correct, forward and backward? If not, what can you fix to make the drawing look better? Start over if you need to.

When you're satisfied with the angles and proportions, add more details. Add details while your pencil is sharp.

Add shading when your pencil is dull. If you have more than one pencil, use a softer one (3B) for shading and a harder one (HB) for details.

Look again at the final drawing. Add any details you've missed.

Remember:
- *Start out lightly!*
- *Turn your drawing as you work. Use a piece of scrap paper to keep your hand off finished parts.*
- *While your pencil is sharp, go over fine details and make lines cleaner. As it gets duller, add shading.*
- *Clean up any smudges with your eraser. Make sure all final lines are crisp and sharp.*

Stand back and admire your creation!

Ruf CTR-2

*Before you start, look carefully at your **reference material** (for now, my finished drawing).*

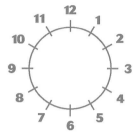

What are the angles formed by the wheels, on the side, and—if you could see them—the two front wheels? Compare these basic angles with the clock face if you need to. Pay special attention to perspective: how much do the lines converge toward the background? How much smaller is the rear wheel?

Draw the ground line, the wheels and the bottom body line.

Draw guide lines for adding depth. Notice how they converge toward a distant vanishing point, because of perspective.

Add curved lines for the fender and roof. Draw the other headlight, the window pillars and the rear view mirror.

When is a Porsche not a Porsche? When it's a Ruf, so completely altered that it actually has a new serial number. Built with a Porsche body shell, this Ruf costs slightly more than a Lamborghini Diablo Roadster. It goes from 0-60 MPH in 3.6 seconds. Which is fast.

***Extremely** fast.*

Always start out *lightly!*

Finishing the drawing takes the most effort, so make sure you're happy with your drawing so far.

Look at it in a mirror, or hold it up to the light and look at it through the back of the paper. Does everything look correct, forward and backward? If not, what can you fix to make the drawing look better? Start over if you need to.

When you're satisfied with the angles and proportions, add more details. Add details while your pencil is sharp.

Add shading when your pencil is dull. If you have more than one pencil, use a softer one (3B) for shading and a harder one (HB) for details.

Look again at the final drawing. Add any details you've missed.

Remember:
- *Start out lightly!*
- *Turn your drawing as you work. Use a piece of scrap paper to keep your hand off finished parts.*
- *While your pencil is sharp, go over fine details and make lines cleaner. As it gets duller, add shading.*
- *Clean up any smudges with your eraser. Make sure all final lines are crisp and sharp.*

Stand back and admire your creation!

Dodge Durango

*Before you start, look carefully at your **reference material** (for now, my finished drawing).*

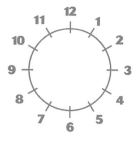

What angles are formed by the wheels, on the side and in the front? Compare these basic angles with the clock face if you need to. Pay special attention to perspective: how much do the lines converge toward the background? How much smaller is the rear wheel?

Draw the ground line, the wheels and the basic body lines.

Draw lines showing depth on the front of the car and windshield. Again, look at the clock face if you find the angles confusing.

Add the curves of the hood, then carefully draw the curves of the front grill and headlights. Observe the amount of clearance in the wheel wells. Draw these. Add the bottom of door lines.

Always start out *lightly!*

Finishing the drawing takes the most effort, so make sure you're happy with your drawing so far.

Look at it in a mirror, or hold it up to the light and look at it through the back of the paper. Does everything look correct, forward and backward? If not, what can you fix to make the drawing look better? Start over if you need to.

When you're satisfied with the angles and proportions, add more details. Add details while your pencil is sharp.

Add shading when your pencil is dull. If you have more than one pencil, use a softer one (3B) for shading and a harder one (HB) for details.

Look again at the final drawing. Add any details you've missed.

Remember:
- *Start out lightly!*
- *Turn your drawing as you work. Use a piece of scrap paper to keep your hand off finished parts.*
- *While your pencil is sharp, go over fine details and make lines cleaner. As it gets duller, add shading.*
- *Clean up any smudges with your eraser. Make sure all final lines are crisp and sharp.*

Stand back and admire your creation!

Plymouth Prowler

*Before you start, look carefully at your **reference material** (for now, my finished drawing).*

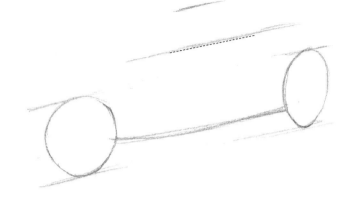

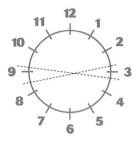

What are the angles formed by the wheels on the side, and in the front? Compare these basic angles with the clock face if you need to. Pay special attention to perspective: how much do the lines converge toward the background? How much smaller is the rear wheel?

Draw the ground line, the wheels and the basic body lines.

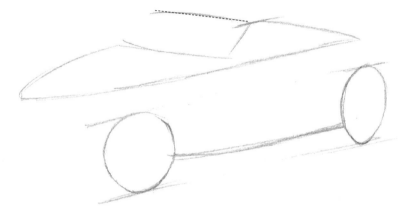

Draw the curved lines that form the pointed front of the car. Add the windshield and back body line. Again, look at the clock face if you find the angles confusing.

Add the other front wheel, the two-part bumper and fenders.

Always start out *lightly!*

Finishing the drawing takes the most effort, so make sure you're happy with your drawing so far.

Look at it in a mirror, or hold it up to the light and look at it through the back of the paper. Does everything look correct, forward and backward? If not, what can you fix to make the drawing look better? Start over if you need to.

When you're satisfied with the angles and proportions, add more details. Add details while your pencil is sharp.

Add shading when your pencil is dull. If you have more than one pencil, use a softer one (3B) for shading and a harder one (HB) for details.

Look again at the final drawing. Add any details you've missed.

Remember:
- *Start out lightly!*
- *Turn your drawing as you work. Use a piece of scrap paper to keep your hand off finished parts.*
- *While your pencil is sharp, go over fine details and make lines cleaner. As it gets duller, add shading.*
- *Clean up any smudges with your eraser. Make sure all final lines are crisp and sharp.*

Stand back and admire your creation!

Formula 1 Racer

*Before you start, look carefully at your **reference material** (for now, my finished drawing).*

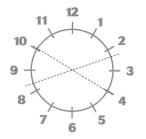

What angles do the wheels form, on one side, and between the two front wheels? Compare these basic angles with the clock face if you need to. Pay special attention to perspective: how much do the lines converge toward the background? How much smaller is the rear wheel?

Draw the ground lines, the wheels, the basic body lines, and in this case the top of the air scoop.

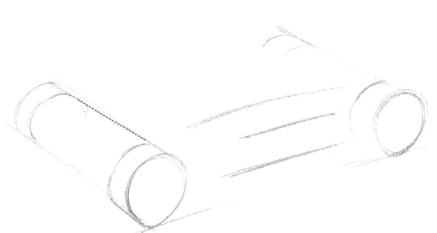

Draw depth guide lines to find the correct placement of the other wheels. Again, look at the clock face if you find the angles confusing.

cowling

Add the rounded point of the front of the car, the rim of the cockpit, and the cowling that covers the engine.

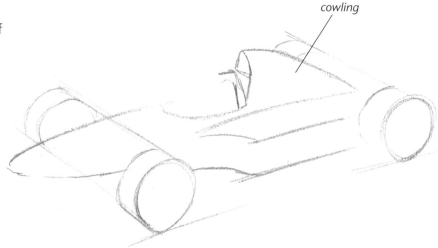

Always start out *lightly!*

Finishing the drawing takes the most effort, so make sure you're happy with your drawing so far.

Look at it in a mirror, or hold it up to the light and look at it through the back of the paper. Does everything look correct, forward and backward? If not, what can you fix to make the drawing look better? Start over if you need to.

When you're satisfied with the angles and proportions, add more details. Add details while your pencil is sharp.

Add shading when your pencil is dull. If you have more than one pencil, use a softer one (3B) for shading and a harder one (HB) for details.

Look again at the final drawing. Add any details you've missed.

Remember:
- *Start out lightly!*
- *Turn your drawing as you work. Use a piece of scrap paper to keep your hand off finished parts.*
- *While your pencil is sharp, go over fine details and make lines cleaner. As it gets duller, add shading.*
- *Clean up any smudges with your eraser. Make sure all final lines are crisp and sharp.*

Stand back and admire your creation!

1957 Chevy

Before you start, look carefully at your reference material (for now, my finished drawing).

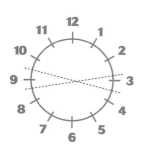

What angles are formed between the wheels on the side, and—if you could see it—between the two front wheels? Compare these basic angles with the clock face if you need to. Pay special attention to perspective: how much do the lines converge toward the background? How much smaller is the rear wheel?

Draw the ground lines, the wheels, and the basic body lines.

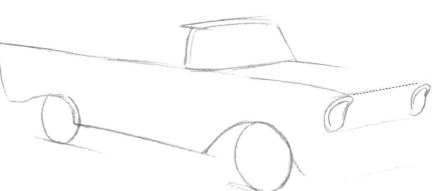

Draw lines showing depth on the front of the car and windshield. Look at the clock face if you find the angles confusing. Add the distinctive headlights, rear end line and flaring wheel wells.

Add the curves of the windshield, side trim, front bumper, and other details you see.

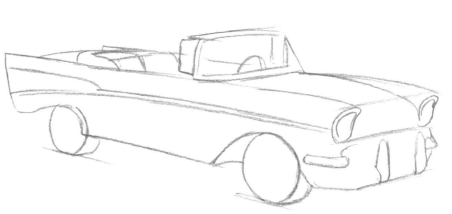

Always start out *lightly!*

Finishing the drawing takes the most effort, so make sure you're happy with your drawing so far.

Look at it in a mirror, or hold it up to the light and look at it through the back of the paper. Does everything look correct, forward and backward? If not, what can you fix to make the drawing look better? Start over if you need to.

When you're satisfied with the angles and proportions, add more details. Add details while your pencil is sharp.

Add shading when your pencil is dull. If you have more than one pencil, use a softer one (3B) for shading and a harder one (HB) for details.

Look again at the final drawing. Add any details you've missed.

Remember:
- *Start out lightly!*
- *Turn your drawing as you work. Use a piece of scrap paper to keep your hand off finished parts.*
- *While your pencil is sharp, go over fine details and make lines cleaner. As it gets duller, add shading.*
- *Clean up any smudges with your eraser. Make sure all final lines are crisp and sharp.*

Stand back and admire your creation!

T Bucket Street Rod

*Before you start, look carefully at your **reference material** (for now, my finished drawing).*

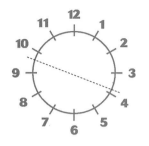

What are the angles formed by the wheels, on one side, and by the two front wheels? Compare these basic angles with the clock face if you need to. Pay special attention to perspective: how much do the lines converge toward the background?

Compare basic body lines with the clock face to be sure they run at the correct angle.

Draw the side wheels, and the basic body lines.

Draw lines for the windshield, and to show depth on the side, front, and top of the car. Draw guide lines to find the correct placement of the other front wheel. Add additional ellipses to add depth to the wheels.

Always start out *lightly!*

Finishing the drawing takes the most effort, so make sure you're happy with your drawing so far.

Look at it in a mirror, or hold it up to the light and look at it through the back of the paper. Does everything look correct, forward and backward? If not, what can you fix to make the drawing look better? Start over if you need to.

When you're satisfied with the angles and proportions, add more details. Add details while your pencil is sharp.

Add shading when your pencil is dull. If you have more than one pencil, use a softer one (3B) for shading and a harder one (HB) for details.

Look again at the final drawing. Add any details you've missed.

Remember:
- *Start out lightly!*
- *Turn your drawing as you work. Use a piece of scrap paper to keep your hand off finished parts.*
- *While your pencil is sharp, go over fine details and make lines cleaner. As it gets duller, add shading.*
- *Clean up any smudges with your eraser. Make sure all final lines are crisp and sharp.*

Stand back and admire your creation!

Funny Car

*Before you start, look carefully at your **reference material** (for now, my finished drawing).*

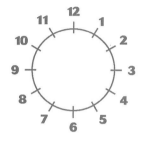

What angles are formed by the wheels, on one side, and by the two front wheels? In this case, almost none. Because this viewpoint is almost at ground level, the lines go practically straight out to the side (and all the wheels appear at the same level as well). Look at how big that rear wheel is!

Draw the ground line and the wheels.

Notice how the bottom of the car lines up with the bottom of the front wheel, but the middle of the rear wheel? Draw the body lines.

Add depth lines on the front of the car and windshield.

Draw the fenders overlapping the wheels.

A funny car is designed to race on a 1/4-mile drag strip. Its engine may produce 5,000 horsepower. In the short time it runs, it consumes 15 gallons of nitromethane fuel at $18 per gallon.

Funny Car

The rear spoiler is made of aluminum and magnesium and capable of producing 5,000 pounds of downward force on the rear tires.

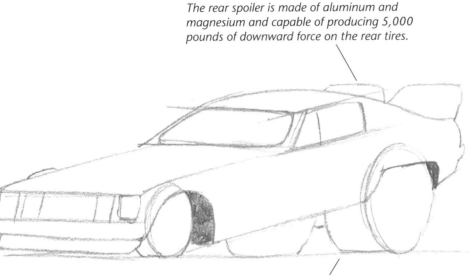

The rear "slicks" are 18 inches wide, nearly ten feet in circumference, and inflated with only four pounds pressure!

Finishing the drawing takes the most effort, so make sure you're happy with your drawing so far.

Look at it in a mirror, or hold it up to the light and look at it through the back of the paper. Does everything look correct, forward and backward? If not, what can you fix to make the drawing look better? Start over if you need to.

When you're satisfied with the angles and proportions, add more details. Add details while your pencil is sharp.

Add shading when your pencil is dull. If you have more than one pencil, use a softer one (3B) for shading and a harder one (HB) for details.

Look again at the final drawing. Add any details you've missed.

Remember:

- *Start out lightly!*
- *Turn your drawing as you work. Use a piece of scrap paper to keep your hand off finished parts.*
- *While your pencil is sharp, go over fine details and make lines cleaner. As it gets duller, add shading.*
- *Clean up any smudges with your eraser. Make sure all final lines are crisp and sharp.*

Stand back and admire your creation!

The Gallery

Here's a weird collection of vehicles to give you ideas. Try drawing them!

A. *Ford Model T - 1920s.*

B. *1933 Ford Model Y - British (note mirror on right side)*

C. *1950s dream car, designed to resemble jet aircraft.*

D. *1,000,000th Volkswagen "Beetle" rolled off the assembly line in 1955*

E. *Exotic car called Isdera from an unusual angle, showing the slope of its side windows and size of its windshield.*

A

B

C

D

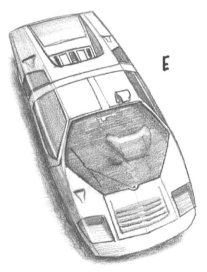

E

Always start out *lightly!*

F

G

F. A concept car called the Ethos, shown at a car show in the hope of selling the design to a car manufacturer.

G A prototype (huge!) minivan that I don't think ever made it into production…

H. Lamborghini Countache – compressed perspective from photo (on the side of a model box!) taken with a telephoto lens.

I. Landrover from a similar angle – interesting comparison to the Lamborghini!

J. Mazda racing prototype. I used to own one of these…

H

I

…just kidding!

J

Tips and Tricks: Some Basics

Use reference material: find pictures in magazines or books when you can't look at actual cars. Look at details, light and dark areas, and the effects of perspective from the camera angle.

Turn your paper as you draw to take advantage of the point of your pencil, and the natural way your hand draws curves.

Put scrap paper under your hand to keep from smearing parts of the drawing you've already finished.

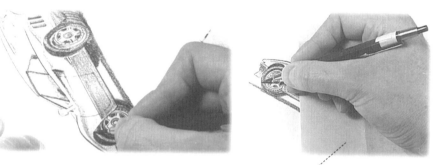

Use your eraser to create highlights and to clean up any smudged areas.

Protective paper keeps drawing clean

Kneadable eraser can be pinched into a point for close work

Use different pencils. Pencils range from 6B (softest and darkest) to 9H (hardest). A normal 2B pencil works well for sketching and shading, but a harder HB makes crisper lines – I even use a 5H, which is very hard, for very fine details.

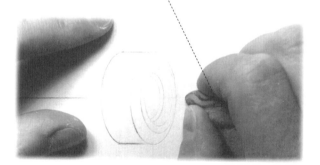

For very smooth shading, use a soft pencil and a *tortillon* (see page 4), a wound-up paper stick made for blending pastels.

Tips and Tricks: Making Wheels Round

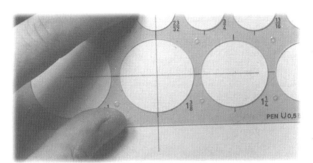

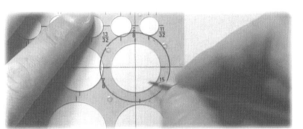

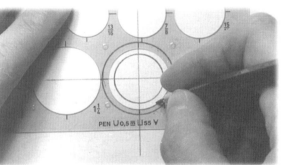

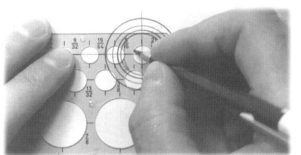

"Aren't wheels always round?" you ask. No, in fact, they're only round when you look at them in exactly the right way. Otherwise they're elliptical (see next page). Round wheels can be both fun and frustrating to draw.

If you want perfect circles, you might want to try a transparent circle template. Make a horizontal and vertical line, then align them with the marks on the template. Then draw circle after circle, using different size holes in the template.

When you start looking at wheel (or hub cap) designs, you'll find a bewildering variety. Most are divided into five spokes or holes. But some have four, some have six, some have none, some have seven, or nine, or eleven, or...well, *count them for yourself!*

The more you look, the more you'll see. Have fun hunting for and drawing cool wheels!

Tips and Tricks: Wheels from an Angle

Although I have a template for ellipses, I don't use it. I prefer to draw freehand.

These photos show how the ellipses go together to make a wheel from an angle.

Starting with a horizontal and vertical line, draw one ellipse. Next, slide the template along the horizontal line, and draw part of a second ellipse, the same size as the first.

Use a ruler to connect them to make the top and bottom of the tire. Now slide the template to the right, slightly beyond the first vertical line, and make a smaller ellipse.

Though you don't have to, you can add another, still smaller ellipse on the same vertical axis. Then slide the template left to the first vertical line for the rim of the wheel.

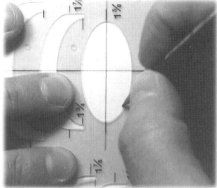
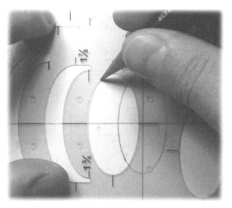

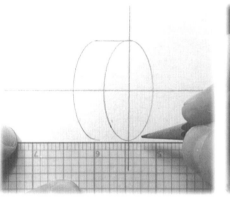
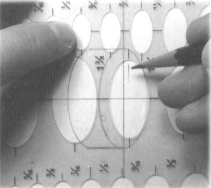

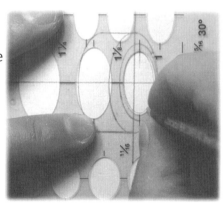
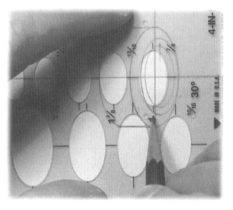

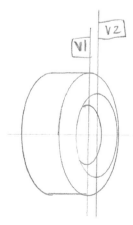

V1=vertical axis used for largest and smallest ellipse

V2=vertical axis used for smallest ellipse

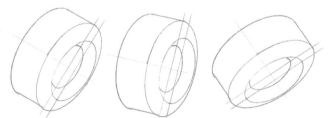

When viewing wheels from above, rotate the axes. Note that they remain perpendicular to each other.

Tips and Tricks: Imagination!

Here's my favorite drawing tip: use your imagination!

A 30-year-old Ford parked behind a warehouse (may not even run) suddenly takes to the air as it crashes over rugged terrain!

A pathetic-looking 1955 Fiat becomes a Lamborghini-stomping terror!

How about a cartoon based on a radio-controlled model?

Imagination: you've got it. Use it!

Learn about other books in
this series online at
www.drawbooks.com!

DRAW
DESERT *Animals*

by

Doug DuBosque

PEEL productions, inc.

For my wife,
friend,
patient editor,
and child of the desert,
Susan Joyce DuBosque

−D.D.

Addax Antelope. 6
Arabian Oryx 8
Arabian Toad-headed Agamid. 10
Bactrian Camel 12
Camel Spider. 14
Caracal Lynx 16
Desert Cottontail 18
Desert Tortoise 20
Diamondback Rattlesnake. 22
Dromedary 24
Egyptian Slit-faced Bat 26
Elf Owl 28
Fat Sand Rat. 30
Fennec Fox 32
Gila Monster. 34
Horned Toad 35
Jerboa 36
Lanner Falcon 38
Pallas's Cat. 40
Roadrunner. 42
Sandgrouse. 44
Scarab Beetle 45
Scorpion. 46
Sidewinder 48
Spotted Skunk. 50
Tarantula 52
Thorny Devil. 54
Trapdoor Spider. 56
Vicuña. 58
Drawing Tips. 60
Saving Your Work. 62

 # A few thoughts before you start...

Deserts – cool!

The deserts, or dry places, of the world hold plenty of surprises for those who explore them. Let's do that with a pencil!

Draw Desert Animals shows you how to draw fascinating creatures, step by step. You may find some of the drawings quite easy. Others will be challenges.

What do you need?

- **PENCIL**
  (2B or 3B will work well)
- **PENCIL SHARPENER**
- **ERASER**
  (kneadable works best)
- **PAPER**
  (test of quality: how easily can you erase on it?)
- **PLACE TO DRAW**
  Good light, no distractions.

What do you **really** need?

- **POSITIVE ATTITUDE**
  Forget *"I can't."*
  Say, "I'm learning." "I'm figuring this out." "I did this part well; now I'm going to work on the harder part...."

"...and I'm not stopping *until I get it RIGHT!*"

Think of drawing in three stages.
First

LOOK carefully at the desert animal you wish to draw! See the shapes and pieces and how they fit together.

Then, **lightly sketch** the shapes in the right place.

When you sketch lightly, you can easily correct any mistakes before they ruin your drawing.

Second

Make sure you have all the shapes and pieces in the right place:

- **adjust** lines
- **redraw** pieces that don't look right
- **erase** sketch lines you no longer need.

Third

Spend as much time as you need to make your drawing jump off the page:

- **darken** lines at emphasis points: joints, feet, points of claws, horns, spikes, eyes...
- add **fur, feathers,** or **scales...**
- add **shading...**
- **clean up** any smudges with your eraser...
- **Date and save** your drawing in a portfolio (see p.62).

Just so you know...

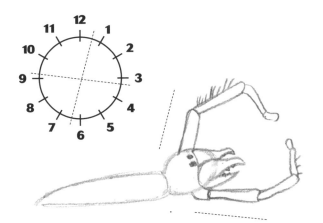

CLOCK FACES appear from time to time. Use them as a reference to see the tilt of ovals, legs, and other angles in the drawing.

LOOK signs point out visual elements of the drawing–in this example, where one part overlaps another.

pedipalps

LABELS will help you identify the parts of the animal mentioned in the text.

And now, let's

DRAW DESERT Animals...

Addax antelope

Addax nasomaculatus

Africa. Height: .9 – 1.2 m (3 – 4 ft)

An addax never drinks, getting all the moisture it needs from its food. Its large, wide-spreading hooves are adapted to walking on soft sand. Addax are nomads, traveling in herds of 20 to 200. They seem to have a special ability to locate the patches of desert vegetation that suddenly sprout after a downpour. Color varies from animal to animal, but they all have a patch of dark brown hair on the forehead.

1) Begin the addax by lightly sketching two ovals. Compare the tilt of the back leg oval to the clock face. Draw lines to connect the ovals, top and bottom.

2) Sketch a circle for the head, centered at the top of the shoulder. Sketch a smaller circle for the nose and mouth. Add ears.

   Draw jagged lines to connect the head to the body.

3) Draw the eyes–**look** at the way one sits on the edge of the circle, and one doesn't. Add curved guide lines for the facial pattern.

   Sketch small, light circles for the leg joints. Draw the front and rear legs. Notice how the tilt of the oval shows you the angle of the top of the rear leg.

   Add the tail.

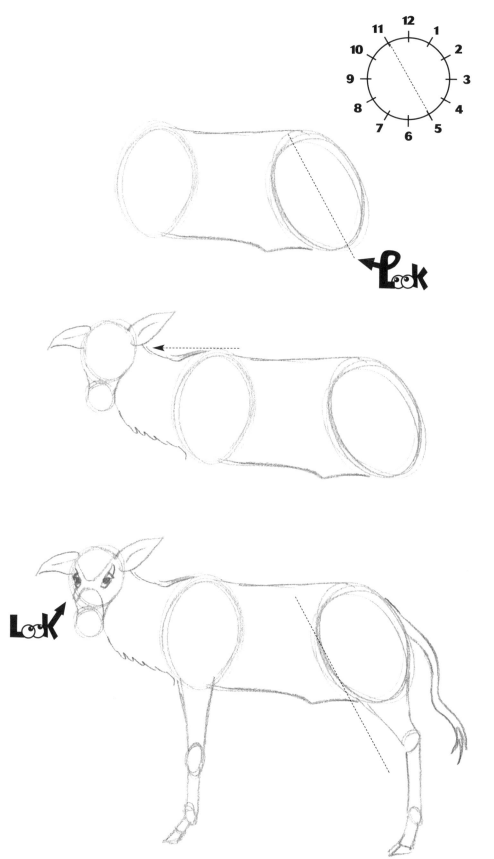

4) Lightly draw the graceful, spiralling horns. Once you have them right, begin to add small curved lines for the ridges on them. Add nostrils and the mouth. Shade the darker area of the face and ear.

Lightly sketch the joints and limbs of the other two legs. Note where each line intersects the overlapping lines of the body or leg.

Carefully erase "leftover" ovals before moving to the final step. If they're too dark—as in this example—you may want to start again, using what you've learned to make the second drawing even better.

5. Because the addax is light colored, you don't need to shade the whole body. Make your pencil strokes get lighter toward highlight areas. In the lightest areas, you don't need to shade at all.

Starting with the darkest areas of the body, add light, short pencil strokes for fur. Leave the belly and side lighter.

Clean up any smudges with your eraser. Put today's date on your drawing and save it in your portfolio!

Draw Desert Animals   **7**

Arabian Oryx

Oryx leucoryx
SE Saudi Arabia.
Size: 2 m (6½ ft) long

The only oryx found outside Africa, this small, rare animal travels widely in extreme desert conditions to find grass and shrubs to eat. It shelters from the sun by scraping a hollow under a bush or on the side of a sand dune. This oryx has been over hunted for its hide, meat and horns. Protected by law, it may be extinct in the wild (the last wild one seen was in 1972). It lives in captivity, though, and hopefully can be reintroduced to its native habitat.

1. This drawing starts out with three ovals tilting in all different directions. The tilt of the ovals will capture the way the animal stands, or moves. The ovals also remind you of the underlying anatomy as you draw. Draw the ovals.

2. Notice the height of the head in relation to the shoulder (just a little bit above). Make a light circle for the head, a smaller one for the nose, and lines to connect them. Add the eye, halfway up the head circle and off to the left. Draw the ears. Draw a line to connect the head with the top of the body, and continue your line along the top—connecting all body ovals. Add the swishing tail. Draw the bottom of the neck.

3. Starting with small circles for the joints, draw the two closest legs. Note the angles of the rear leg.

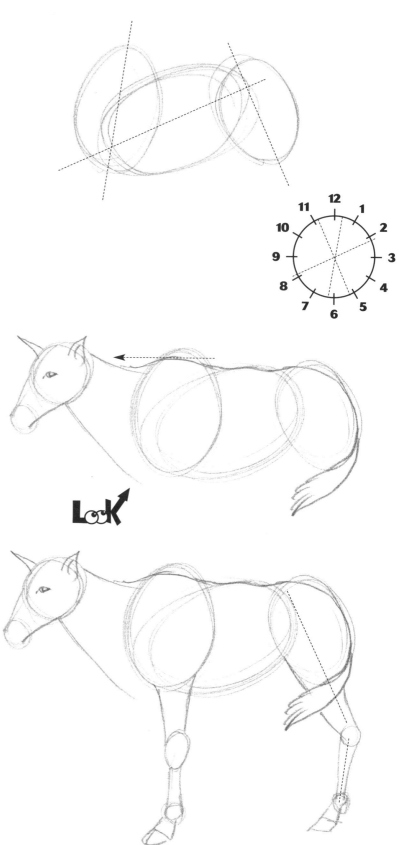

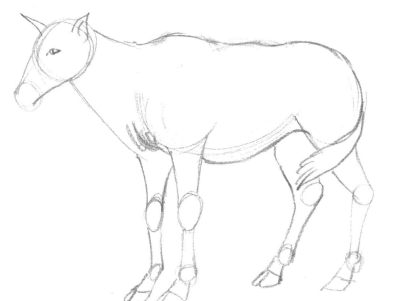

4. Starting with light circles for the joints, draw the other two legs. Notice how the bottom of the neck meets the front leg. Connect the belly and the rear leg.

5. Draw the long, curved horns–lightly at first *(of course!)*.

A couple of hints:

When drawing the horns, turn the paper so that the curve comes naturally. If you're left handed, you may need to turn your paper sideways to make the curve comfortable.

To keep from smudging, place a piece of clean paper over the part you've already drawn. Rest the heel of your hand on this. Keep the paper still, or it might smudge the drawing underneath.

Add the mouth and nose. Carefully shade the face to make the facial patterns.

6. Using short pencil strokes, continue shading the body. Pay attention to the direction of the lines and their darkness. Leave the belly light. Darken the hooves and add a little bit of grass. Make a couple of lines for distant sand dunes behind the oryx.

Orsome Oryx! Clean up any smudges with your eraser, put today's date on your drawing and save it in your portfolio!

Draw Desert Animals   **9**

Arabian Toad-Headed Agamid

Phrynocephalus nejdensis

SW Asia. Size: up to 12.5 cm (5 in)

This burrowing lizard digs short tunnels for shelter. It can also bury itself in sand by wriggling from side to side. It eats mainly insects but also some flowers and leaves. If alarmed, it will stand high on its legs, and roll and unroll its tail; this is its defensive posture.

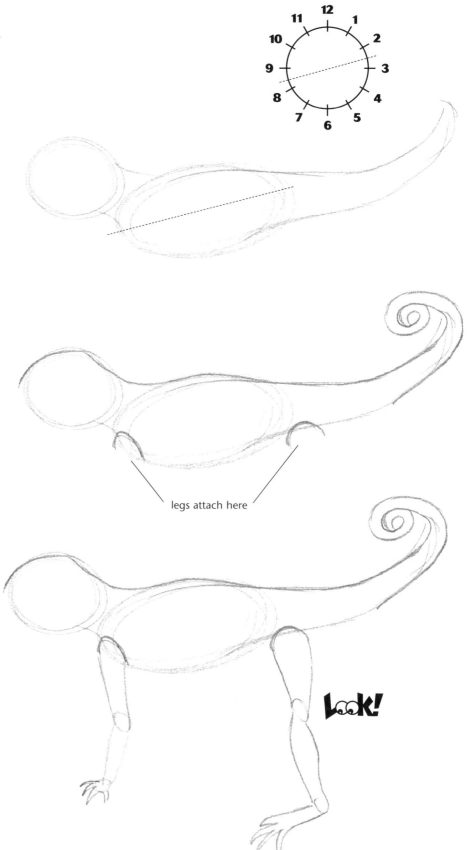

legs attach here

Look!

1. Begin your drawing by lightly sketching the tilted horizontal oval of the body. Compare the tilt of the oval to the clock face: this forward angle helps convey the defensive posture. To the oval, add gently curving lines for the tail. At the other end, draw a rounder oval for the head, and connect it to the body with two short lines for the neck.

2. Draw one smooth line over the top of the head, neck, and back, connecting the ovals and the tail. Draw small curves to locate the attachment points for the legs. Carefully add the spiralling tip of the tail.

3. As always when drawing limbs, use small, light circles to mark the joints. Add curved lines to finish the legs. Notice the distinct curves in the rear leg. Draw the feet.

right rear leg

Refine the details before adding shading and finishing touches.

4. Draw the tilted eye with its thick eyebrow above. Add the mouth, swooping down and back into the jaw line. Draw the small visible parts of the two legs on the far side of the lizard. Refine the bottom of the neck, belly, and tail, adding the curved flaps just behind the rear leg.

If your drawing looks good to you, continue. Otherwise, save it as a practice sketch, putting it in your portfolio with today's date.

5. To complete our friend the toad head, lightly outline the stripes on the legs and tail, and the spots on the back. Carefully shade from one end to the other and back again, looking for any details you missed. Add the *cast shadow* beneath.

Go over the outline with a sharpened pencil. Clean up any smudges with your eraser.

Toadally cool, dude! Put today's date on your drawing and save it in your portfolio!

Draw Desert Animals **11**

Bactrian camel

Camelus ferus

Central Asia, Northern Africa, Middle East. Size: 3m (10) long, 2m (7 ft) high at shoulder

Bactrian camels have two humps–think of the letter B turned on its side. The humps store fat to help them survive when food is scarce. They eat grass, and foliage of bushes and trees. Their long, shaggy hair keeps them warm in the winter, but they shed it in the summer. They move slowly with a rolling gait, able to lift two legs on the same side at the same time.

1. Start out by lightly sketching the large, slightly tilted oval of the body. *Intersecting* it, draw the small, narrow oval of the hip. Notice how it tilts. Add a U shape for the shaggy front leg, dropping down below the body.

2. Add two humps on the back. Sketch a circle for the head. Where does it lie in relation to the first oval you drew? Add a short line connecting it to the back, and draw a long, shaggy, U shape for the neck. Draw the tail.

3. Three-fourths of the way up the head, draw a horizontal line. Fill in, above the line, with spiked hair. *(Nice hair!)*. Halfway up the head, draw an ear on either side. Level with the top of the ears, draw the nostrils. Level with the bottom of the ears, draw the top of the mouth. Add more lines on the nose and mouth.

   Draw the eyes between the nostrils and ears, and use short pencil strokes to make the shaggy hair on the face and neck.

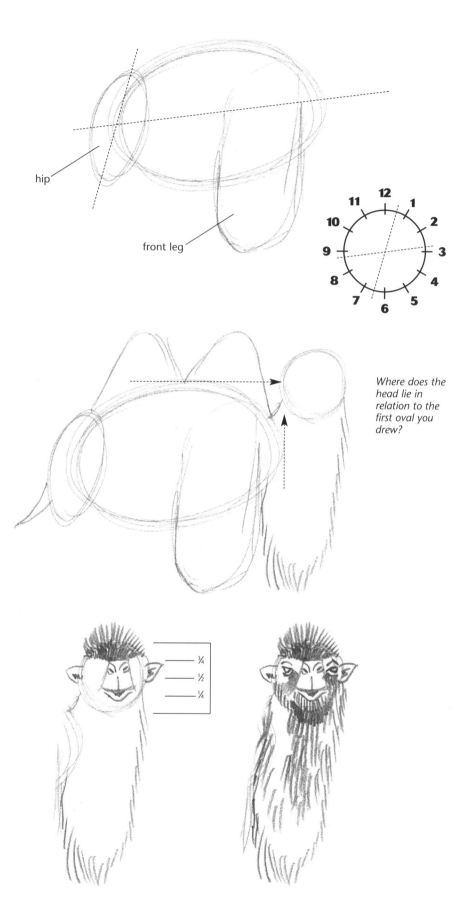

Where does the head lie in relation to the first oval you drew?

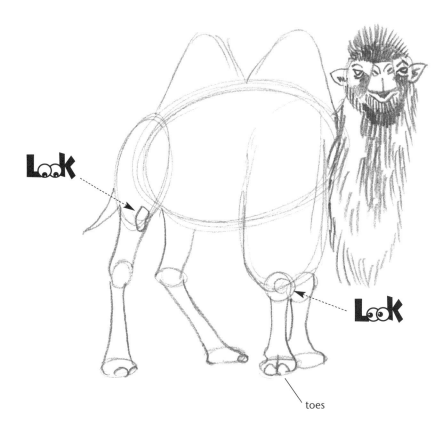

Look

Look

toes

4. At the bottom of the front leg U, draw small ovals for the leg joints. Draw wide, low ovals for the hooves, and curving lines connecting them to the top part of the leg. Notice how one leg overlaps part of the other. Add toes.

   Using similar ovals and lines, complete the rear legs. Add the tail.

   Look: *where the camel kneels, thick callus builds up on the legs. On your body, the calluses on the rear leg would be on your knees; the ones in front on the back of your wrists.*

5. Finish your drawing by carefully adding short pencil strokes to shade the body and add texture.

   Take your time. Which parts are darkest? Which are lightest? What direction do the lines run on each part of the body? You'll improve quickly if you get in the habit of asking these questions often as you draw.

   Add a small *cast shadow* under the camel. Clean up any smudges with your eraser.

   Oh, by the way, camels spit. Does your camel look like it's spitting at you? Whether or not, put today's date on your drawing and save it in your portfolio!

Draw Desert Animals   **13**

Camel spider (Wind scorpion)

Solifugida, or *Solipugida*

Africa, Orient, America, Southern Spain. Size: up to 15 cm (6 in) span across outstretched legs

These hairy, fast-moving *arachnids* (spider relatives) hunt for insects at night, sometimes eating lizards, small mammals and birds. They have strong *chelicerae* (that's what an arachnid's "jaws" are called), with which they chop, squash and chew the victim, which ends up a formless lump. They may move as fast as 16 km/h (10 mph). Also known as wind scorpions or sun spiders, they like the drier parts of the desert and stay away from oases.

Yikes! This one looks complicated! Start with the simplest shapes, and add one piece at a time...

1. Sketch the two main body parts: one long and bullet-shaped; the other almost a circle.

2. Add two dots for eyes. Draw the huge jaw on the closer side of the head, and the little bit of jaw visible on the other side.

3. Just behind the jaw, add the first segment of the first *pedipalp* (feeler: like legs but without claws), then the next segment.

4. Add remaining segments, and four visible segments of the other pedipalp.

5. Draw the second set of feeler legs. Notice how they go *under* the first set, adding *depth* to your drawing (**look**).

6. The third set of legs supports the spider. These walking legs go straight out to the side. Draw them thicker, and stronger.

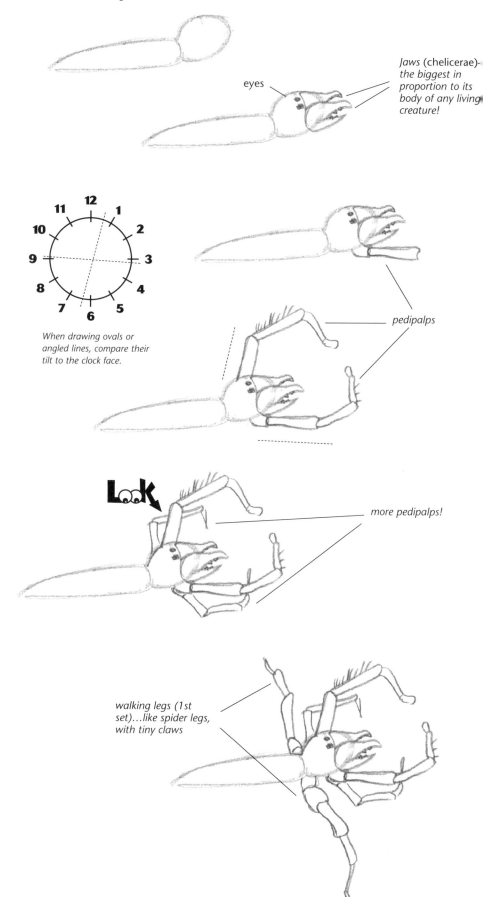

eyes

Jaws (chelicerae)- the biggest in proportion to its body of any living creature!

When drawing ovals or angled lines, compare their tilt to the clock face.

pedipalps

more pedipalps!

walking legs (1st set)...like spider legs, with tiny claws

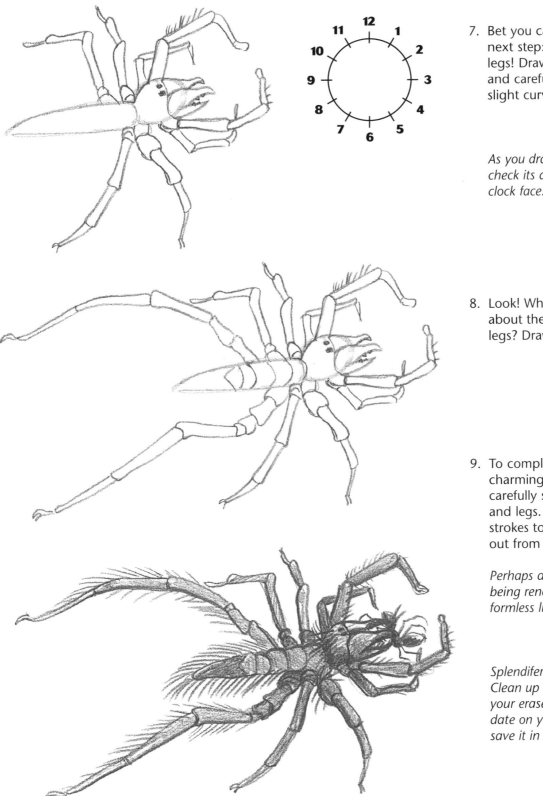

7. Bet you can't guess the next step: another set of legs! Draw them slowly and carefully. Notice the slight curves and angles.

As you draw each segment, check its angle against the clock face.

8. Look! What's different about the last set of legs? Draw them!

9. To complete this charming character, carefully shade the body and legs. Use short pencil strokes to make the hairs, out from the body.

Perhaps add a hapless ant, being rendered into a formless lump…

Splendiferous arachnid! Clean up any smudges with your eraser, put today's date on your drawing and save it in your portfolio!

Caracal

Felis caracal

Africa, Middle East to India.
Size: .8 – 1.2 m (33 – 47 in)
including tail

The solitary caracal patrols a home range, preying on mammals from mice to medium sized antelopes, including birds, reptiles, and smaller domestic animals. Females bear litters of 2-3 young, who don't become independent until they've reached the age of 9-12 months.

1. Before you draw, **look** at how much room divides the two ovals of the cat's body. Now sketch one round oval; make the other narrower and slightly tilted. Add the curving lines for the top and bottom of the body.

2. Sketch a small circle for the head, level with the top of the shoulder. Draw the ears with their tufts of hair at the end. Connect the head to the body with short, curved neck lines. Sketch a smaller circle for the nose.

3. In the upper right of the small nose circle, draw the dark triangle of the nose, with whiskers sticking out either side. **Look** at the difference between the two eyes. Add a line curving up and back, with the round eye underneath. Draw the small visible bit of the other eye.

4. Sketch small circles to locate the joints on the back leg. Draw the leg, paying careful attention to the angle of each section.

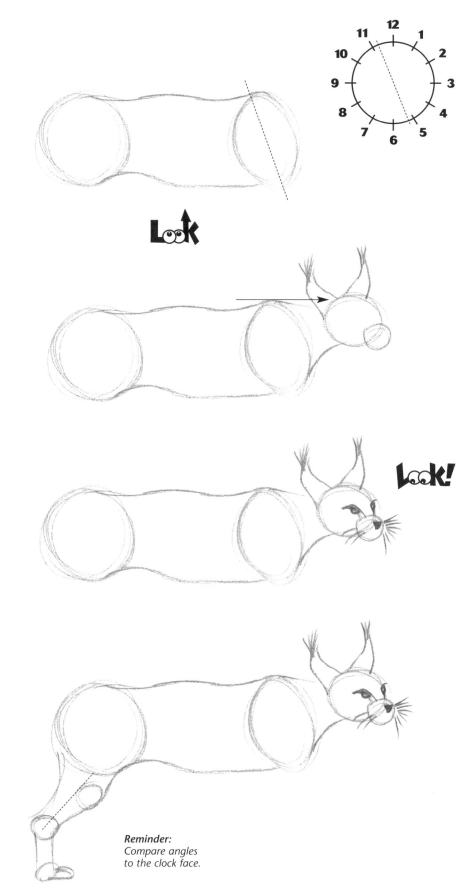

Reminder:
Compare angles
to the clock face.

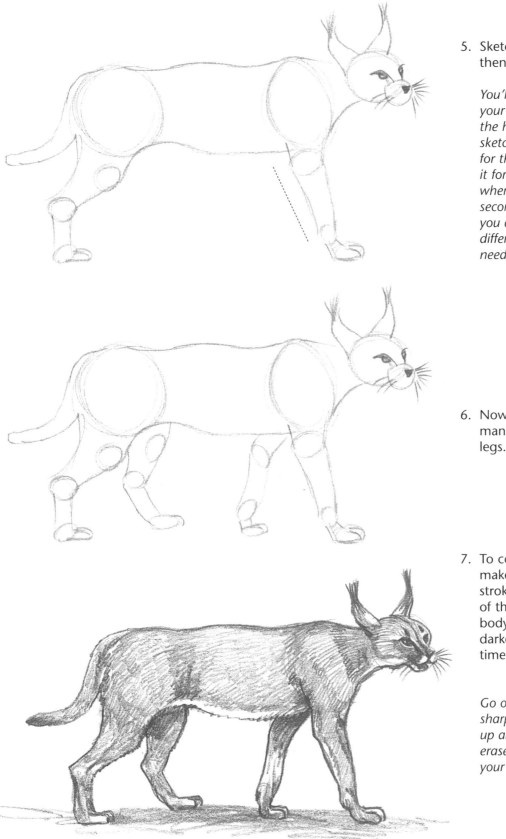

5. Sketch the front leg ovals, then draw the front leg.

   You'll find it very helpful in your drawing if you get in the habit of lightly sketching those little circles for the joints. For one thing, it forces you to figure out where the limb bends. A second reason: it also helps you draw the limbs in different positions if you need to.

6. Now, in a similar manner, add the other legs.

7. To complete the caracal, make short pencil strokes—in the direction of the fur—over the entire body. Note lighter and darker areas. Take your time.

   Go over the outline with a sharpened pencil, and clean up any smudges with your eraser. Put today's date on your drawing and save it!

Draw Desert Animals   17

Desert Cottontail

Sylvilagus auduboni

North America.
Size: 35 — 45 cm (9-11 in) incl. tail

Desert cottontails make their shelter in a burrow or shallow depression in the ground. Most active in the late afternoon and evening, they stay close to cover, When alarmed, they dart away quickly, flicking up their tails as they run, showing the white underside. The young are born blind and helpless after a gestation period of 26-30 days.

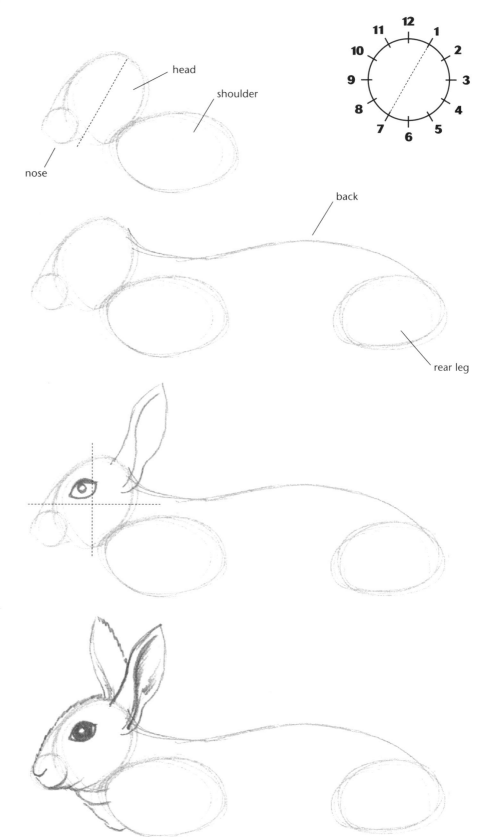

1. Sketch a horizontal oval for the rabbit's shoulder, and a tilted oval for the head. Sketch a small circle for the nose and connect it to the head with lines.

2. Sketch another horizontal oval to begin the rear leg. Connect it to the head with the long, swooping line of the back.

3. Notice where the eye appears in the head. Draw the eye with a circle for the highlight. Add the ear. Make it about as long as the rest of the head.

4. Draw the second ear. Darken the eye (except for the small circle). Add lines for the nostril and mouth, and lines for the chin and throat.

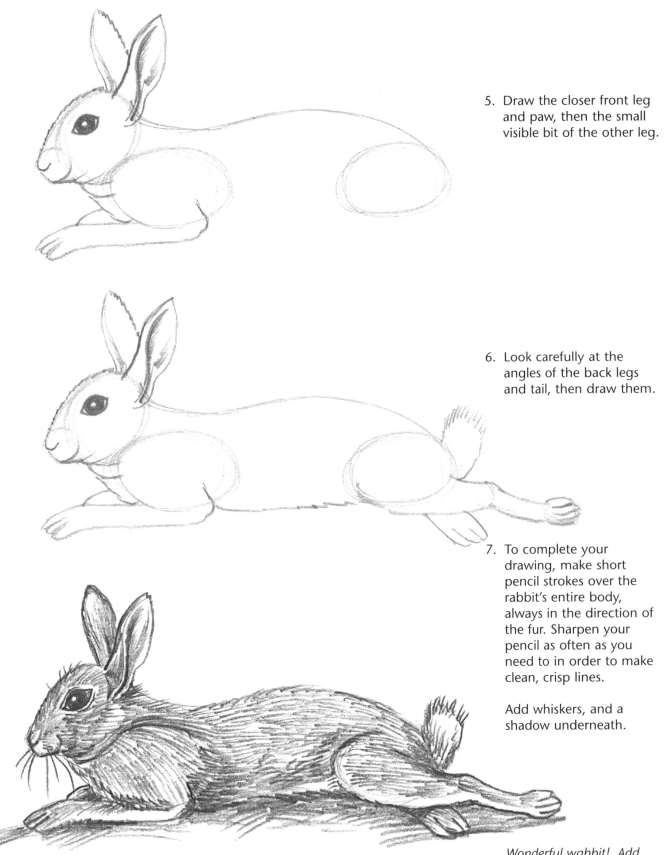

5. Draw the closer front leg and paw, then the small visible bit of the other leg.

6. Look carefully at the angles of the back legs and tail, then draw them.

7. To complete your drawing, make short pencil strokes over the rabbit's entire body, always in the direction of the fur. Sharpen your pencil as often as you need to in order to make clean, crisp lines.

   Add whiskers, and a shadow underneath.

   Wonderful wabbit! Add today's date and save your drawing!

Desert Tortoise

Gopherus agassizi
SW United States.
Size: up to 51 cm (20 in) long

During the heat of the day, the desert tortoise stays in an underground burrow, which may be up to 9 M (30 ft) long. It gets all its water from plants it eats, such as cactus and succulents. A desert tortoise can exist an entire dry season without water!

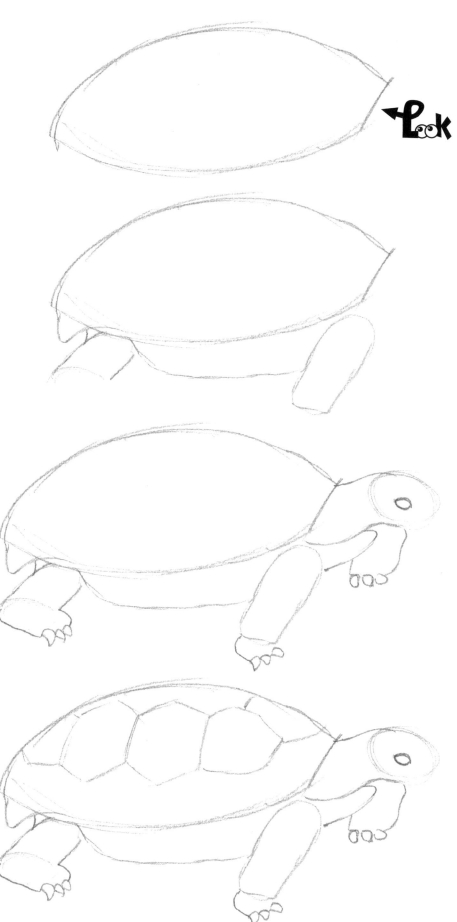

1. Sketch an upward arc and a downward arc for the top and bottom of the shell. Note the straight section at the neck.

2. Lightly sketch the front and rear legs, and the lower part of the shell, including the point behind the rear leg.

3. Sketch an oval for the head. Add the neck, eye, and the part of the shell underneath the head, and the visible portion of the other front leg. Draw the feet. Don't forget claws!

4. Carefully lay out the row of hexagons (six-sided shapes) on the top of the shell.

5. Continue laying out the hexagon pattern on top of the shell, above the row of hexagons, and the rectangle shapes on the bottom of the shell.

6. Shade the bottom part of the shell. Add shadows to create the folds on the neck. Darken the eye, leaving a small white area. Draw small scaly patterns on the head, front leg, and feet.

7. Light and dark contrasts make the tortoise drawing come to life. Look at the dark areas; see which areas stay light.

   Add lots and lots and lots of small lines in the patterns of the shell—some lighter, some darker. Add more small scaly patterns on the head, neck, legs and feet.

   Draw a shadow on the ground, and a few small marks for pebbles.

   Torrific tortoise! Clean up any smudges with your eraser, put today's date on your drawing and save it in your portfolio!

Diamondback Rattlesnake

Crotalus atrox

Southwest US & northern Mexico.
Size: .76 – 2.25 m (2½ – 7½ ft)

The markings on the western diamondback aren't as distinct as you'd think from the name: on the back you'll see diamond-shaped or hexagonal markings, but you may have to look carefully *(and by the time you get that close, the snake is probably rattling its tail at you in warning!)*. Overall, the snake has a speckled or dusty appearance. The tail is set off by broad black and white rings. When rattlesnakes strike, their fangs pierce the victim just for a split second, enough time to inject poison. Then they retreat to their hiding place. Later they look for their kill.

Have fun with this drawing. Enjoy practicing the swooping curves!

1. Sketch gentle, curving lines for the top and bottom of the snake's body. Join them in an upward curve for the fang, and add an extending lower jaw.

2. Look at the rear portion— then carefully draw it. Add the other fang, and mouth details.

3. Extend the body downward. Study how each line curves. Two of them even run into each other (**look**).

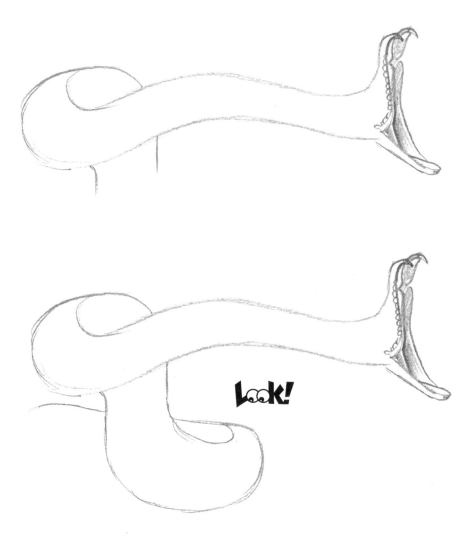

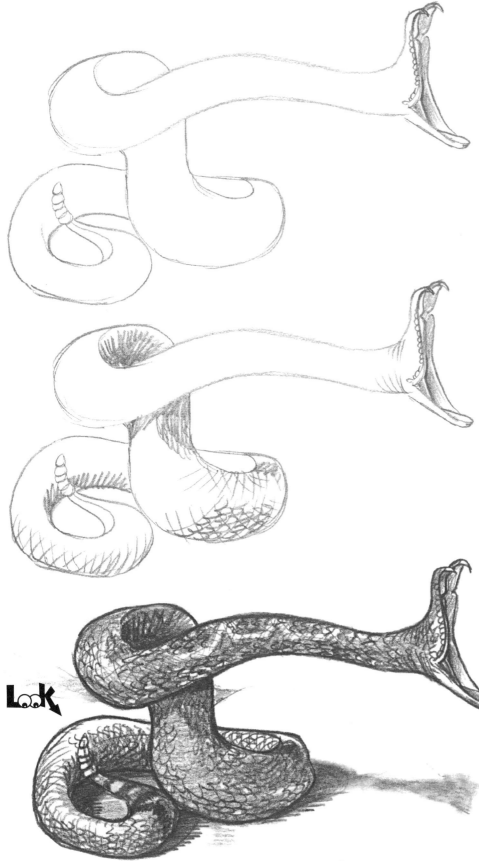

4. Draw curving lines to finish the body and the tail. Draw small ovals for the rattles.

Before you go on, look at your drawing. Is your snake shape smooth and flowing? If not, try again, practicing nice, smooth, connecting curves. Get comfortable with drawing the snake before you spend time adding scales and shading. Save your sketches (with today's date!) in your portfolio!

5. Add *crosshatching* (crisscrossing lines), curving around the *contour* to create guide lines for scales. Use short pencil strokes to darken the shadows.

6. Shade the whole body—except, of course, for highlights **(look)** and the faint pattern on the back. Continue shading and adding scales. Go over the outline with a sharpened pencil. Add the distinct light and dark bands on the tail.

Draw a *cast shadow* on the ground. Soften it by rubbing it with your finger or a piece of paper.

Clean up any smudges with your eraser. Put today's date on your drawing and save it in your portfolio!

Look

Draw Desert Animals 23

Dromedary

Camelus dromedarius

North Africa, Middle East.
Size: body 2.2 – 3.4 m (7¼ – 11 ft);
tail 50 cm (19¾ in)

Not a wild animal! People who know think the one-humped camel has been domesticated since 4,000 BC. Today, you'll find two types: heavy, slow-moving beasts of burden, and graceful, fast racers used for riding. They feed on grass and other available plants, and can withstand long periods in areas of tough, sparse vegetation without drinking, thanks to adaptations in their stomach linings and kidneys. In one experiment, a thirsty camel drank 104 liters (27 US gallons) of water in ten minutes! The hump stores fat, not water. Females breed every other year. The long gestation period (365-440 days) results in a single young that can walk after a day.

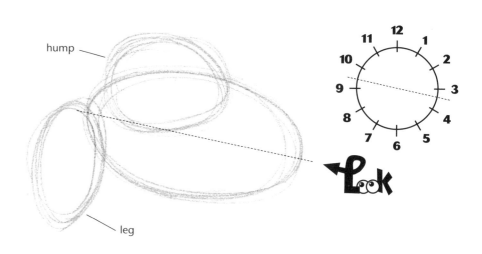

1. Sketch a large, slightly tilted, oval. Sketch a smaller oval, off-center, for the hump. Add a vertical oval for the rear leg.

2. Level with the top of the hump, sketch a small circle for the head. Add lines to form the front of the head. Draw the mouth and nostril. Add the eye and the ear. Draw the gently curving (and slightly shaggy) lines for the neck.

3. Draw the callused knee at the bottom front of the leg oval. Sketch circles for the leg joints. Add curving lines to complete the rear legs. Draw wide, almost triangular shapes for the camel's spreading hoofs.

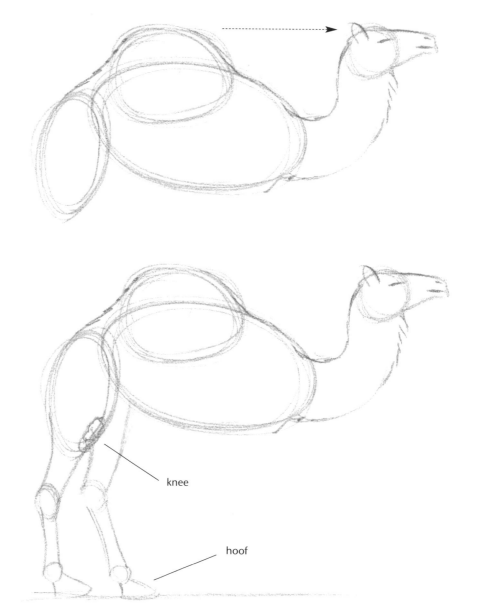

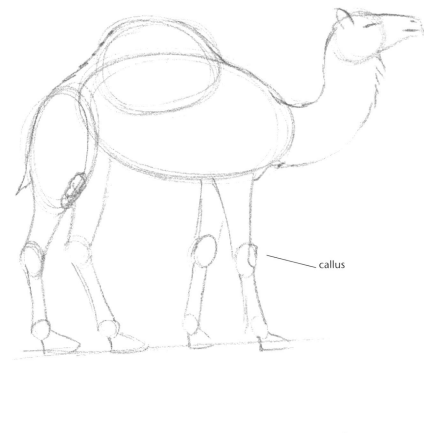

callus

4. Next, add the front legs. Notice the callus on the front of the front leg. The callused areas on the front and rear legs are from kneeling, to lie down and get up again.

   A camel folds its legs underneath to reduce exposure to the hot desert sun (see sketch of Bactrian camels on page 62.). Also, the camel's food store—the fat-filled hump on its back—helps insulate the body underneath from the sun's heat.

5. Using your eraser, carefully clean up sketch lines you no longer need.

   Add pencil strokes—always in the direction of the hair and contours of the body—to shade *just* the shadow areas.

   Go over the outline with a sharpened pencil. Add a *cast shadow* beneath, and *(why not?)* a couple of pyramids in the distance.

   Dazzling dromedary! Clean up any smudges with your eraser, put today's date on your drawing and save it in your portfolio!

Egyptian Slit-Faced Bat

Nycteris thebaica

Middle East, Africa south of Sahara.
Size: body 4.5 – 7.5 cm (1¾ – 3 in);
wingspan 16 – 28 cm (6¼ – 11 in)

Hang around ancient Egyptian temples, and you just may run into a few of these! Slit-faced bats like to catch a variety of invertebrates for supper. Scorpions seem to be a favorite! The bats usually give birth to a single young in January or February; they may do the same later in the year.

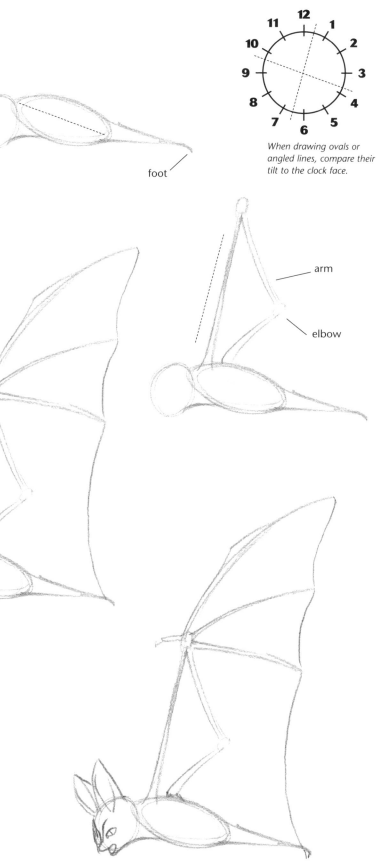

foot

When drawing ovals or angled lines, compare their tilt to the clock face.

arm

elbow

1. Sketch a flat, slightly tilted oval for the bat's body. Sketch a circle at one end for the head. Add a neck line to connect it to the body. Draw two lines tapering to the foot.

2. Draw the front of the wing, up from the top of the body (compare the angle with the clock face). Sketch tiny circles and lines for the bent arm holding it out.

3. From the point where the arm and wing lines meet, draw the bat's long thin "fingers" spreading out to make triangular shapes. Draw the back edge of the wing, connecting it to the tapered end of the foot.

4. Look closely at the bat's facial features—mouth, nose, the little sensing organ on top of the nose, eyes and eye slits. Add them. Draw the ears.

   These facial features are part of their "radar," picking up signals, making it possible for them to move and hunt with precision.

5. Add small lines inside the ears. Behind them, draw a slight hump in the back where the other wing attaches. Look at the wing angles. Draw the second wing.

6. Look at the contrast of light and dark in this final drawing.

   Use *crosshatching*, to carefully shade the closer wing. Use short pencil strokes to create the fur on the body. Continue shading, watching for light and dark areas, until you're through. Then take a sharpened pencil and go over lines you want to emphasize.

   Clean up any smudges with your eraser, put today's date on your drawing and save it in your portfolio!

Elf Owl

Micrathene whitneyi

Southwest US & Mexico.
Size: Body 12.5 – 15 cm (5 – 6 in)

Though one of the smallest owls in the world, the elf owl has a loud voice. It lives in wooded canyons and deserts with saguaro cactus, where it roosts in abandoned woodpecker holes. Elf owls use their feet to catch insects in flight; they also catch food on the ground, including grasshoppers and scorpions (they remove or crush the stinger), and sometimes small snakes and lizards.

1. Sketch a horizontal oval for the owl's head. Beneath it, add the slightly tilted vertical oval of the owl's body.

2. Toward the side of the face, draw the curved beak. On either side, draw two curved lines for eyes.

3. Darken the inside of the eyes, leaving a small refelective spot. Near the owl's right eye, draw a jagged line to show texture on the outline of the head. Add short pencil strokes, up and away from the eye, to shade the head.

4. Add more shading, with short pencil strokes, around the eyes and on the head. Draw the wing, lightly outlining the feathers.

5. Shade the wing, leaving some feather areas white. Draw short, curling strokes to create feathers on the breast and belly.

6

7

6. Look closely at the owl's legs—where they attach to the body, and the directions of each section. Draw the owl's legs. Add two lines for the branch on which the owl perches.

   Draw the tail feathers.

7. Darken the outlines of the feet and branch. Outline the wing and tail feathers. Go over your owl, top to bottom and side to side, adding feathers and shading, and making areas lighter or darker as needed.

Elf owls perch in trees and bushes when they're looking for food or resting. When it's time to nest, they find an old woodpecker hole in a cactus. Try drawing your elf owl nesting in a saguaro cactus!

Clean up any smudges with your eraser, put today's date on your drawing and save it in your portfolio!

Fat Sand Rat

Psammomys obesus

Algeria, east to Saudi Arabia.
Size: body 14 – 18.5 cm (5½ – 7¼
in); tail 12 – 15 cm (4¾ – 6 in)

What do you do if you can't be sure
when you'll find food? If you're a fat
sand rat, you lay down a thick layer
of fat all over your body while food
is abundant, then live off it when
food is scarce. *(What other desert
animals store fat?)* This gerbil is
active day and night, collecting
seeds and other vegetation to carry
back to its burrow.

head

1. Sketch two light
   overlapping ovals for the
   head and face of the rat.
   Behind the head, sketch
   part of another oval—the
   front part of the body.
   Upward from that oval,
   sketch the rounded back
   curving down into the
   rear leg. Draw a curved
   line for the belly.

2. Sketch an oval for the
   nose and mouth. Outline
   the top of the head,
   making a smooth
   connection between the
   ovals. Just above the
   middle of the head, draw
   the eye. To the side of it,
   add the ear.

3. Darken the eye, leaving a
   small white reflective spot.
   Draw the nostrils and
   mouth. Outline the front
   of the face.

4. With a sharp pencil, draw
   lines above and below the
   eye. Add two short legs,
   tilting towards the front.
   Draw feet, then claws.

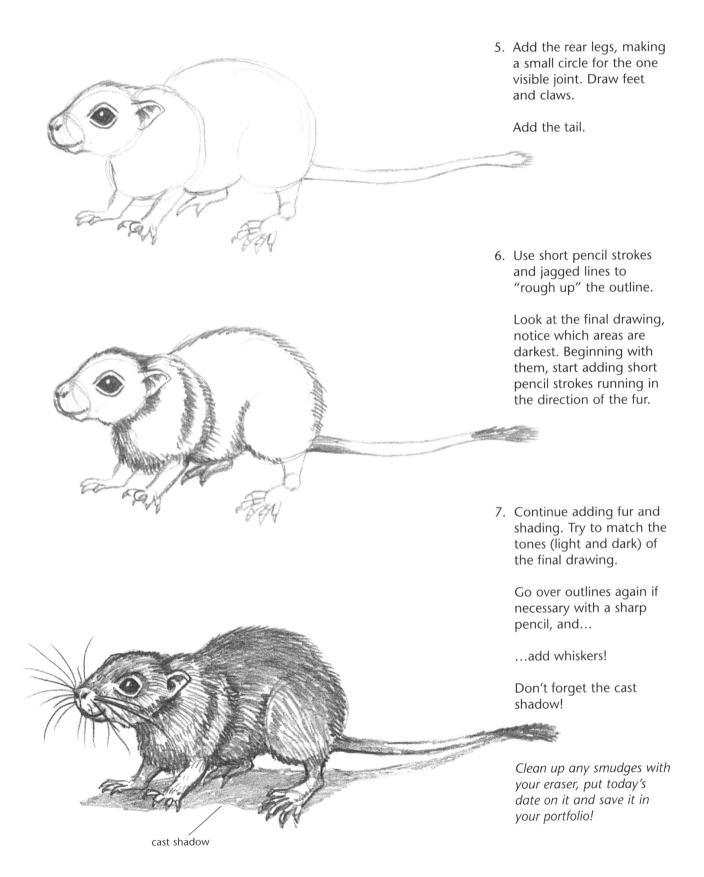

5. Add the rear legs, making a small circle for the one visible joint. Draw feet and claws.

   Add the tail.

6. Use short pencil strokes and jagged lines to "rough up" the outline.

   Look at the final drawing, notice which areas are darkest. Beginning with them, start adding short pencil strokes running in the direction of the fur.

7. Continue adding fur and shading. Try to match the tones (light and dark) of the final drawing.

   Go over outlines again if necessary with a sharp pencil, and…

   …add whiskers!

   Don't forget the cast shadow!

   Clean up any smudges with your eraser, put today's date on it and save it in your portfolio!

cast shadow

Draw Desert Animals   **31**

Fennec fox

Vulpes zerda

North Africa, Arabia.
Size: body 36 – 40 cm (14½ – 16 in);
tail 20 – 20 cm (8 – 12 in)

Fennec foxes live in groups of up to ten, and feed at night on small animals and insects. Small and agile, they live in burrows. In soft sand, they dig so quickly it can look like they're just sinking into the ground!

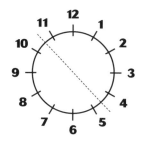

Compare the tilt of ovals and other angles with the clock face.

1. Begin by sketching the body of the fox—two tall ovals connected with curving lines.

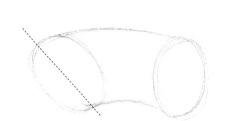

2. Sketch a light circle for the head, noting where it lies in relationship to the shoulder (arrow). Add the nose and mouth. Notice that the neck lines curve outward on both top and bottom. Draw lines for the neck.

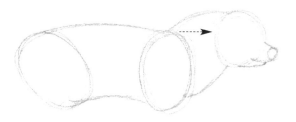

3. Darken the nose and mouth. Add the eye, with a small circle that will remain white. Draw the distinctive large ears.

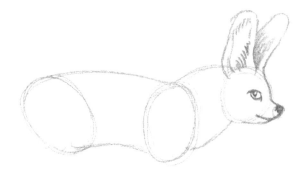

4. Draw squiggly lines to form the bushy tail.

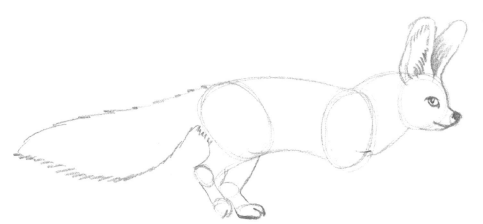

5 Sketch small circles for the leg joints. Draw the rear legs and feet. Add emphasis to the farther one, which is supporting the fox's entire weight.

6. Likewise, draw the front legs and feet. Notice that neither is completely on the ground.

7. Look at the variations in the tones (light and dark). Use short pencil strokes to create the fur of the fennec fox. Leave some areas light. Go over the outline, adding emphasis at points you think need it.

Add a slight *cast shadow* underneath the fox. Draw whiskers! Clean up any smudges with your eraser.

Fine fox! Put today's date on your drawing and save it!

Draw Desert Animals   **33**

Gila Monster

ALWAYS SKETCH **LIGHTLY** AT FIRST!

Heloderma suspectum
Southwest United States.
Size: 60 cm (23 in)

The slow-moving Gila (pronounced "heela") moves about mainly at night, looking for birds' eggs, small reptiles and small rodents to eat. The large tail is used to store fat, since food in the desert is not always abundant *(what other desert animals store fat?)*. Gila monsters and their relatives, Mexican Beaded Lizards, are the only venomous lizards. They take shelter under rocks or in burrows. The females lay eggs once a year, in a hole, in autumn or winter. The eggs hatch about 30 days later.

1. Sketch three flat ovals to begin your Gila drawing.

2. Add two legs with claws. Draw the small visible section of the other front leg (behind the head). Refine the shape of the head, and join the ovals together with smooth curved lines.

3. When all the parts of your Gila are in place, erase unnecessary guide lines. (A kneadable eraser works best; you can dab and twist with it, forming a point to get into tight areas.) Draw the forked tongue, eye, and mouth. Add the short pencil lines on the feet.

4. Look at the patterns on the Gila's tail—bands of light and dark, with dark or light squarish spots in them. Draw the patterns. Add scales in the light areas.

5. The body has a less regular pattern. Have fun drawing it! Add a shadow beneath the Gila, and draw some rocks and twigs near it.

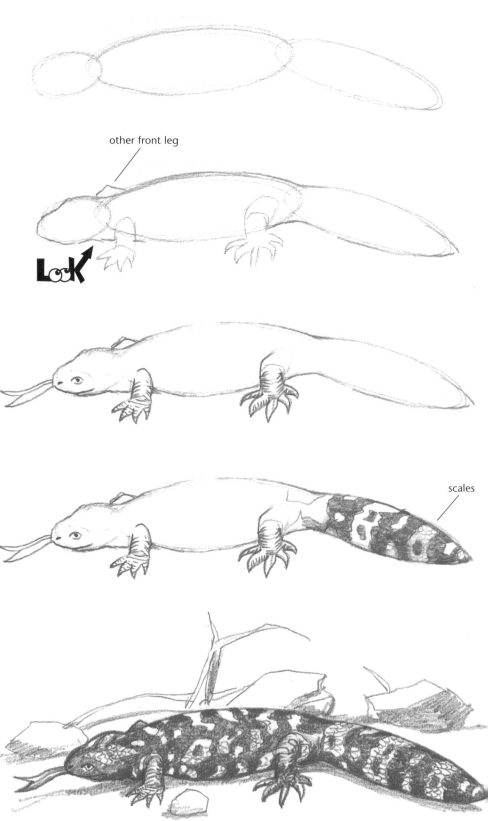

other front leg

scales

Put today's date on your drawing and save it!

34 Draw Desert Animals

Horned Toad

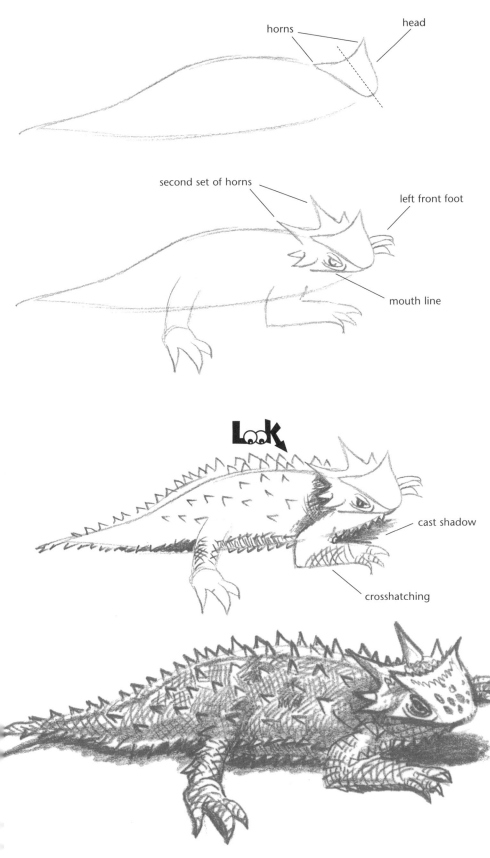

horns

head

second set of horns

left front foot

mouth line

L**oo**K

cast shadow

crosshatching

Phrynosoma douglasii

North America.
Size: 4 — 13 cm (1.6 — 5.2 in)

"That's not a toad!" you say. You're right. The name horned toad is given to a lizard, with horns or spikes on the back of the head (the only other horned lizard is the Thorny Devil of Australia). At night, it wriggles below the sand, during the day it moves about slowly and feeds on insects and ants. Horned toads (also called Texas horned lizards) lie very flat and motionless when disturbed, but can also inflate themselves, jump forward and hiss. And–who knows how–they can even squirt blood from their eyes!

1. Lightly sketch curved lines for the top and bottom of the body. Add the tilted shape that makes the top of the head—rounded at the front and pointed at the back for the horns.

2. Add the second set of horns. Draw the eye and the mouth line. Lightly sketch the two visible legs, with claws. Draw the claws of the left front foot.

3. *Now look at the details!* Add a row of spikes along the back and scattered on the body. Add a *cast shadow* for contrast under the chin and behind the horns. Use *crosshatching* to create scales.

Following this example, add more shading, shadows, and *crosshatching*. Leave the head lighter than the body. This makes the head, eye, and spikes, the focal point of the drawing.

Put today's date on your drawing and save it!

Draw Desert Animals **35**

Jerboa

Dipus sagitta (northern three-toed)

North Africa, Asia.
Size: body 10-13 cm (4 – 5¼ in);
tail 15 – 19 cm (6 – 7½ in)

Like the kangaroo rat of the United States, jerboas live in a burrow, coming out only at night when the surface temperature has cooled off from the heat of the day. In autumn, they dig a deeper burrow to hibernate. In the spring, they may have two litters, with 2-5 young each. A jerboa gets all the water it needs from its food, which includes seeds, roots, and insect larvae.

1. Lightly sketch a horizontal, slightly tilted oval for the jerboa's body. Sketch the oval of the leg overlapping the oval of the body. Add another, smaller, almost round oval for the head.

2. From the leg oval, draw the first section of leg, with a small circle for the ankle joint. From there, draw the next section and the foot. Sketch a small circle for the elbow, and draw the front paw.

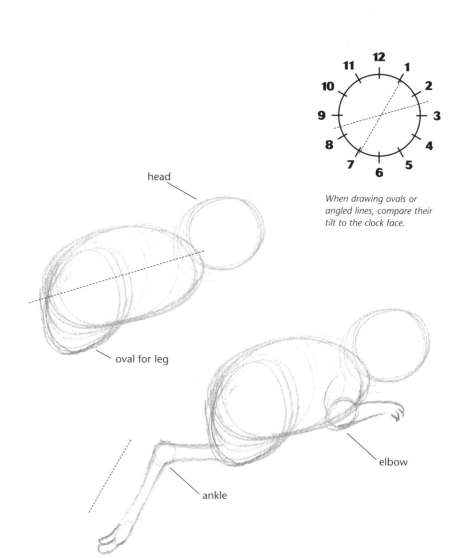

When drawing ovals or angled lines, compare their tilt to the clock face.

head

oval for leg

ankle

elbow

Climate control
By digging beneath the scorching hot surface of the desert, jerboas and their relatives, kangaroo rats, manage to stay cool during the day. At night, when the surface cools, they emerge to search for food.

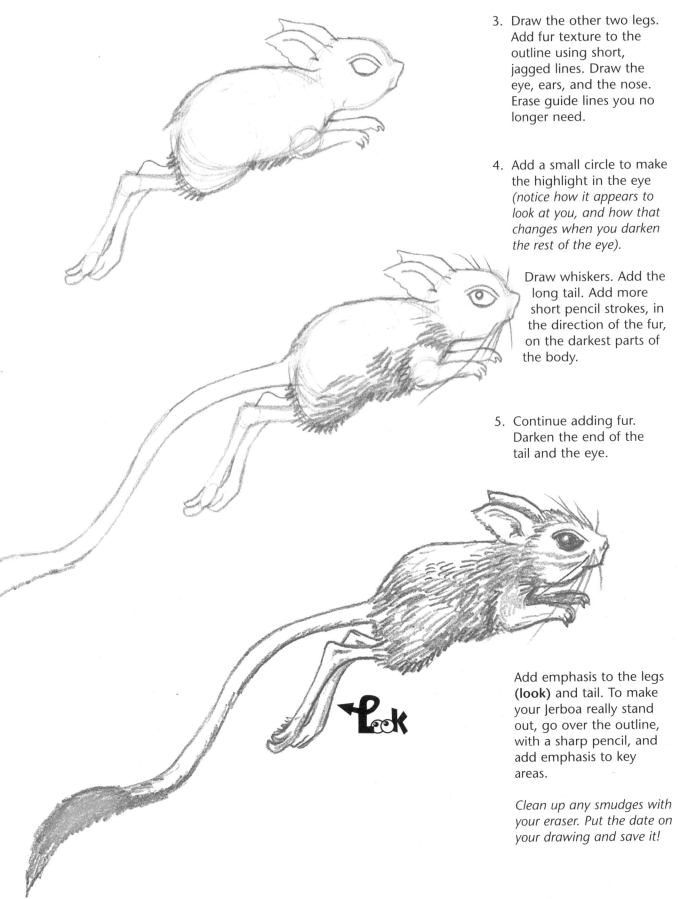

3. Draw the other two legs. Add fur texture to the outline using short, jagged lines. Draw the eye, ears, and the nose. Erase guide lines you no longer need.

4. Add a small circle to make the highlight in the eye *(notice how it appears to look at you, and how that changes when you darken the rest of the eye).*

Draw whiskers. Add the long tail. Add more short pencil strokes, in the direction of the fur, on the darkest parts of the body.

5. Continue adding fur. Darken the end of the tail and the eye.

Add emphasis to the legs **(look)** and tail. To make your Jerboa really stand out, go over the outline, with a sharp pencil, and add emphasis to key areas.

Clean up any smudges with your eraser. Put the date on your drawing and save it!

Draw Desert Animals   **37**

Lanner Falcon

Falco biarmicus

North Africa, Middle East.
Size: Body 40 – 45 cm (16 – 18 in);
wingspan 70 – 80 cm (25 – 27 in)

Falco means sickle, and refers to the curved claws of falcons. Falcons swoop down and grab birds out of the air. People have trained them for thousands of years, to catch food and also as a sport. Falcons don't build nests; they either take over an abandoned nest from another bird, or lay their eggs on high ledges.

1. *Lightly* sketch the tall, slightly tilted oval of the falcon's body. Above it, add a small oval for the head. Leaving space for the shoulder **(look)**, add the curving lines.

2. Draw the curving beak, with the characteristic double notch of a falcon. Draw a line back for the mouth. In the center of the head, draw the curve of the eyebrow, and then the round eye under it.

3. Sketch the two legs, each with a thick feathered portion. Sketch the feet with claws. Add a jagged line to make the top of a rock for the falcon to perch on.

4. Study the falcon's shoulders and wings before drawing them. Add the shoulder beneath the falcon's beak, then the outside and inside of the wing beneath it. Draw the curve of the wing on the other side—see how it extends behind, to the other side of the body. Draw lines for the tail feathers.

When drawing ovals or angled lines, compare their tilt to the clock face.

outside of wing

inside of wing

tail feathers

5. Erase guide lines you no longer need.

   Very carefully, with a sharp pencil, shade the head with short strokes radiating from the mouth and beak.

   Shade the tail feathers. Go over the outlines of the wings, legs and feet with a sharp pencil. Add jagged lines where feathers stick out slightly at the edge of the leg.

6. Notice the details and shading in this drawing. With a sharp pencil, add details: the marks on the breast feathers, claws, or details on the rock. As your pencil becomes duller, add the softer shading.

   Every once in a while, sit back from your drawing and take stock—really look at it and appreciate your progress. Do you see any other details you need to add? Add them.

   Falco fabuloso! Clean up any smudges, date and save your drawing!

Draw Desert Animals   39

Pallas's Cat

Felis manul

Central Asia.
Size: 71 – 86 cm (28 – 38 in)

This elusive cat lives in caves, rock crevices, or burrows taken from other animals such as marmots. It only comes to hunt at night, preying on mice, birds, and small hares. The fur color varies from pale gray to yellowish to reddish-brown. Pallas's cat has the longest, densest fur of any wild cat.

Here's a good example of using form to add realism to a drawing. The shape of the cat's body may look like a sack of potatoes, but there are bones and muscles underneath the skin. Understanding a little about them is the key to having your drawing not look like "Pallas's Potato Sack."

1. Sketch three light, overlapping circles. You don't need to sketch the hidden part of each circle.

2. The body is fairly easy, but the face may be tricky, so complete it first. Near the center of the head circle, draw a small triangular nose; above it, to either side, draw the expressive eyes.

3. Draw the distinctive dark markings on the cheeks. Add the mouth, with a shadow underneath. Draw a line connecting the mouth to the nose.

4. From the nose, go up and out, straight past each eye, and draw the short ears. From the nose up, use short upward pencil strokes for fur. Add spots on the forehead. Continue adding fur lines radiating outward around the face.

top of rear leg

ankle

5. Sketch a tall, tilting oval for the top of the rear leg. Sketch a small circle for the ankle joint and add the rear leg and paw. Draw the front leg and paw. Add a little shading with short pencil strokes to remind you of the form of the leg under the fur, even though you can't really see it.

Finish shading the face, and add whiskers.

6. Sketch the tail, with its dark rings. Carefully add the visible part of the other two legs.

7. Paying close attention to dark and light areas, go over the entire cat with short pencil strokes in the direction of the fur. Add the stripe marks on the back and side, showing the round *contour*. Draw a *cast shadow* underneath. **Look** at the way lines create texture in the *cast shadow*.

Purrfect! Clean up any smudges with your eraser. Date and save your drawing in your portfolio!

Draw Desert Animals 41

Roadrunner

Geococcyx californianus

North America.
Size: 58 cm (23 in) including tail

The roadrunner is a species of cuckoo. It makes quick dashes, then stops suddenly and looks around. If it sees food–a lizard, small snake, grasshopper or insect–it dashes after it, making quick turns if necessary. Roadrunners make neat nests in trees or cactus clumps, lining them with leaves, feathers, even snake skins and bones!

1. Look carefully at the angle of each oval, and compare its tilt to the clock face. Lightly sketch the two ovals. Connect them with curved lines to make the roadrunner's neck.

2. Draw the long and slightly curved beak. Add the eye. Notice the direction the scraggly neck feathers point. Draw them. Add the dark patch behind the eye.

3. See the limp lizard hanging from the roadrunner's beak? Notice how the legs of the lizard hang and point downward. Also notice that part of this lizard's tail is missing…!

   Draw the lizard and *then* draw the lower part of the beak.

42   **Draw Desert Animals**

4. Draw a line showing the edge of the wing. Add feathers. On the bird's belly, add short lines to make it look fluffy, in contrast to the neck feathers. Look carefully at the angles of the leg and foot. From the back of the body, draw one leg and foot, with three of its four claws visible.

5. Add the second leg, at a different angle than the first leg. Draw the branch on which the roadrunner sits. Draw long pencil strokes to begin the tail.

6. Draw the tail roughly the length of the body. Outline and darken the wing and tail feathers. Add shading and contour lines to the legs and feet. Use varied pencil lines to add texture to the branch.

fluffy feathers

edge of wing

OK, roadrunner— thanks for posing. You can eat your supper now!

Put today's date on your drawing and save it!

43

Sandgrouse

Syrrhaptes paradoxus

Central Asia, southern Siberia, southern Mongolia – northern China. Size: 25 – 48 cm (10 – 19 in)

Sandgrouses are related to doves and pigeons. The desert dwellers eat only very dry seeds, so they need to drink every day. After drinking their fill at a watering spot, they then soak their bellies in water and fly back (as far as 30 km (19 miles!) to their young, which drink the water from the belly feathers. Pallas's sandgrouse performs "eruptions" every once in a while: suddenly large numbers leave their home and fly tens of thousands of kilometers east or west. No one knows why.

Leave room for the tail!

throat

1. Look at the finished drawing. As you start your drawing, remember to leave room for the tail! Sketch two light ovals, for the body and head.

2. Add the beak, eye, and facial markings. Draw short, curving pencil strokes for the feathers of the throat.

3. Add swooping lines for the upward curving wing and tail. Look carefully at the feet, and draw them.

4. The last step involves observation, patience, and time. Carefully observe the location, direction, and shading of the various wing and tail feathers. Do "soft" shading when your pencil gets dull; use your freshly sharpened point to go over outlines.

Clean up any smudges with your eraser, put today's date on your drawing and save it in your portfolio!

Scarab Beetle

family Scarabaeidae, Africa.

Scarab beetles, also known as dung beetles, roll dung into balls larger than themselves. The female lays eggs in it, and it provides nourishment for the larva after they hatch. The ancient Egyptians considered scarab beetles sacred, since the dung balls reminded them of the sun.

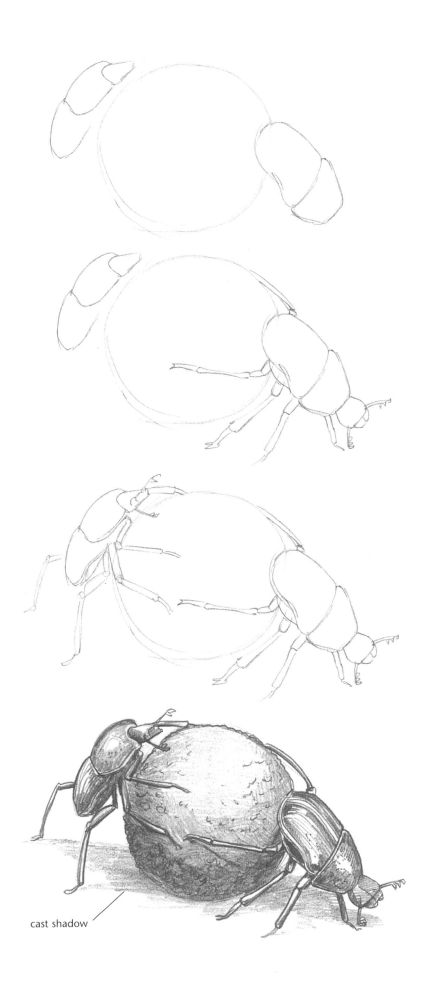

cast shadow

1. Possibly the most difficult part of this drawing is getting the dung ball round! Start by lightly sketching the circle for the dung ball, and see if you can get it as round as the beetles do! Next, add the main body parts of each beetle.

2. Look at the front beetle. See the angle of each section of each leg. Add the segmented legs, a head and antennae to the front beetle.

3. See the rear beetle. As with the front beetle, pay close attention to the angle of each section of each leg. Add its legs, head and antennae.

4. Notice how the beetles shine, while the dung ball looks dull. As you add shading and details, pay close attention to light and dark. Add a *cast shadow* beneath.

   Clean up any smudges with your eraser, put today's date on your drawing. and save it in your portfolio.

   You dung good!

Scorpion

order *Scorpiones*
Size: body 3 mm – 8 cm (⅛ in – 3 in)

About 600 different species of scorpion are known. They have one main part of their body, then five segments forming the "tail," at the end of which is the poisonous stinger. Scorpions live in cracks, but can dig their own resting places as well. At night, they eat beetles, cockroaches, and other arthropods. With their pincers (pedipalps) they bring prey to their chelicerae (jaws), which they use to tear it apart. They only sting when they need to subdue large or struggling prey. American and North African desert scorpions have the worst sting – one Sahara scorpion's sting can kill a dog in a few seconds.

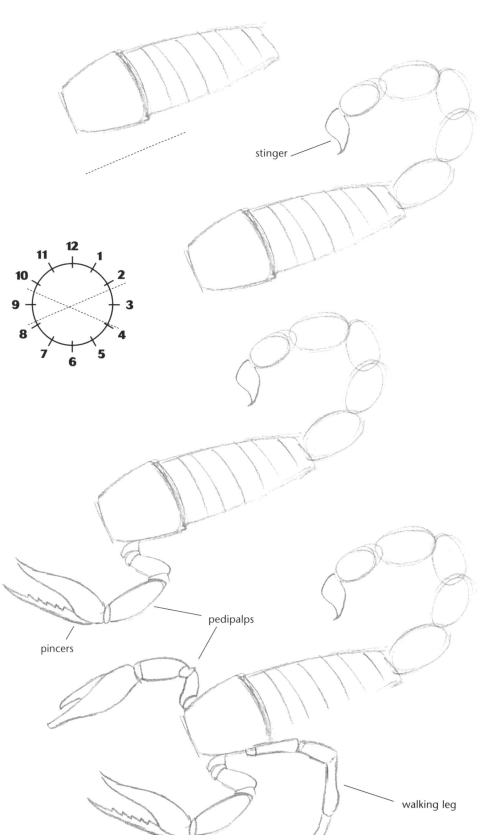

stinger

pedipalps

pincers

walking leg

1. Sketch the two main parts of the body at an angle (compare with clock face).

2. Sketch five connected ovals for the tail, and the stinger at the end.

3. Notice the three main sections of the pedipalp, with smaller connecting sections. Carefully observe the angle of each section *before drawing*.

   Draw the first of the two pedipalps, with the large pincers at its end.

4. Add the other pedipalp, and the first of the walking legs.

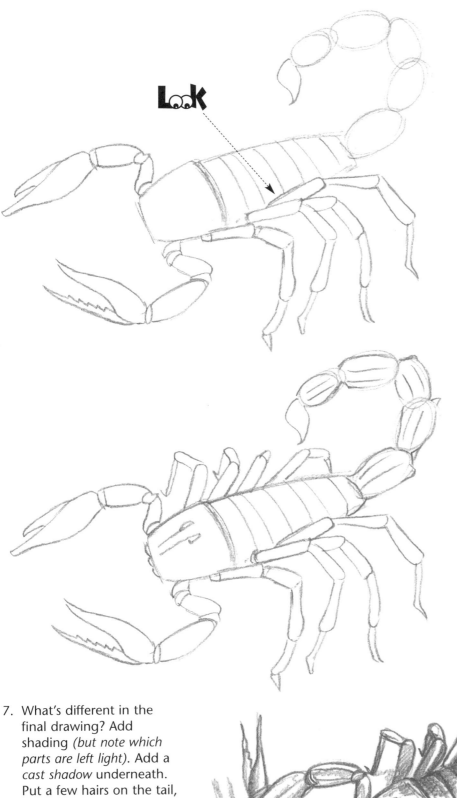

L👀K

5. Do you see how the remaining three walking legs *overlap* (**look**) one another? While more difficult to draw, this helps make your drawing look more real, because *overlapping* adds *depth*.

Draw the remaining three walking legs on the scorpion's left side.

6. On the far side, fewer segments of each leg are visible. Look carefully, and draw them.

Compare angles to the clock face to keep your lines running in the right direction.

Add lines on the tail sections.

7. What's different in the final drawing? Add shading *(but note which parts are left light)*. Add a *cast shadow* underneath. Put a few hairs on the tail, and—what has the scorpion caught? Draw part of the pedipalp of another scorpion, which has just lost a fight to yours.

Put today's date on your drawing and save it!

Sidewinder

Crotalus cerastes

Southwest United States.
Size: 60 – 70 cm (24 – 28 in)

The sidewinder rattlesnake moves uniquely through the desert sand: only two parts of its body touch the ground at once! Sidewinding leaves a series of J-shaped marks in the sand. Usually sidewinders hunt at night for small lizards and rodents, and rest during the day–under a bush or in another animal's burrow.

1. Start your drawing with two curving lines. Make the top line connect to the middle of the bottom line.

2. Add a second curved line below each of the first two. Draw the outline of the sidewinder's head.

3. Add upward-curving lines to connect the ends of the first lines you drew. Make sure the lower curve aligns with the other curving side.

4. Add two more small upward-curving lines to complete the other side of the snake's body. Add the end of the tail, with rattles on the tip.

5. Look carefully at the curves representing the bottom of the snake. Add contour lines to the snake's underside.

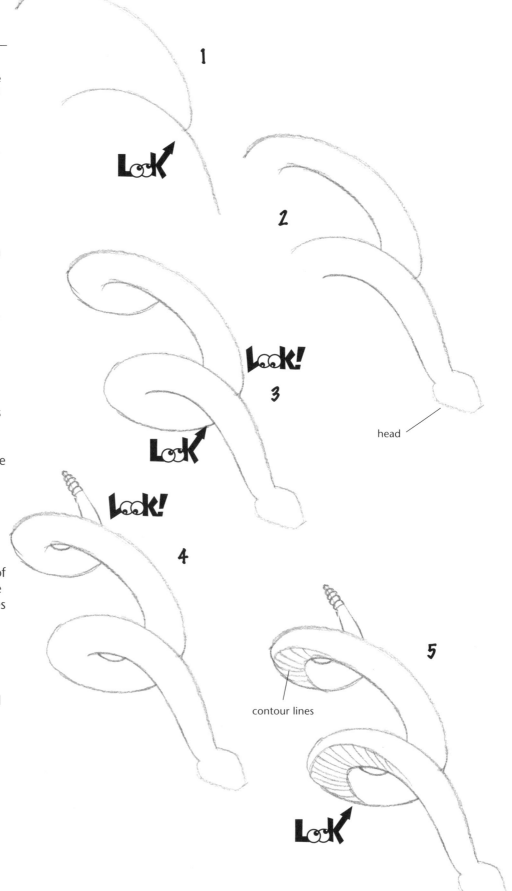

head

contour lines

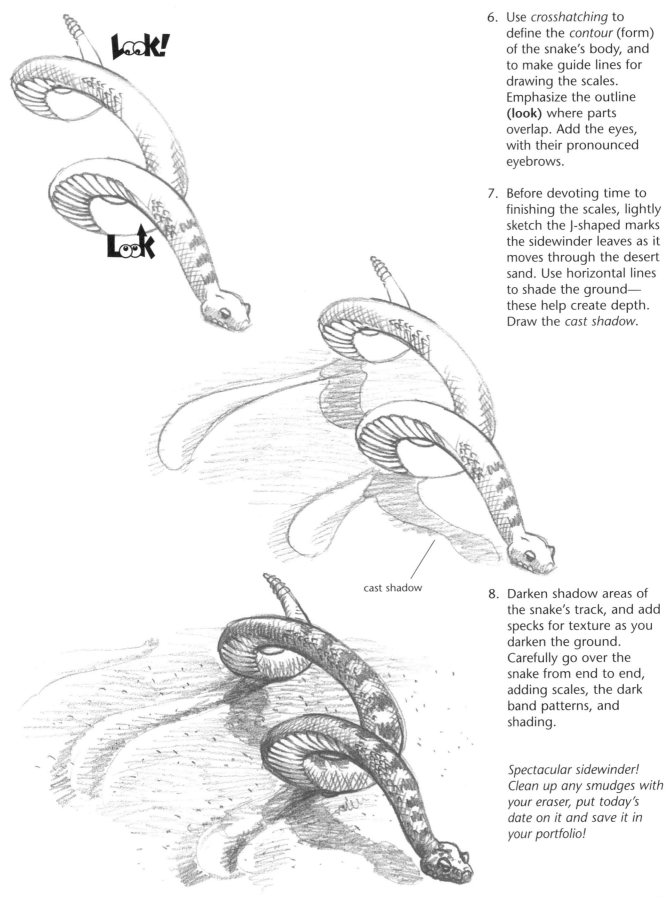

6. Use *crosshatching* to define the *contour* (form) of the snake's body, and to make guide lines for drawing the scales. Emphasize the outline **(look)** where parts overlap. Add the eyes, with their pronounced eyebrows.

7. Before devoting time to finishing the scales, lightly sketch the J-shaped marks the sidewinder leaves as it moves through the desert sand. Use horizontal lines to shade the ground— these help create depth. Draw the *cast shadow*.

cast shadow

8. Darken shadow areas of the snake's track, and add specks for texture as you darken the ground. Carefully go over the snake from end to end, adding scales, the dark band patterns, and shading.

Spectacular sidewinder! Clean up any smudges with your eraser, put today's date on it and save it in your portfolio!

Spotted Skunk

Spilogale gracilis
North America.
Size: 33 – 56 cm (13 – 22 in)

Spotted skunks usually den underground, but also climb trees. No two skunks have exactly the same color pattern. They eat rodents, birds, eggs, insects, and fruit. In the southern part of their range (central Mexico) they give birth any time of the year. Farther north, they give birth in the spring to 4-5 young, after a gestation of 4 months. Before spraying its unpleasant smelly spray, a spotted skunk warns its enemies by doing a handstand.

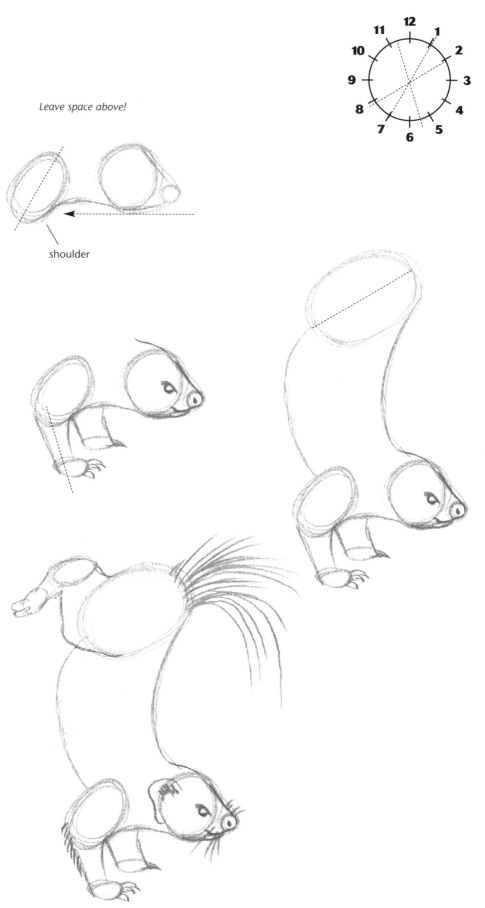

Leave space above!

shoulder

1. Before you draw, note that the shoulder oval lies slightly lower than the head oval. Lightly sketch the two small ovals. Leave room above for the rest of the body! Connect the two ovals with a curved line for the neck. Sketch a small circle for the nose, and draw lines to connect it to the head.

2. From the shoulder oval, draw two lines at a slight angle for the leg. Add an oval for the foot. Draw claws. Draw the other leg and foot. Draw the eye, nose and mouth.

3. Far above the head and leg, sketch a larger, tilted oval. Draw two curved lines to connect the back leg oval with the head and shoulder ovals.

4. Sketch ovals for the rear leg joints. Add the leg and claws. With curving pencil strokes, draw the hairs of the tail, pointing up, then falling back down. Add the ear, whiskers, and short pencil strokes on the front leg for hair.

50   **Draw Desert Animals**

5. With a sharp pencil, go over the outline, using short back and forth movements–almost like scribbles–to add texture to places where fur sticks out. Lightly "map out" the white spots and stripes for your skunk–remember, each is unique!

6. Look! Notice how the dark areas don't appear completely black. Using short back and forth pencil strokes, always in the direction of the fur, make the whole skunk, except for the white spots, dark. Leave highlight areas slightly lighter; make shadow areas slightly darker. When the tones are correct, add a few more crisp pencil strokes to emphasize the texture of the fur.

Question:
What do you say to a spotted skunk doing a handstand?

Answer:
"Goodbye."

OK, another:
How do you say "goodbye" to a skunk doing a handstand?

Answer:
As fast as you can!

Did you pick up some smudges on your drawing? It's easy to do, and also easy to avoid. Get in the habit of putting a piece of clean paper under your hand to protect parts you've already drawn.

Put today's date on your drawing and save it in your portfolio!

Draw Desert Animals 51

Tarantula

North America.
Size: body up to 7.5 cm (3 in) long;
leg span to 30 cm (12 in)

The tarantula is a kind of wolf spider *(Lycosa)*. When threatened, a tarantula might rear up on its hind legs and make a hissing noise. Unlike other spiders, the jaws of the tarantula move up and down instead of sideways. While it is a big, scary looking spider, the tarantula's bite is not as bad as people sometimes think: it's similar to a wasp sting.

1. Lightly sketch a horizontal oval for the spider's abdomen, and a rounder one for the cephalothorax. Add the eight eyes, and the visible part of the jaws (the fangs point down, so you don't see them from this angle).

2. Draw the two most extended legs first, starting with the coxa and trochanter, thence proceeding to depict the femur, patella, tibia, metatarsus, and tarsus. (!)

3. The other two legs are *foreshortened* (coming toward you in the picture), so you don't see the full complement of parts *(I'll bet that's OK with you!).*

   Draw them as you see them, using the clock face as a guide for angles.

4. Add a little more definition to the cephalothorax by making slight rounded indents where each leg attaches. Draw the thick pedipalps.

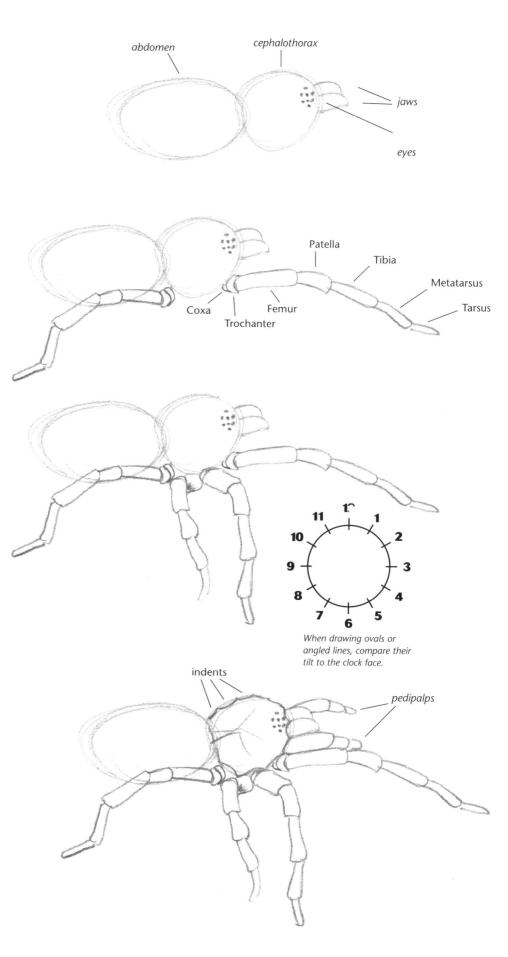

When drawing ovals or angled lines, compare their tilt to the clock face.

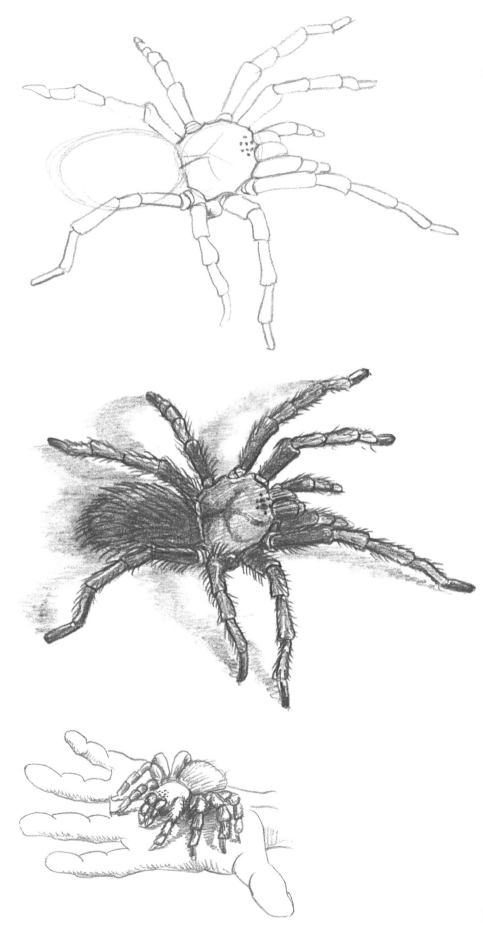

5. You'll find the legs on the other side easier to draw, since there is little *foreshortening.* Add them one segment at a time.

   As you can see, the last step involves some time. Are you ready to keep going on this drawing, or do you want to keep it as a practice sketch and start another? Your choice. Put the date on this drawing and save it if you do decide to start over.

6. Finish your tarantula by shading the body parts with a dull pencil, then adding short pencil strokes for hairs when the pencil is sharp.

   With a dull pencil (and perhaps smearing it a bit with your finger or a small wad of paper), add the *cast shadow* beneath.

   You can have fun adding a hand to your drawing to show scale. Don't know how to draw a hand? Maybe you want to practice on a separate sheet, and draw it before you draw the spider!

   Tantalizing tarantula! Clean up any smudges with your eraser, put today's date on it and save it in your portfolio!

Draw Desert Animals   **53**

Thorny devil

Moloch horridus

Australia. Size: 15 cm (6 in)

This small desert lizard (also known as the *Australian moloch*) looks larger because of the points all over its body. The points keep predators away (would *you* eat something that thorny?). It moves slowly, and likes to eat ants—one at a time, sitting for hours by an ant nest. At night, dew drops form on the lizard's skin: this is how the Thorny Devil gets water to drink!

1. Sketch a long, slightly tilted oval for the body. Sketch a smaller oval for the head, tilting the opposite way. Connect them with lines for the neck.

2. Add lines for the legs and claws. Draw the tail.

   Add a line underneath for the ground.

3. Look at this thorny devil! At the front of the head, draw the eye and mouth. Add spikes on the chin and top of the head.

   Add a jagged edge to the bottom of the tail. Draw spikes on the front and rear leg. Make smaller spikes on each of the claws.

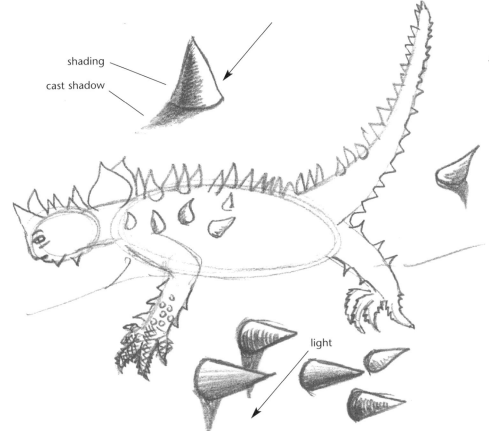

shading

cast shadow

light

4. Before you start going wild with spikes, take a moment to study the various cones you see here. The rounded spikes on the Moloch's back are really little cones; you don't have to draw them as carefully as these examples, but you'll find it helpful to see how the shadows of the cones look.

Draw more spikes along the lizard's back, and start adding those little cone-shaped spikes.

On the legs, make small circles, tightly packed together, for scales.

5. Go wild with spikes! Then add shading and the darker areas of the lizard's camouflage pattern. Make a *cast shadow* beneath.

Mahvelous Moloch! Clean up any smudges with your eraser. Put the date on your drawing and save it!

cast shadow

Trapdoor Spider

family Ctenizidae
Worldwide.

Trap-door spiders dig burrows, covering the opening with a hinged flap made from silk and dirt. Then they sit and wait until an unwary insect wanders close to the door, and ZIP!—they push the door open, jump on the insect, and drag it back into the tunnel to kill and eat it.

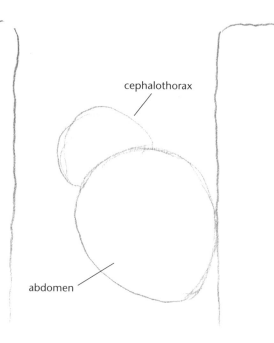

1. Start your drawing with two upside-down L shapes for the tunnel. Lightly draw the two ovals of the spider's body—the abdomen and cephalothorax.

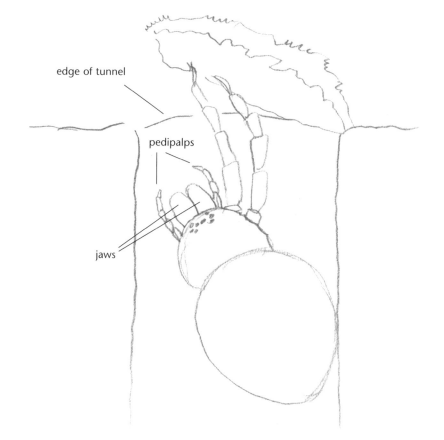

2. From the cephalothorax, draw two segmented legs reaching upward. Add the pedipalps, eight tiny eyes, and jaws (in this top view, you can't see the fangs).

    Look at the squiggly shaped trap door. Draw the trap door and a line for the edge of the tunnel.

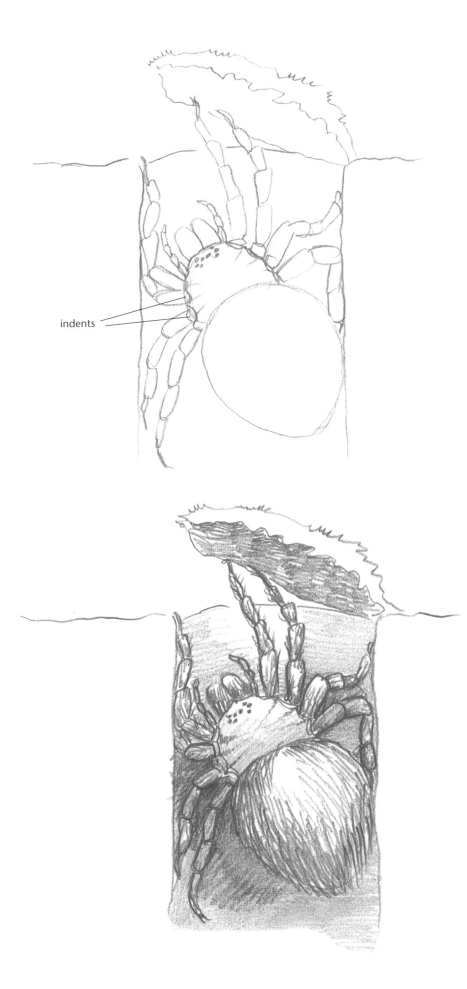

indents

3. Add the remaining legs, one at a time. Draw indents on the cephalothorax at the point where each leg attaches.

4. With a sharp pencil, make short strokes to shade the hairy abdomen and legs. As your pencil gets dull, add to the softer shading of the tunnel and trap door.

Go over outlines, darkening as necessary.

Clean up any smudges with your eraser. Put the date on your drawing and save it in your portfolio!

Knock knock.

Who's there?

Draw Desert Animals   **57**

Vicuña

Vicugna vicugna

South America: Peru, northern Chile.
Size: 1.4 m long (4.5 ft), 1 m (3 ft)
high at shoulder

This smallest member of the camel
family lives high in the Andes
Mountains, at the edge of the desert
near grasslands. Vicuñas are fast,
graceful animals who live in groups
of up to 15, either one male and
females or all male. The females give
birth to one young after a gestation
period of about ten months. Though
long hunted for their wool and
meat, it appears that their
population is increasing.

1. Sketch two *overlapping*
   circles for the body.
   Sketch two smaller circles
   for the head and nose.
   Connect head and body
   with long, curving lines of
   the neck.

2. Add eyes and nose,
   paying close attention to
   where they lie within their
   circles. Draw a small
   curved line for the mouth,
   and add ears.

3. Darken the eye, shade the
   face, darken the jaw line
   and make a shadow on
   the neck. Add jagged lines
   for the shaggy fur on the
   chest.

4. Sketch small circles for the
   leg joints. Draw the front
   legs and hoofs.

5. Add a rear leg.

6. Draw the other rear leg. Add the tail. Use short pencil strokes to outline the back. Add hair under the belly.

7. Pay attention to darker and lighter areas as you carefully shade the rest of the body. Add emphasis to outlines. Draw a cast shadow with some rocks and grass on the ground.

Vabulous Vicuña! Clean up any smudges with your eraser, put today's date on it and save it in your portfolio!

Draw Desert Animals 59

Drawing Tips

Start out loose and light

You've seen it enough times in this book: *Always sketch lightly at first.*

Sketching means trying out ideas, trying out variations, and basically not worrying too much whether the finished product is perfect.

Sketching can vastly improve your drawing skill. Try to do a number of quick sketches to get a feel for the animal: from life, from pictures, or from videos or TV. Then, using your sketch as a guide, carefully put together your final drawing.

You may find—as perhaps all illustrators and artists do—that your lightly drawn sketches have more energy, and capture more of the spirit of the animal, than your final drawing.

So save every drawing, always with the date you drew it!

Timed Drawings

Here's a challenge: pick a subject, and do timed drawings: first, **five seconds** (really, it's possible!). Next, do a 30-second drawing. One more: give yourself two minutes. Now take as long as you need—ten minutes, a half an hour, a day…feel the difference in each? Which is the most fun?

ALWAYS SKETCH **LIGHTLY** AT FIRST!

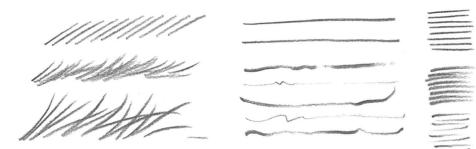

Drawing Tips

Lines make a difference

Lines are not all created equal. Some lines can make your animal come to life. Try making your lines interesting. Learn to use lines to capture the feel of the animal you're drawing. Here are some suggestions.

- ## Make outlines expressive

  How is the outline *of the animal different in each camel? Do you see a technique you can use to make your own drawing more lifelike?*

- ## Create texture with lines

  What about texture–which drawing gives you an idea what the camel might feel like if you touched it?

- ## Use lines to show form

  In addition to showing texture, how do lines help show the form (three-dimensional shape)? Can you see how lines on one of these two Bactrian camels make the drawing look more three-dimensional?

Draw Desert Animals 61

A final thought...

Save your work!

Whenever you do a drawing–or even a sketch–put your initials (or autograph!) and the date on it. Save it. You don't have to save it until it turns yellow and crumbles to dust, but do keep your drawings, at least for several months. Sometimes, hiding in your portfolio, they will mysteriously improve! I've seen it happen often with my own drawings, especially the ones I knew were no good at all, but kept anyway....

Do-it-yourself portfolio

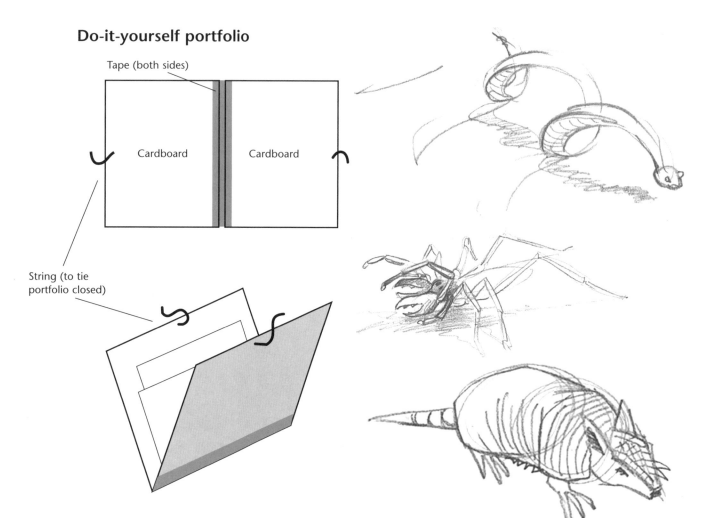

Tape (both sides)

Cardboard   Cardboard

String (to tie portfolio closed)

Index

Addax antelope 6
Agamid, Arabian toad-headed 10
Antelope, addax 6
Arabian oryx 8
Arabian Toad-headed agamid 10
Bactrian camel 12
Bat, Egyptian slit-faced 26
Beetle, scarab 45
Camel, bactrian 12
Camel, dromedary 24
Camel spider 14
Caracal lynx 16
Cat, Pallas's 40
Desert cottontail 18
Desert tortoise 20
Diamondback rattlesnake 22
Dromedary 24
Egyptian slit-faced bat 26
Elf owl 28
Falcon, Lanner 38
Fat sand rat 30
Fennec fox 32
Fox, fennec 32
Gila monster 34
Horned toad 35
Jerboa 36
Lanner Falcon 38
Lizard, moloch 54
Lizard, Texas horned 35

Lizard, thorny devil 54
Lynx, caracal 16
Moloch 54
Oryx, Arabian 8
Owl, elf 28
Pallas's cat 40
Pallas's sandgrouse 44
Rabbit, desert cottontail 18
Rat, fat sand 30
Rattlesnake, sidewinder 48
Rattlesnake, diamondback 22
Roadrunner 42
Sand rat 30
Sandgrouse 44
Scarab beetle 45
Scorpion 46
Scorpion, wind 14
Sidewinder 48
Skunk, spotted 50
Spider, camel 14
Spider, trapdoor 56
Spotted skunk 50
Tarantula 52
Thorny devil 54
Tortoise, desert 20
Trapdoor spider 56
Vicuña 58
Wind scorpion 14

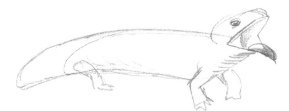

Learn about other books in
this series online at
www.drawbooks.com!

DINOSAURS

by Doug DuBosque

PEEL productions, inc.

Contents

Rods and joints 4

How to make arms and legs look real!

Supplies 6

What you need to start your dino-drawing adventures

Linosaurs..7

For an easy start, draw one line at a time

Ovalsaurs 21

For more flexibility, build from this basic shape

Trianglesaurs 39

Sometimes, triangles will jump out at you. Draw them!

Solidsaurs..51

For maximum effect, build forms into your drawing

Index 63

Rods and Joints

Look carefully at this *Tyrannosaurus* skeleton.

Can you find the shoulder joint? The knee?

Can you see where the legs and arms bend?

To make the legs of a dinosaur look good in your drawing, learn about the skeleton. Look at one whenever you can when drawing a dinosaur.

Draw *rods* (lines) to show parts of arms and legs. Draw *joints* (circles) where they bend.

rod

joint

hip

From this angle, one hip joint lies directly behind the other, so you can only see one.

Always draw rods and joints very lightly, so you can either erase them or cover them with shading. You don't want them as part of your final drawing, but they do give you a powerful tool to use along the way!

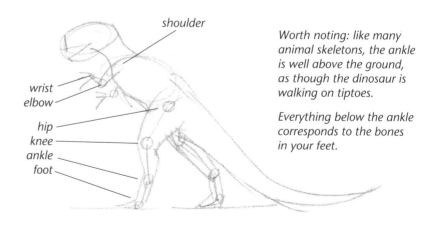

shoulder

wrist
elbow

hip
knee
ankle
foot

Worth noting: like many animal skeletons, the ankle is well above the ground, as though the dinosaur is walking on tiptoes.

Everything below the ankle corresponds to the bones in your feet.

Always start out *lightly!*

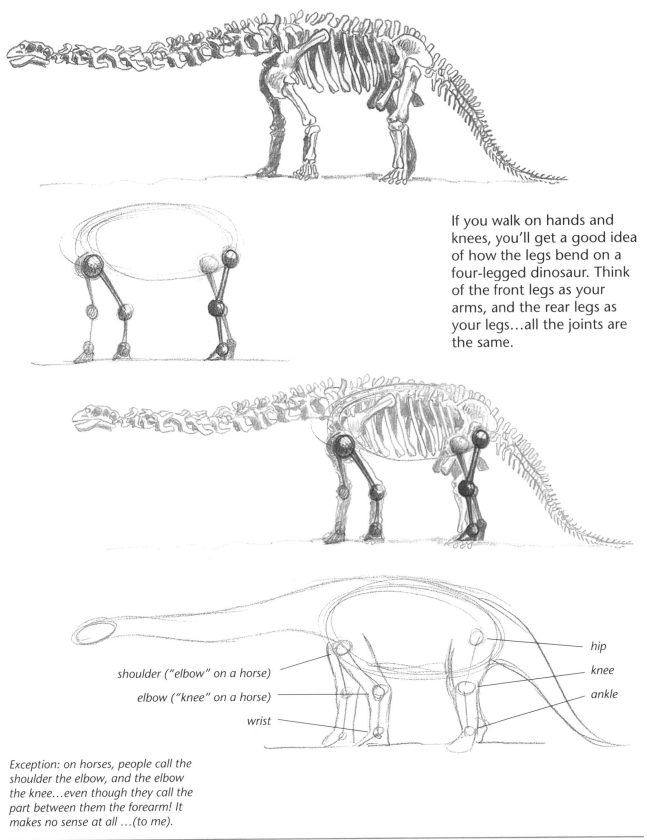

If you walk on hands and knees, you'll get a good idea of how the legs bend on a four-legged dinosaur. Think of the front legs as your arms, and the rear legs as your legs...all the joints are the same.

shoulder ("elbow" on a horse)

elbow ("knee" on a horse)

wrist

hip

knee

ankle

Exception: on horses, people call the shoulder the elbow, and the elbow the knee...even though they call the part between them the forearm! It makes no sense at all ...(to me).

Supplies...

You can draw with just about anything.

People in caves used dried clay and black stuff out of the fire pit, and we're still talking about their drawings 25,000 years later! But caves, charcoal, mud and torches do not make for an optimal drawing environment. So find a comfortable place to draw – with decent light, so you can see what you're doing.

Draw with a pencil that's longer than your finger.

 Find an eraser – the one on your pencil will disappear quickly.

Plan to keep your drawings – you'll find instructions for a simple portfolio on page 62.

For practice drawings, use recycled paper – for example, draw on the back of old photocopies or computer printouts.

Sharpen your pencil when it gets dull!

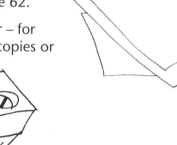

Positive attitude!
Persistence!
Practice!

CHAPTER 1
LINOSAURS

Sometimes, you can make a dinosaur starting with simple lines.

Can you spot the dinosaurs lurking in these curves?

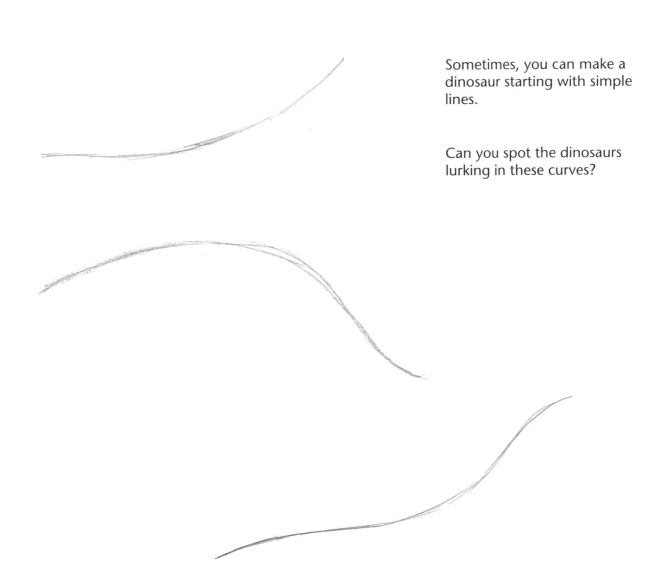

Camarasaurus

CAM-**AR**-A-**SAW**-RUS

"Chambered lizard." Late Jurassic;
Colorado, Wyoming, Utah and
Oklahoma USA. Up to 60 feet (18m)
long; weighed perhaps 20 tons.
Because of long nasal openings on the
top of its skull, some people think it had
a trunk like an elephant (draw that if
you want)!

Draw a long, swooping line.

Add a partial circle hanging
from the middle of it.

Draw another line to
complete the tail.

Add another line for the
neck. Draw the mouth.

Always start out *lightly!*

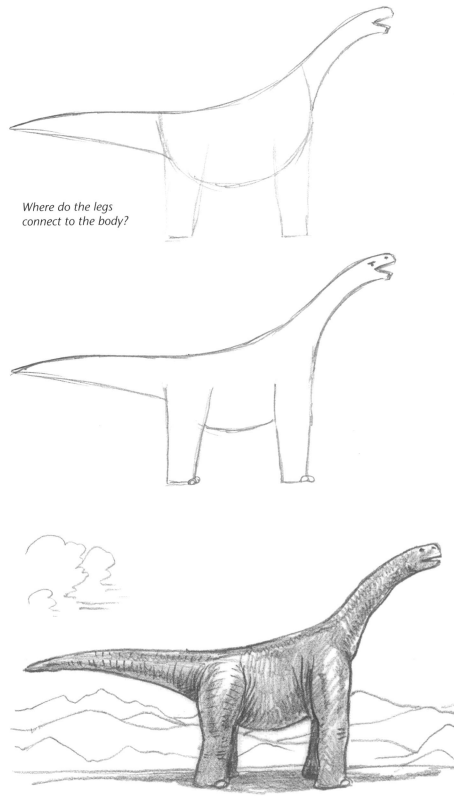

Where do the legs connect to the body?

Now draw the legs. Since the legs are straight, you don't really need rods and joints to draw them.

Add the eye, a nostril and toe nails. Carefully erase lines you no longer need: in the legs, on the tail and on the neck.

- Finish your drawing by adding texture, shading, and background. (See pages 60-61 for ideas.)

- Look at your drawing in a mirror (or through the back of the paper) to spot areas you can improve.

- While your pencil is sharp, go over fine details and make lines cleaner. As it gets duller, add shading.

- Turn your drawing as you draw to avoid smudging it with your hand.

- Finally, clean up any smudges with your eraser.

Allosaurus

AL-o-SAW-rus

"Other lizard." Late Jurassic; North America, Africa, Australia, perhaps Asia. Up to 39 feet (12m) long; weighed 1-2 tons. Lived long before Tyrannosaurus, and had longer arms with strong claws to hold its prey while it tore at it with teeth serrated like steak knives.

Start this drawing with a swooping line. Draw lightly!

Draw another line above the first, starting at one end and ending in the middle.

From the top line, add a smooth, curving line to complete the tail. At the other end, add lines for the neck and head. Make a bump where the eye will go. Leave room for the mouth.

Now lightly draw the leg. You may find it helpful to start with *rods and joints* (see pages 4-5).

The leg looks complex, but actually it bends just the way your own leg bends, at the knee and at the ankle.

back of knee   front of knee

Add the other leg. Now your dinosaur looks as though it's moving!

Draw the arm.

Draw the other arm. Now add nose, eye and mouth.

- Finish your drawing by adding texture, shading, and background. (See pages 60-61 for ideas.)

- Look at your drawing in a mirror (or through the back of the paper) to spot areas you can improve.

- While your pencil is sharp, go over fine details and make lines cleaner. As it gets duller, add shading.

- Turn your drawing as you draw to avoid smudging it with your hand.

- Finally, clean up any smudges with your eraser.

Awesome Allosaurus!

Stenonychosaurus

STEN-OH-NIKE-O-SAW-RUS

"Narrow claw lizard." Cretaceous; southern Alberta, Canada. 6 feet (2m) long; weighed 60-100 lbs (27-45 kg). Has been called the most intelligent dinosaur because of its large brain size (relatively speaking), which probably gave it fast reflexes for catching small prey.

Start with a long slanting and curving line. Draw another curved line under it.

Using circles for the joints, add the top part of the leg.

Now add the thinner bottom of the leg, and the foot. Pay close attention to the details of the foot!

When you've completed the first leg, draw the second.

Notice that each foot has a sickle claw that sticks up.

Always start out *lightly!*

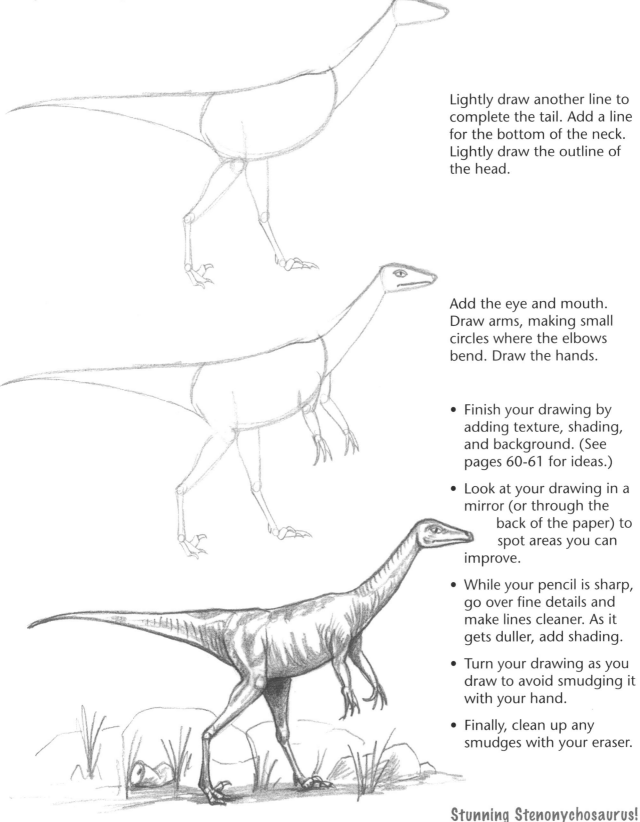

Lightly draw another line to complete the tail. Add a line for the bottom of the neck. Lightly draw the outline of the head.

Add the eye and mouth. Draw arms, making small circles where the elbows bend. Draw the hands.

- Finish your drawing by adding texture, shading, and background. (See pages 60-61 for ideas.)

- Look at your drawing in a mirror (or through the back of the paper) to spot areas you can improve.

- While your pencil is sharp, go over fine details and make lines cleaner. As it gets duller, add shading.

- Turn your drawing as you draw to avoid smudging it with your hand.

- Finally, clean up any smudges with your eraser.

Stunning Stenonychosaurus!

Ouranosaurus

OO-**RAN**-O-**SAW**-RUS

"Brave monitor lizard." Early cretaceous; Niger, West Africa. Ate plants. 23 feet (7m) long. Had a tall fin along its back and tail, probably for regulating body temperature. Closely related to Iguanodon, and like it had spike-like thumbs.

Start with a long, swooping line for the back. Add a curving line underneath for the bulk of the body.

Draw two lines for the neck. Add another line to make the bottom of the tail.

Lightly draw the head. Add mouth and eye.

Look at the leg–see how it bends in two places? Draw it, very lightly at first, starting with *rods and joints* (see pages 4-5).

Look!

Always start out *lightly!*

Add the other leg. Draw the arms and hands. Add the curving fin, running from the neck to the tip of the tail.

- Finish your drawing by adding texture, shading, and background. (See pages 60-61 for ideas.)

- Look at your drawing in a mirror (or through the back of the paper) to spot areas you can improve.

- While your pencil is sharp, go over fine details and make lines cleaner. As it gets duller, add shading.

- Turn your drawing as you draw to avoid smudging it with your hand.

- Finally, clean up smudges with your eraser.

Anchiceratops

AN-KI-SER-A-TOPS

"Close-horned face." Cretaceous; Alberta, Canada. Ate plants. 20 feet (6m) long. Had a long neck frill and one long horn above each eye, with a smaller one on the nose. The frill was probably for display, not for defense.

Always start out *lightly!*

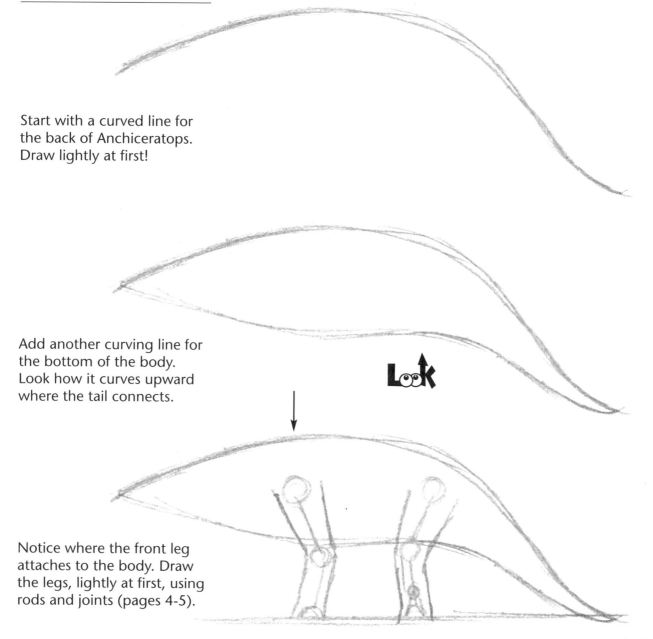

Start with a curved line for the back of Anchiceratops. Draw lightly at first!

Add another curving line for the bottom of the body. Look how it curves upward where the tail connects.

L**oo**k

Notice where the front leg attaches to the body. Draw the legs, lightly at first, using rods and joints (pages 4-5).

Notice that the legs bend toward each other.

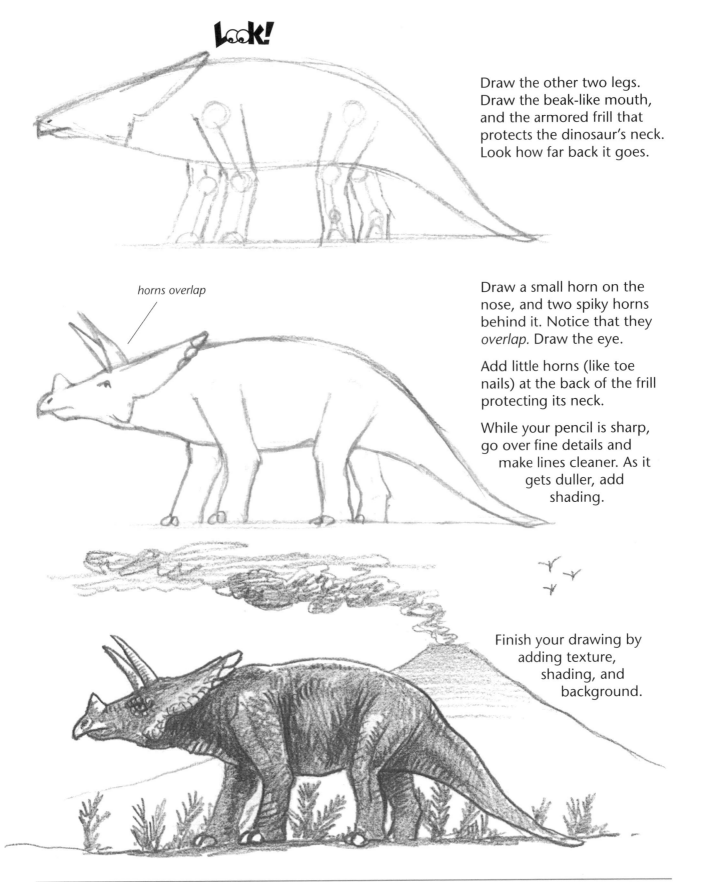

Look!

Draw the other two legs. Draw the beak-like mouth, and the armored frill that protects the dinosaur's neck. Look how far back it goes.

horns overlap

Draw a small horn on the nose, and two spiky horns behind it. Notice that they *overlap.* Draw the eye.

Add little horns (like toe nails) at the back of the frill protecting its neck.

While your pencil is sharp, go over fine details and make lines cleaner. As it gets duller, add shading.

Finish your drawing by adding texture, shading, and background.

Tuojiangosaurus

TWA-JAN-GO-SAW-RUS

"Tuojiang lizard." Late Jurassic; south-central China. Ate plants, probably grazing like a horse. 20 feet (6m) long. Of all Stegosaurus-type skeletons found in Asia, this one is the best preserved.

Draw a long line, curving up from the tail and back down to the end of the nose. Add another curve for the belly.

Draw additional lines to complete the head and tail.

Draw legs. Make the back legs bigger and longer than the front legs.

Always start out *lightly!*

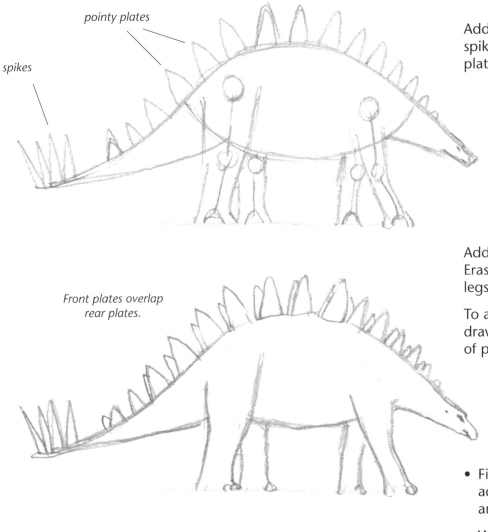

spikes

pointy plates

Front plates overlap
rear plates.

Add two more legs. Draw
spikes on the tail and pointy
plates on the back.

Add the eye and mouth.
Erase lines where tail and
legs overlap the body.

To add depth to your
drawing, make a second row
of pointy plates.

- Finish your drawing by
  adding texture, shading,
  and background.

- While your pencil is sharp,
  go over fine details and
  make lines cleaner. As it
  gets duller, add shading.

- Turn your drawing as you
  draw to avoid smudging it
  with your hand.

- Finally, clean up any
  smudges with your eraser.

Dsungaripterus

TSUN-GA-RIP-TER-US

Early Cretaceous. Skull 16 inches (41cm) long. Unusual upward-curving beak – for eating shellfish and snails? Who knows?

Start with a slanting line for the main axis of the body.

At a *right angle*, draw the curving lines of the head.

Add lines for the top of the wings, and the fingers where the wing bends.

Add curved lines for the bottom of each wing. Draw feet, and the oval at the end of the tail.

Finally, draw the lines of the arms and a few veins in the wing. Add shading.

Dsungaripterus was a type of Pterosaur (TER-o-sor). Pterosaurs weren't actually dinosaurs, they were flying reptiles.

CHAPTER 2

OVALSAURS

It's great to be able to draw a dinosaur in one position. But what if you want to draw it moving around?

How could you make it reach for food in a tree?

Or walk?

You'll gain flexibility in drawing different dinosaur poses when you start your drawing with ovals....

Apatosaurus

A-PAT-O-SAW-RUS

"Deceptive reptile." Late Jurassic; Colorado, Oklahoma, Utah and Wyoming, USA. Ate plants. 70 feet (21m) long; weighed 33 tons. One of the best-known dinosaurs. Has also been called *Brontosaurus* ("thunder reptile). Shorter than *Diplodocus* but much heavier.

Lightly draw two overlapping ovals for the body.

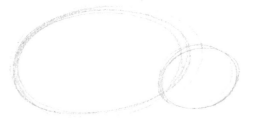

Make a much smaller, tilted oval for the head. Notice how far it is from the body.

From the top of the head, draw a smooth curving line touching the tops of larger ovals to make the back.

Add the line for the bottom of the neck. Add details to the face.

Always start out *lightly!*

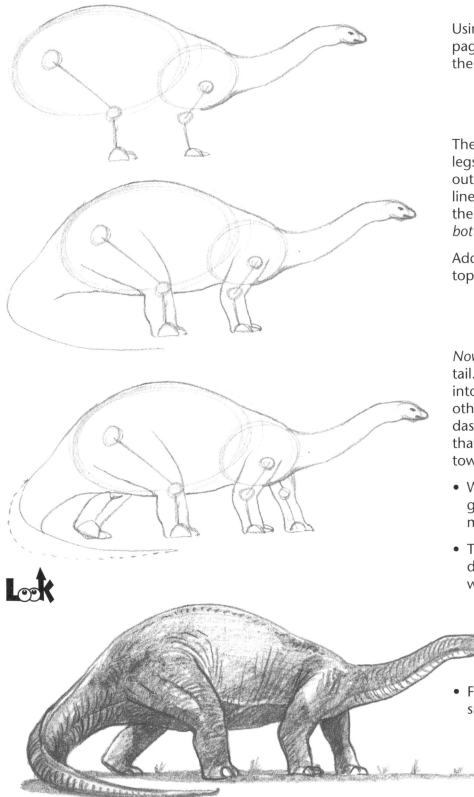

Using rods and joints (see pages 4-5), place the legs in the first two ovals you drew.

Then add thickness to the legs by making their outlines. Extend the belly line back to the beginning of the tail. *Don't draw the bottom of the tail yet!*

Add the curving line of the top of the tail.

Now add the bottom of the tail. Look at the way it runs into the other line. Draw the other line (shown with dashes) and you've got a tail that looks like it's curving toward you!

- While your pencil is sharp, go over fine details and make lines cleaner.

- Turn your drawing as you draw to avoid smudging it with your hand.

- Finally, clean up any smudges with your eraser.

Triceratops

TRI-**CER**-A-TOPS

"Three-horned face." Cretaceous; North America, from Alberta and Saskatchewan to Colorado and South Dakota. Up to 30 feet (9m) long; weighed 6 tons. Cores of the horns measure up to 3 ft (90cm); actual horns may have been much longer.

Draw a light, horizontal oval.

Using rods and joints (see pages 4-5), construct the front and rear leg. Make the hip higher than the shoulder. Notice how the legs bend toward each other.

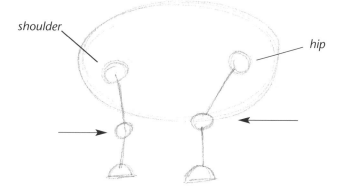

shoulder

hip

Carefully outline the legs and draw the toes. Then lightly erase the rods and joints.

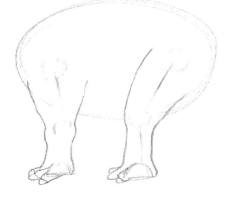

Now draw the other legs.

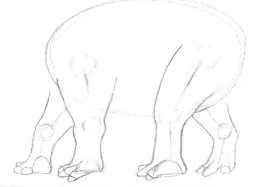

Always start out *lightly!*

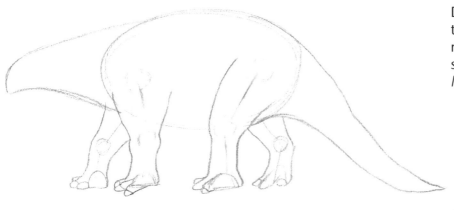

Draw the tail, making the top and bottom of it blend right into the oval. Draw the shape of the head—*very lightly!*

Add the eye, nose and mouth. Draw the three horns. Make the curved frill above the neck.

- Finish your drawing by adding texture, shading, and background. (See pages 60-61 for ideas.)

- Look at your drawing in a mirror (or through the back of the paper) to spot areas you can improve.

- While your pencil is sharp, go over fine details and make lines cleaner. As it gets duller, add shading.

- Turn your drawing as you draw to avoid smudging it with your hand.

- Finally, clean up any smudges with your eraser.

T'riffic Triceratops!

Parasaurolophus

PAR-A-SOR-O-LO-FUS

"Beside Sauralophus." Cretaceous; Alberta, Utah and New Mexico. 33 feet long (10m). The long (up to 6 ft/1.8m) crest on its head was probably a visual signal to other dinosaurs. It might have supported brightly colored skin connected to the neck, like a flag or banner. It wasn't a snorkel!

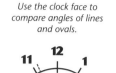

Use the clock face to compare angles of lines and ovals.

Lightly draw an oval, with one end higher than the other.

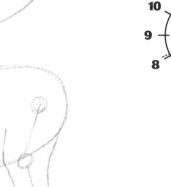

Draw the closest two legs, using rods and joints (pages 4-5). Notice how much bigger the rear leg is than the front leg.

Add the other two legs, and the straight, pointed tail.

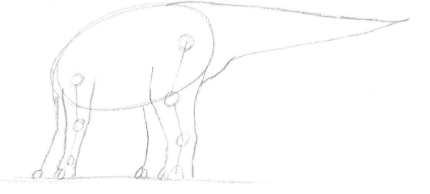

Lightly draw a circle for the head. Add the curving neck lines, then the crest on top and the jaws.

Always start out *lightly!*

Now carefully erase lines where legs, neck and tail overlap or join the body. Add eye and mouth. Begin shading in the darkest areas, on the far legs. Next…

…Wait a minute! What's going on here? It's turned around and stood up to take a better look at you!

What can we do now?

No problem: it's easy to draw dinosaurs in different positions when you start with ovals!

- Look at your drawing in a mirror (or through the back of the paper) to spot areas you can improve.

- While your pencil is sharp, go over fine details and make lines cleaner. As it gets duller, add shading.

- Turn your drawing as you draw to avoid smudging it with your hand.

- Finally, clean up any smudges with your eraser.

Ankylosaurus

AN-**KY**-LO-**SAW**-RUS

"Fused lizard." Late Cretaceous; Alberta, Canada; Montana, USA. Up to 35 feet (10.7m) long. Built like an army tank. Swung its tail as a weapon, but with its armor plating, could have done well to simply hunker down when things started to get ugly. Some ankylosaurs had spikes along the sides; others didn't.

Draw a horizontal oval for the body. Add a pointed head on one end. Draw the tail, two curving lines ending with an oval.

Use rods and joints (see pages 4-5) to draw the legs, then add their outlines. Don't forget the toenails!

Add the other two legs - notice where they join the body. Draw a line for the edge of the armor plating, all along the side. Draw eye and mouth, and horns on the face.

Carefully erase the rods and joints in the legs. Erase the main oval where the neck and tail join. Add a checkerboard pattern for the armor plates of the back, with a small bump in each square. Draw larger bumps on the neck and base of tail. Add a small row of bumps on the nose and tail.

Always start out *lightly!*

Add a cast shadow on the ground underneath.

What is the darkest part of the dinosaur? Where is the lightest part?

- Finish your drawing by adding texture, shading, and background. (See pages 60-61 for ideas.)

- Look at your drawing in a mirror (or through the back of the paper) to spot areas you can improve.

- While your pencil is sharp, go over fine details and make lines cleaner. As it gets duller, add shading.

- Turn your drawing as you draw to avoid smudging it with your hand.

- Finally, clean up any smudges with your eraser.

Use your knowledge of ovals, rods and joints to make your ankylosaurus in different settings: perhaps using its tail as a weapon…

…or trying NOT to become someone's lunch!

Pachycephalosaurus

PAK-EE-SEF-O-LO-SAW-RUS

"Thick-headed lizard." Cretaceous; western North America. 15 feet (4.6m) long. Scientists have decided that the extraordinarily thick (10 inch/25cm) skulls served as crash helmets, and that male dinosaurs would butt heads to establish dominance, as males of some species still do today.

Use the clock face to compare angles of lines and ovals.

Begin by drawing a slanted oval for the dinosaur's body.

Add two swooping lines for the tail. Draw a vertical oval for the head, and two lines for the neck.

Using rods and joints (see pages 4-5), draw the hip, knee, ankle and foot of the leg. Then draw the joints of the shoulder, elbow, and hand.

Add a line for the ground.

Outline the leg and arm.

Always start out *lightly!*

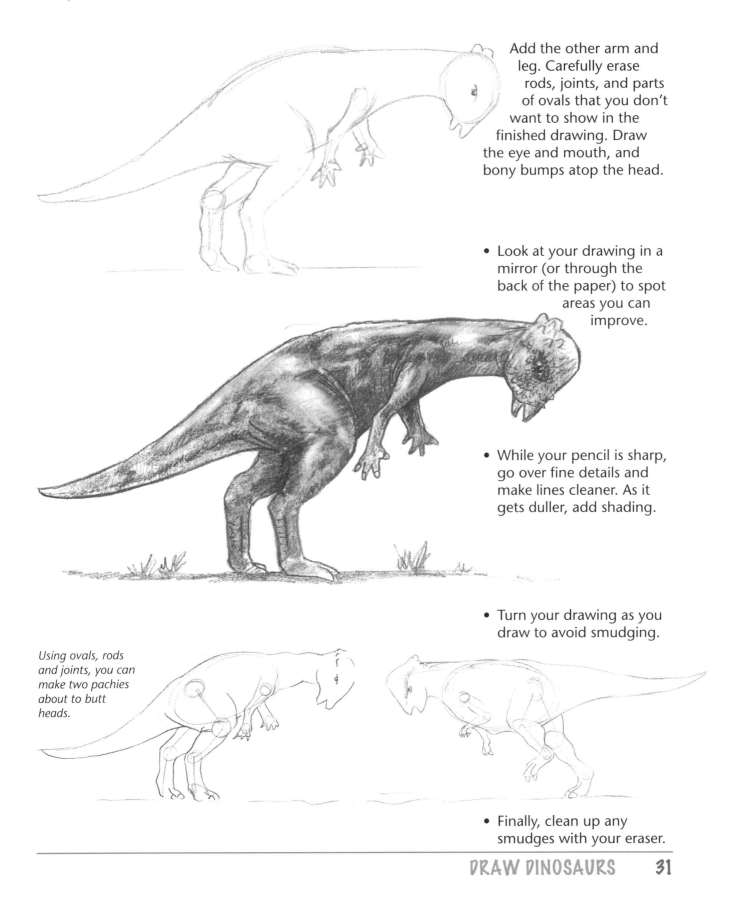

Add the other arm and leg. Carefully erase rods, joints, and parts of ovals that you don't want to show in the finished drawing. Draw the eye and mouth, and bony bumps atop the head.

• Look at your drawing in a mirror (or through the back of the paper) to spot areas you can improve.

• While your pencil is sharp, go over fine details and make lines cleaner. As it gets duller, add shading.

• Turn your drawing as you draw to avoid smudging.

Using ovals, rods and joints, you can make two pachies about to butt heads.

• Finally, clean up any smudges with your eraser.

Stegosaurus

STEG-O-SAW-RUS

"Roof lizard." Biggest known stegosaurid. Late Jurassic; Colorado, Oklahoma, Utah and Wyoming, USA. Up to 30 feet (9m) long; weighed up to 2 tons. Spikes on end of tail for defense. Scientists still debate what those big plates did, and whether they were staggered or in even pairs.

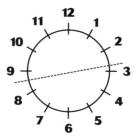

Use the clock face to compare angles of lines and ovals.

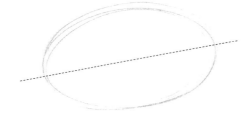

Draw a tilted, horizontal oval.

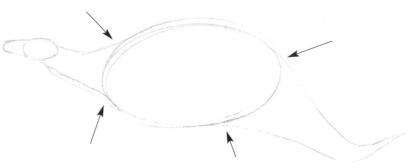

Draw a small, flat oval for the head, with a bump for the nose. Add two curving lines for the neck. Notice how the lines join the bottom of the big oval. They seem to flow right into it. Add lines for the tail, coming to a point at the end.

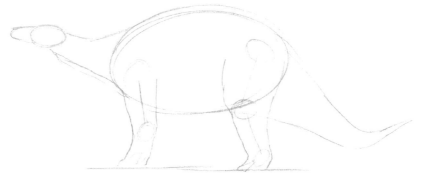

Using rods and joints (see pages 4-5), place the legs, then add outlines.

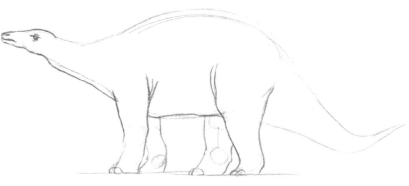

Add the remaining two legs. Draw the eye, nose and mouth. Carefully erase rods and joints, and parts of ovals that overlap. Darken the bottom outline.

Always start out *lightly!*

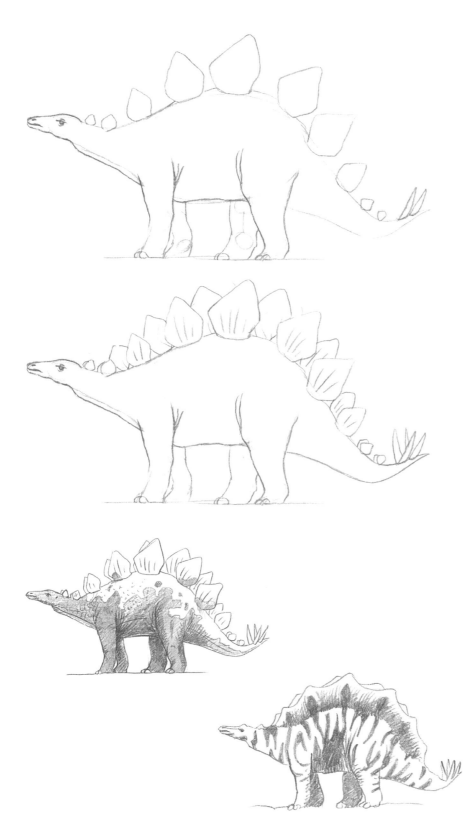

Draw a line of diamond-shaped armor plates along the back. Draw two tail spikes.

Add another row of plates. Make vertical lines on them. Draw the remaining two spikes on the tail.

- Finish your drawing by adding texture and shading. Use your imagination! Did Stego have a camouflage pattern? Or perhaps stripes, like a zebra? And were those plates really bare, or perhaps supporting a fin on the back? *Who knows?*

- Look at your drawing in a mirror (or through the back of the paper) to spot areas you can improve.

- While your pencil is sharp, go over fine details and make lines cleaner. As it gets duller, add shading.

- Turn your drawing as you draw to avoid smudging it with your hand.

- Finally, clean up any smudges with your eraser.

Kentrosaurus

KEN-TRO-SAW-RUS

"Pointed lizard." Late Jurassic; Tanzania, East Africa. 17 feet (5m) long. Stegosaurus-like plates become spikes farther back. Extra spikes stuck out sideways from the hip.

Lightly draw a tilted oval.

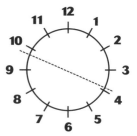

Use the clock face to compare angles of lines and ovals.

Add two long, swooping lines for the tail, then draw a small oval for the head, and two lines for the neck. Draw the eye and mouth.

The bottom of the tail and the top of the neck are level.

Draw a line for the ground, and use rods and joints (see pages 4-5) to create the front leg.

Add the rear leg, using rods and joints (see pages 4-5).

Always start out *lightly!*

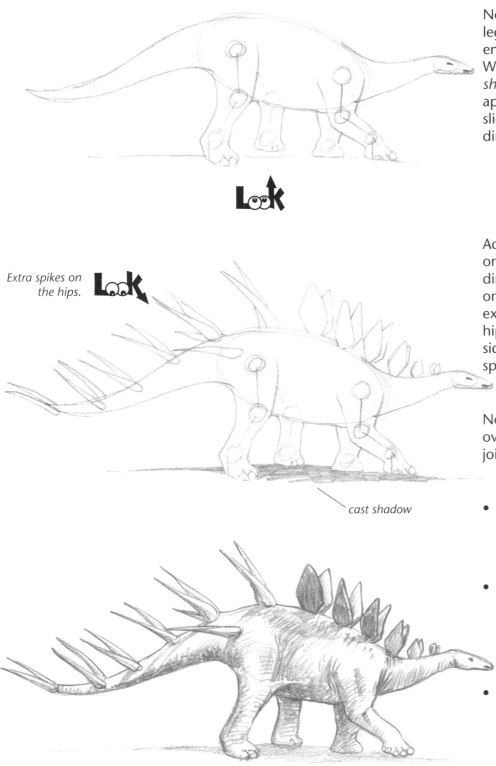

Now draw the other two legs. Look how one rear leg ends *above* the ground line. When you add the *cast shadow* underneath, it will appear that you're looking slightly down at the dinosaur.

Lᴏᴏᴋ

Extra spikes on the hips.

Lᴏᴏᴋ

Add pairs of pointed plates on the front half of the dinosaur, and pairs of spikes on the back. Notice the extra pair of spikes on the hip. Try turning your paper sideways when you draw the spikes.

Now, carefully erase overlapping ovals, rods and joints. add the *cast shadow.*

cast shadow

- Look at your drawing in a mirror (or through the back of the paper) to spot areas you can improve.

- While your pencil is sharp, go over fine details and make lines cleaner. As it gets duller, add shading.

- Finally, clean up any smudges with your eraser.

Kool kentrosaur!

Maiasaura

MY-A-SOR-A

"Good mother lizard." Cretaceous; Montana, USA. Up to 30 feet (9m) long. In 1978 scientists discovered fossilized baby Maiasaura and eggs around a mound-shaped nest, the first evidence of dinosaurs with organized family structure.

Start with a a tilted oval for the dinosaur's body.

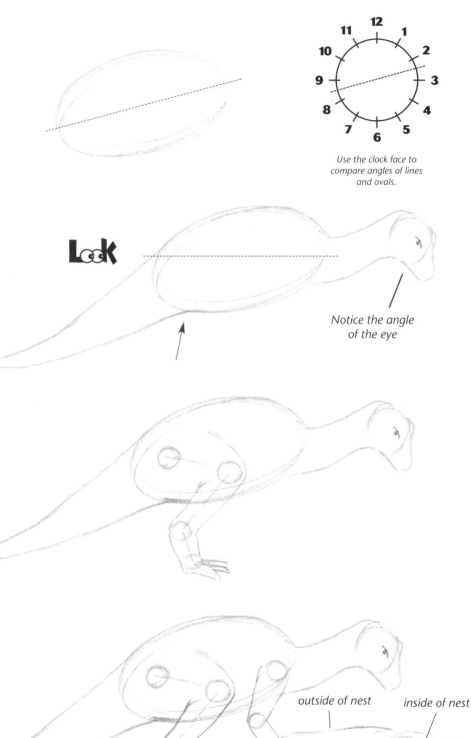

Use the clock face to compare angles of lines and ovals.

Look where the top of the tail joins the body. From that point, draw the line for the top of the tail. Then add the bottom of the tail, which flows smoothly into the bottom of the oval.

Notice the angle of the eye

Draw a circle for the head. Place the eye inside it. Add the curving lines of the neck, flowing into the ovals at either end.

Using rods and joints (see pages 4-5), draw the hip, knee, ankle and foot. Lightly add the outline of the leg.

Repeat for the arm. Make the hand higher than the foot. Draw lines for the inside and outside of the nest. Draw eggs in the nest.

outside of nest   *inside of nest*

You only see part of each egg.

Always start out *lightly!*

Now add the other leg and arm. Draw the mouth and nostril

Carefully erase rods and joints, and overlapping sections of the main oval. Then go over the outlines and begin to add details.

Finish your drawing by adding texture, shading, and background. (See pages 60-61 for ideas.)

Clean up any smudges with your eraser.

Mahvelous Maiasaura!

Plesiosaurus

PLEES-EE-O-SAW-RUS

"Ribbon reptile." Jurassic; Germany, England. 6-28 feet long (2-9m). Swam by flapping front flippers up and down. Probably moved its neck very quickly to catch fish. Alas, not a dinosaur but a swimming reptile.

Draw a horizontal oval for the body, and a smaller one for the head.

Draw the swooping lines of the neck. Add the tail.

Draw the centerline of the back.

Add limbs, with flippers instead of feet.

Draw the mouth and eye. Carefully erase the original oval at neck and tail.

Add shading to add form to the body, and you have a...

...pleasing Plesiosaurus!

CHAPTER 3

TRIANGLESAURS

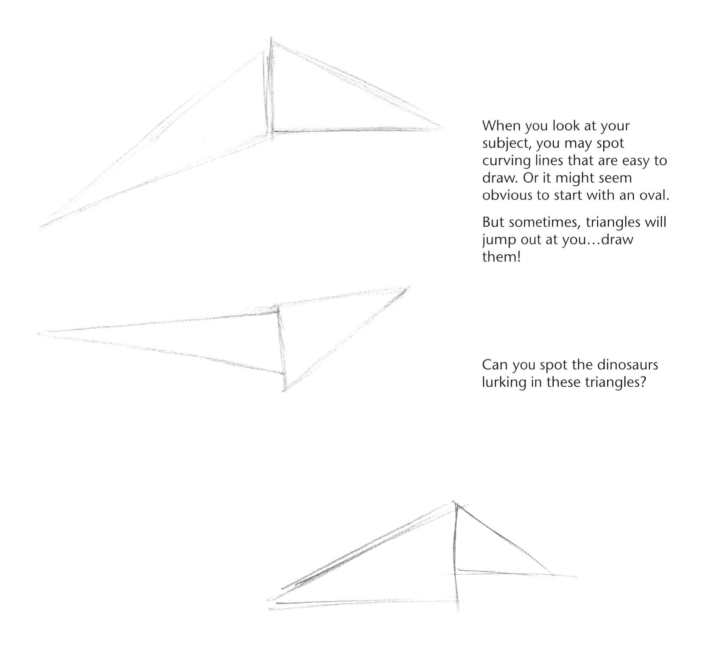

When you look at your subject, you may spot curving lines that are easy to draw. Or it might seem obvious to start with an oval.

But sometimes, triangles will jump out at you…draw them!

Can you spot the dinosaurs lurking in these triangles?

Looking for Triangles

When artists and illustrators sit down to draw a realistic picture, they almost always have some sort of *reference material.* In other words, they look at something as they draw it.

But no people see things exactly alike.

One person might see big swooping lines and start the drawing as a linosaur.

Another person might start with an oval for the body, making an ovalsaur.

And a third person might see triangles, and use them to begin the drawing.

Triangles are everywhere. When you look at your subject, look for curving lines and look for ovals...but also look for triangles.

Always start out *lightly!*

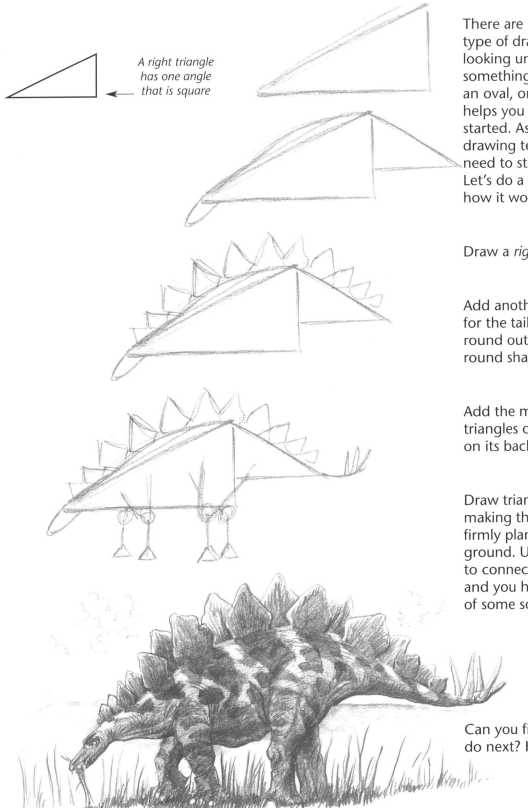

A right triangle has one angle that is square

There are no rules to this type of drawing. Just keep looking until you find something – whether a line, an oval, or a triangle – that helps you get your drawing started. As with the other drawing techniques, you need to start out very lightly! Let's do a quick sketch to see how it works.

Draw a *right triangle*.

Add another right triangle for the tail. Draw a curve to round out the back. Add a round shape for the head.

Add the most obvious triangles of all – the plates on its back.

Draw triangles for feet, making them look very firmly planted on the ground. Use open triangles to connect with the knees, and you have the beginning of some solid-looking legs!

Can you figure out what to do next? Keep going!

Tyrannosaurus

TIE-RAN-O-SAW-RUS

"Tyrant lizard." Cretaceous; western North America, china. Ate meat. Lots of it. 39 feet (12m) long; 18.5 feet (5.6m) tall; weighed 7 tons—as much as an African elephant. Skull measured 4 feet (1.2m). Saw-edged teeth could be 7 inches (18cm) long.

A right triangle has one angle that is square

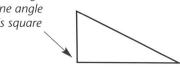

Start by drawing (very lightly!) a *right* triangle.

Draw another long triangle connecting to it and pointing downward.

Using more triangles, make the shape of the thigh and calf of the dinosaur. Add part of a triangle for the other leg. Notice how the triangles look like legs already!

Make single lines for the bottom part of the leg, and small triangles for the feet. Draw one foot at an angle and slightly higher.

The dinosaur is pushing with this foot to get leverage as it pulls with its jaws.

Always start out *lightly!*

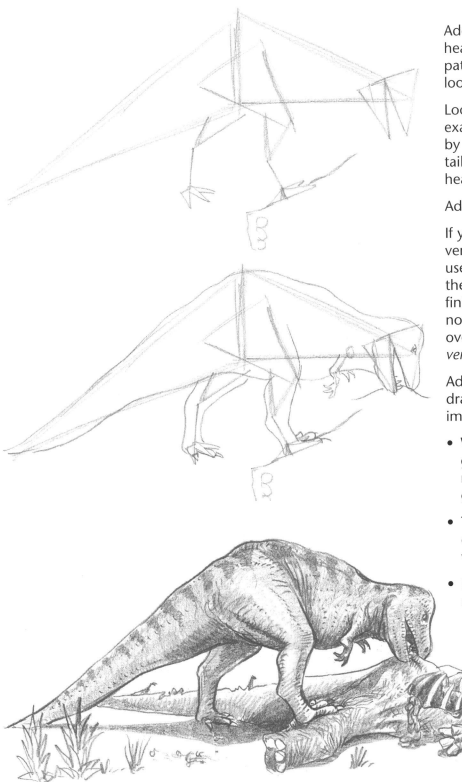

Add two triangles for the head. You now have a pattern of triangles that looks like Tyrannosaurus!

Looking at the finished example, round the triangles by making outlines of the tail, back, belly, legs, and head.

Add the arms.

If you drew your triangles very lightly, you can carefully use your eraser and make them disappear before finishing your drawing. If not, you may want to start over—making the triangles *very* light this time!

Add details to your finished drawing. Use your imagination!

- While your pencil is sharp, go over fine details and make lines cleaner. As it gets duller, add shading.

- Turn your drawing as you draw to avoid smudging it with your hand.

- Finally, clean up any smudges with your eraser.

Velociraptor

VEL-OS-I-RAP-tor

"Swift plunderer." Late Cretaceous; Mongolia, china, and Khazakhstan. 6 feet (1.8m) long. Probably hunted in packs, attacking with claws and teeth. In 1971 a specimen was found that had died while attacking a Protoceratops.

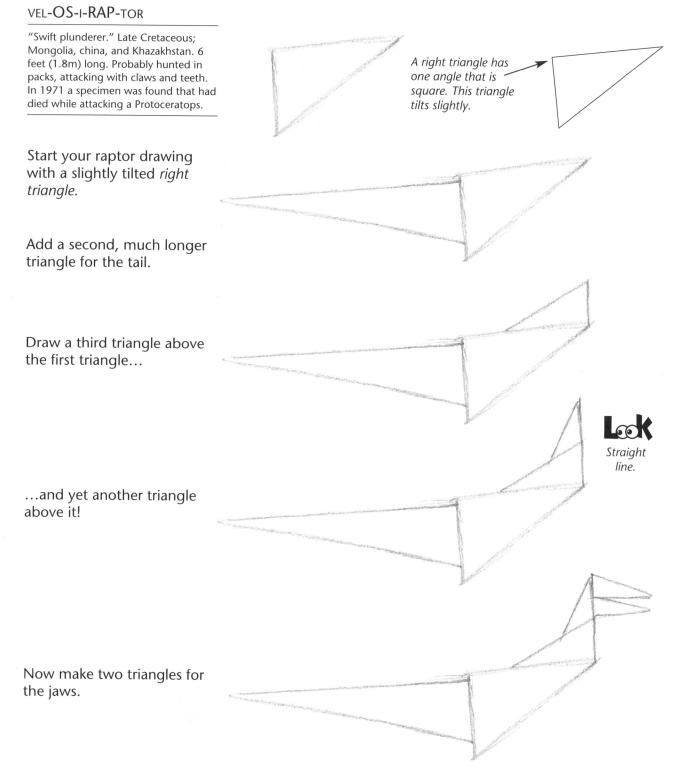

A right triangle has one angle that is square. *This triangle tilts slightly.*

Start your raptor drawing with a slightly tilted *right triangle.*

Add a second, much longer triangle for the tail.

Draw a third triangle above the first triangle…

Look
Straight line.

…and yet another triangle above it!

Now make two triangles for the jaws.

Origamisaurus?

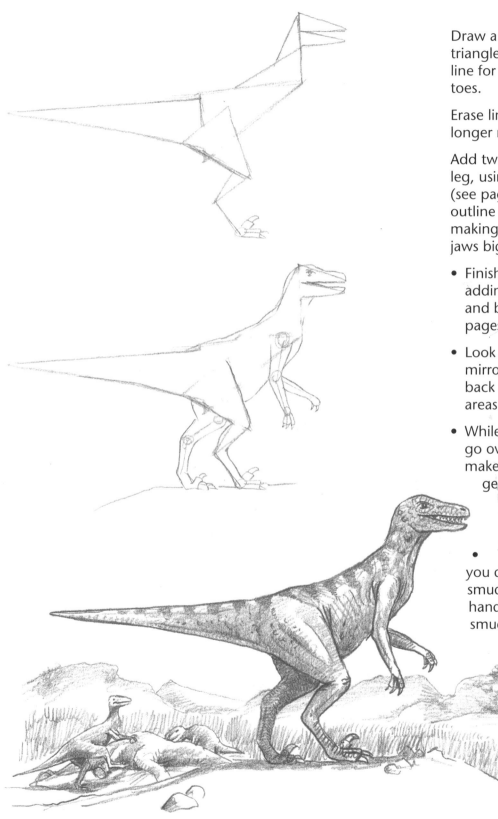

Draw a big and a small triangle for the leg. Add a line for the lower leg, and toes.

Erase lines that you no longer need.

Add two arms, and the other leg, using rods and joints (see pages 4-5). Enhance the outline of the dinosaur by making the belly, neck and jaws bigger.

- Finish your drawing by adding texture, shading, and background. (See pages 60-61 for ideas.)

- Look at your drawing in a mirror (or through the back of the paper) to spot areas you can improve.

- While your pencil is sharp, go over fine details and make lines cleaner. As it gets duller, add shading.

- Turn your drawing as you draw to avoid smudging it with your hand. Clean up any smudges with your eraser.

Compsognathus

KOMP-sog-NATH-us

"Pretty jaw." Jurassic; southern Germany, southeast France. Ate small animals. Up to 2 feet (60cm) long. This chicken-sized dinosaur probably lived and hunted in small herds, possibly attacking larger animals in a group.

A right triangle has one angle that is square. This triangle tilts slightly.

Start by lightly drawing a right triangle.

Add another right triangle pointing the other direction. Make the tops of both form a straight line.

From the end of the first triangle, make another triangle sticking up for the neck…

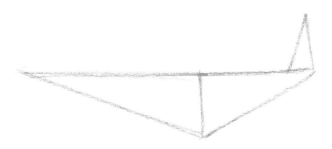

…and from it, a triangle sticking out for the head.

Lightly draw a titling triangle to make the top of the leg.

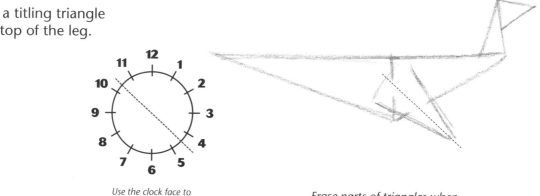

Use the clock face to compare angles.

Erase parts of triangles when you no longer need them, or if they become confusing.

Always start out *lightly!*

Complete the leg with rods and joints (see pages 4-5). Add rods and joints for the other leg and arm.

Now add the round curves of the outline, following the example.

- Finish your drawing by adding texture, shading, and background. (See pages 60-61 for ideas.)

- Look at your drawing in a mirror (or through the back of the paper) to spot areas you can improve.

- While your pencil is sharp, go over fine details and make lines cleaner. As it gets duller, add shading.

- Turn your drawing as you draw to avoid smudging it with your hand.

- Finally, clean up any smudges with your eraser.

What a cute little fellow! I wonder if he's friendly…?

Deinonychus

die-no-NIKE-us

"Terrible claw." Early Cretaceous; Montana, USA. 10-13 feet (3-4m) long. Larger then *Velociraptor,* it could kick into the belly of an animal and tear it open with its large (5 inch/12.7cm) scythe-like claw. There were also three heavy claws on each hand, with powerful arm muscles to make them effective weapons. This would be a dinosaur to avoid!

Always start out *lightly!*

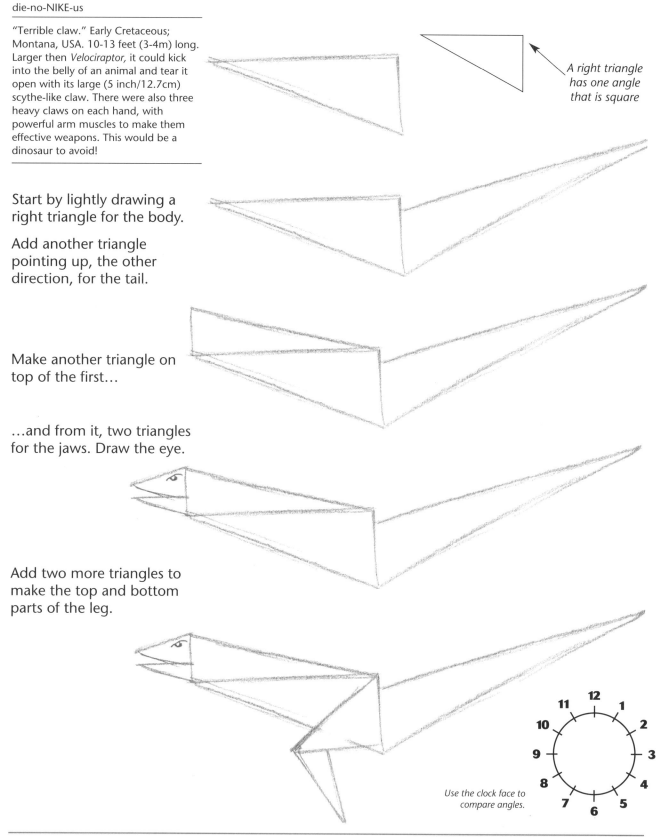

A right triangle has one angle that is square

Start by lightly drawing a right triangle for the body.

Add another triangle pointing up, the other direction, for the tail.

Make another triangle on top of the first…

…and from it, two triangles for the jaws. Draw the eye.

Add two more triangles to make the top and bottom parts of the leg.

Use the clock face to compare angles.

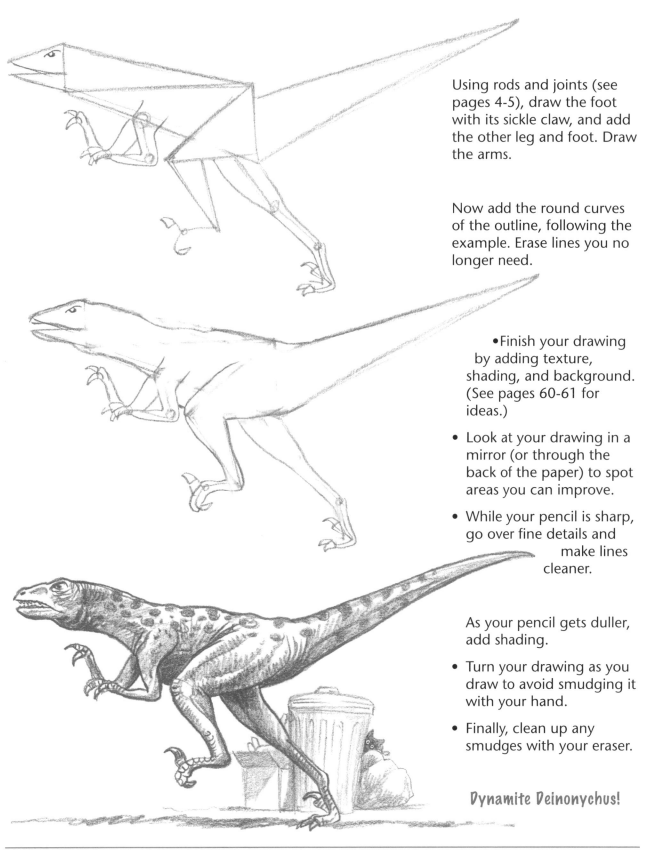

Using rods and joints (see pages 4-5), draw the foot with its sickle claw, and add the other leg and foot. Draw the arms.

Now add the round curves of the outline, following the example. Erase lines you no longer need.

• Finish your drawing by adding texture, shading, and background. (See pages 60-61 for ideas.)

• Look at your drawing in a mirror (or through the back of the paper) to spot areas you can improve.

• While your pencil is sharp, go over fine details and make lines cleaner.

As your pencil gets duller, add shading.

• Turn your drawing as you draw to avoid smudging it with your hand.

• Finally, clean up any smudges with your eraser.

Dynamite Deinonychus!

Pteranodon

TER-AN-O-DON

"Winged toothless." Late Cretaceous; Wyoming, USA. Wing span of 23 feet (7m); greater than any known bird. Probably only weighed about 37 lbs (17kg). Long, toothless jaw was counterbalanced by bony crest at top of head. Probably scooped fish out of the ocean, as pelicans do today – and probably had a pelican-like pouch as well.

There's no right or wrong way to using triangles in drawing. Just remember that they can be a handy tool.

For example, you may not need all the triangles I used in the Pteranodon's wing. Use as many as you find helpful!

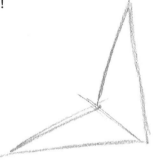

- Look at your drawing in a mirror (or through the back of the paper) to spot areas you can improve.

- While your pencil is sharp, go over fine details and make lines cleaner. As it gets duller, add shading.

- Turn your drawing as you draw to avoid smudging it with your hand.

- Finally, clean up any smudges with your eraser.

CHAPTER 4
SOLIDSAURS

As your dinosaur drawings improve, you may want the extra challenge of making dinosaurs that look as though they're coming right toward you.

In order to do this, it helps to understand basic forms and how to draw them.

Basic forms

To draw solidsaurs, you'll find three forms most useful: cylinders, cones, and rounded forms based on ovals.

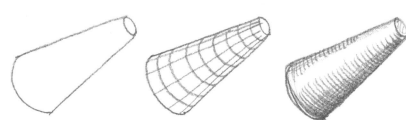

Cylinder

Shading makes your solid form look solid.

But for shading to work, it needs to follow the *contours* of the form. The middle drawing of each form shows *contour lines.* When you add shading, make the lines of the shading follow these lines.

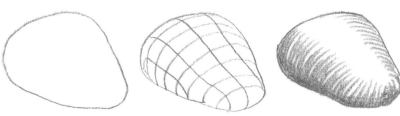

Cone

Combined, the forms can make bodies, legs, and more….

Rounded form

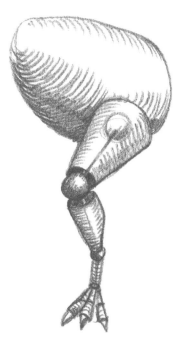

Using solid forms, you can choose whether to do serious, realistic drawings or make funny drawings and cartoon characters. In any case, understanding forms and contour lines will help make your drawings look more three-dimensional.

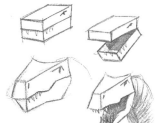

These heads were drawn using a box, another common form.

Lambeosaurus

LAM-be-oh-SAW-rus

"Lambe's lizard" Cretaceous; western North America. About 50 feet (15m) long. The tall, showy head crest was a hollow bone. The nostrils ran up from the snout through the crest.

Start with a vertical, slightly tilted oval for the body. Add the lines for the tail. Draw the oval for the head, with eye and crest. Add almost vertical neck lines. Draw the centerline of the body.

Use a combination of cylinders and cones to draw the leg, with curving lines showing the contours. Add more contour lines on the tail and belly.

Add the other leg and arms.

Always start out *lightly!*

Finish details in the head and neck, and add more shading to round out the body.

- Finish your drawing by adding texture, shading, and background. (See pages 60-61 for ideas.)

- Look at your drawing in a mirror (or through the back of the paper) to spot areas you can improve.

- While your pencil is sharp, go over fine details and make lines cleaner. As it gets duller, add shading.

- Turn your drawing as you draw to avoid smudging it with your hand.

- Finally, clean up any smudges with your eraser.

Lovely Lambeosaurus!

Scelidosaurus

SKEL-**IDE**-OH-**SOR**-US

"Limb lizard." Early Jurassic; southern England, Tibet. 13 feet (4 m) long. Probably a slow-moving dinosaur, it had very sturdy legs and was armored with bony knobs on its back. It's one of the few dinosaurs where fossils show an impression of the skin!

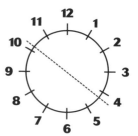

Use the clock face to compare angles of lines and ovals.

Draw a flat, tilted oval with contour lines showing the form.

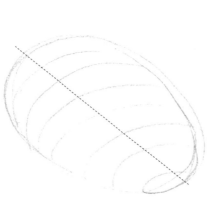

Add the neck and head. Use contour lines wrapping around the neck to create *foreshortening* (making it look like it's coming toward you). Add other lines where the rows of bumps will be on the back.

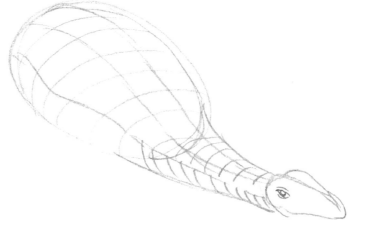

Using cylinders, draw the front leg.

Always start out *lightly!*

With more cylinders, draw the rear leg and the small visible portion of the front leg.

Draw the tail. Lightly erase lines you no longer need, then add the rows of bumps on the back.

- Finish your drawing by adding texture, shading, and background. (See pages 60-61 for ideas.)

- Look at your drawing in a mirror (or through the back of the paper) to spot areas you can improve.

- While your pencil is sharp, go over fine details and make lines cleaner. As it gets duller, add shading.

- Turn your drawing as you draw to avoid smudging it with your hand.

- Finally, clean up any smudges with your eraser.

Segnosaurus

SEG-no-SAW-rus

"Slow lizard." Cretaceous; southeast Mongolia. May have been 30 feet (9m) long. This dinosaur is known only from a partial skeleton. The best guess is that it might have been a swimmer and fed on fish.

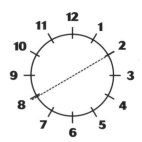

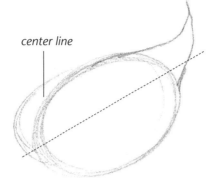

center line

Draw a tilted oval. Add the center line of the body, and extend it to make the top of the tail. Add the bottom line of the tail.

With cylinders, rods and joints, draw the back leg. Make contour lines wrapping around the leg and the body.

Add the arm. Shade the area behind it to make a dark shadow. The *contrast* of the dark makes the light arm appear closer.

Add the other arm and leg in a similar manner.

Always start out *lightly!*

Draw the neck and head. Use contour lines to show the form of the neck.

- Finish your drawing by adding texture, shading, and background.

- Look at your drawing in a mirror (or through the back of the paper) to spot areas you can improve.

- While your pencil is sharp, go over fine details and make lines cleaner. As it gets duller, add shading.

- Turn your drawing as you draw to avoid smudging it with your hand.

- Finally, clean up any smudges with your eraser.

Sensational Segnosaurus!

Finishing Touches

Before you add shading or texture, carefully remove lines that you don't want in the finished drawing.

It's OK if you erase some of the "good" lines. You'll go over them again to "sharpen" them.

Some paper erases well. Some paper doesn't. Don't be discouraged if erasing messes up your drawing, but do try to find a good "erasing" paper. Draw more lightly next time so you don't have as much to erase!

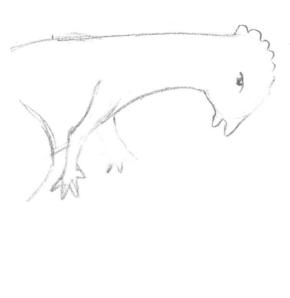

Erase lines you don't need in the final drawing: rods and joints, and where parts overlap.

A kneadable eraser starts out square, but you bend and twist it so you can erase small areas…a great help if you can find one.

Next, build tones (light and dark) by shading with a dull pencil. Don't just scribble with your pencil in every direction: follow the *contours* of the form.

A blending stump looks like a pencil made of paper. Use it or a rolled-up wad of paper to smooth shaded areas

With a blending stump or small rolled-up wad of paper, you can smudge the shading to make it very smooth.

While your pencil is sharp, add details and texture. Go over lines, making them sharper and stronger.

Add patterns to the skin, making them follow the *contours* of the body whenever possible.

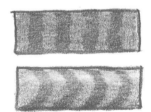

Follow contours when you shade. In the lower box, the stripes and shading show a curved contour, similar to the curve of an arm for leg. In contrast, the upper box looks flat.

Backgrounds

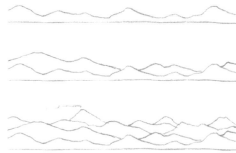

Adding background details can make your drawing much more fun to look at. For a quick background, draw a squiggly line of mountains. Add another, and another. Notice how the hills in front *overlap* those further away.

Add plants, simple or complicated:

A

B

C

A. *Simple pencil strokes suggest grass, and create a sense of scale for this small dinosaur.*

B. *Bushier plants make this dinosaur look larger.*

C. *Plants getting smaller create a sense of depth.*

D

E

D. *Broad, leafy plants as tall as the dinosaur add realism to the drawing.*

E. *Plants that hardly reach its knees make the dinosaur look bigger. But the volcano looks bigger still! Notice overlapping.*

Use your imagination!

Some final thoughts

Remember...

One of the great secrets of our world is that behind every success there's always plenty of practice. The people who do amazing feats of daring, skill, or ingenuity have been practicing, often for much longer than you'd imagine. They've probably failed more often than you can imagine, too, so don't waste time being discouraged. If your drawings don't look exactly the way you'd like them to (especially the first try), stop, look, and try again!

Save your drawings!

Whenever you do a drawing—or even a sketch—put your initials (or autograph!) and date on it. And save it. You don't have to save it until it turns yellow and crumbles to dust, but do keep your drawings, at least for several months. Sometimes, hiding in your portfolio, they will mysteriously improve! I've seen it happen often with my own drawings, especially the ones I *knew* were no good at all, but kept anyway.

If you don't have your own portfolio, here's a way to make one inexpensively (or you can buy one at an art supply store).

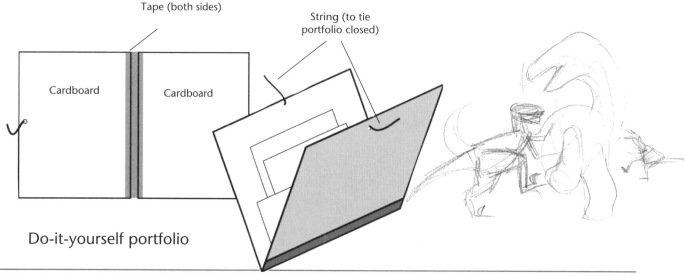

Tape (both sides)

String (to tie portfolio closed)

Cardboard   Cardboard

Do-it-yourself portfolio

Index

Allosaurus......................................10

Anchiceratops 16

Ankylosaurus.............................28

Apatosaurus 22

Camarasaurus..............................8

Compsognathus.....................46

Deinonychus 48

Dsungaripterus.........................20

Kentrosaurus 34

Lambeosaurus 54

Maiasaura...................................36

Ouranosaurus............................14

Pachycephalosaurus 30

Parasaurolophus 26

Plesiosaurus................................38

Pteranodon 50

Scelidosaurus..............................56

Segnosaurus................................58

Stegosaurus........................32, 40

Stenonychosaurus 12

Triceratops 24

Tuojiangosaurus 18

Tyrannosaurus.............................42

Velociraptor................................44

Learn about other books in
this series online at
www.drawbooks.com!

by Doug DuBosque

PEEL productions, inc.

DRAW RAINFOREST Animals

Contents

Basilisk Lizard.....................6

Chimpanzee........................8

Emerald Tree Boa.................10

Flying Squirrel....................12

Frog 1 (Arrow Poison) 14

Frog 2 (Flying)...................15

Frog 3 (Tree) 16

Gorilla............................18

Hoatzin...........................20

Howler Monkey...................22

Iguana............................24

Jaguar 26

Kinkajou..........................28

Ruffed Lemur 30

Macaw 32

Margay 34

Okapi 36

Orangutan........................38

Ouakari 40

Pangolin..........................42

Quetzal 44

Slender Loris.....................46

Sloth 48

Spider Monkey....................50

Tamandua.........................52

Tapir 54

Toucan...........................56

Vine Snake.......................58

Other Ideas & Drawing Tips.......60

Index 63

 # A few thoughts before you start...

Rainforests – cool!

The rainforests, or jungles, of the world hold plenty of surprises for those who explore them. Let's do that with a pencil!

Draw Rainforest Animals shows you how to draw fascinating creatures, step by step. You may find some of them quite easy. Others present more challenges.

What do you need?

- **pencil**
  (2B or 3B will work well)
- **pencil sharpener**
- **eraser**
  (kneadable works best)
- **paper**
  (test of quality: how easily can you erase on it?)
- **place to draw**
  Good light, no distractions.

And don't forget...

- **positive attitude**
  Forget *"I can't."*
  Say, *"I'm learning."*

You drawings may not be perfect the first time. Keep working on them!

Think of drawing in three stages.

First

Read the instructions. LOOK carefully at the animal you wish to draw! See the shapes and pieces and how they fit together.

Then, lightly sketch the shapes in the right place.

When you sketch lightly, you can easily correct any mistakes before they ruin your drawing.

Second

Once you have the basic shapes and lines right,
- add more complicated parts,
- add shading,
- add detail, and
- erase lines you no longer need.

Third

Make your drawing jump off the page!
- add more shading,
- sharpen details,
- clean up with your eraser, and
- date and save your drawing in a portfolio *(see p.62).*

Just so you know...

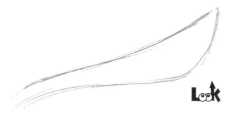

Clock faces appear from time to time. Use them as a reference to see the tilt of ovals, legs, and other angles in the drawing.

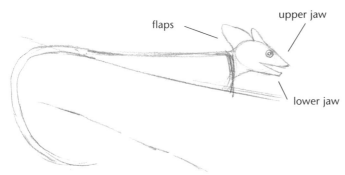

Look signs point out visual elements of the drawing – in this example, a curve turns almost vertical.

flaps — upper jaw

lower jaw

Labels will help you identify the parts of the animal mentioned in the text.

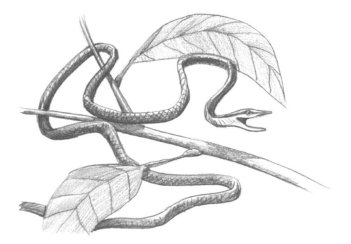

And now, let's

DRAW
RAINFOREST Animals

Basilisk Lizard

Basiliscus plumifrons: South America. Size: 80 cm (31 inches). Feeds on fruit and small animals during the day. Few four-legged animals can run on two legs the way this lizard does. It can even run a short distance across water!

1. Start with two slanting lines for the branch. Lightly draw a long triangle for the lizard's body. Add the long, curving tail.

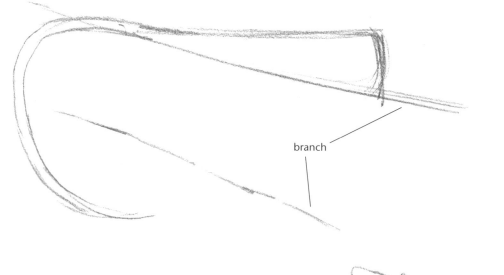

branch

2. Still drawing very lightly, make an oval for the head. Add the upper and lower jaws at one end. Draw the neck and flaps on top of the head. Carefully place the eye, above the back of the mouth.

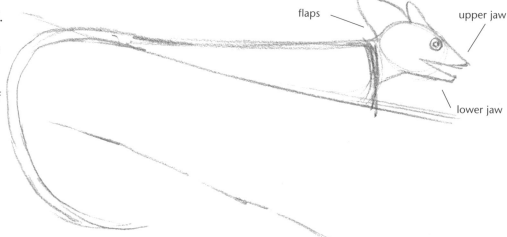

flaps

upper jaw

lower jaw

3. Look closely at the legs grabbing the branch. Draw the legs – one piece at a time.

   Draw lightly at first!

Sit back, take a deep breath, and really look at your drawing. Do all the proportions look correct? Is there anything you need to improve before continuing?

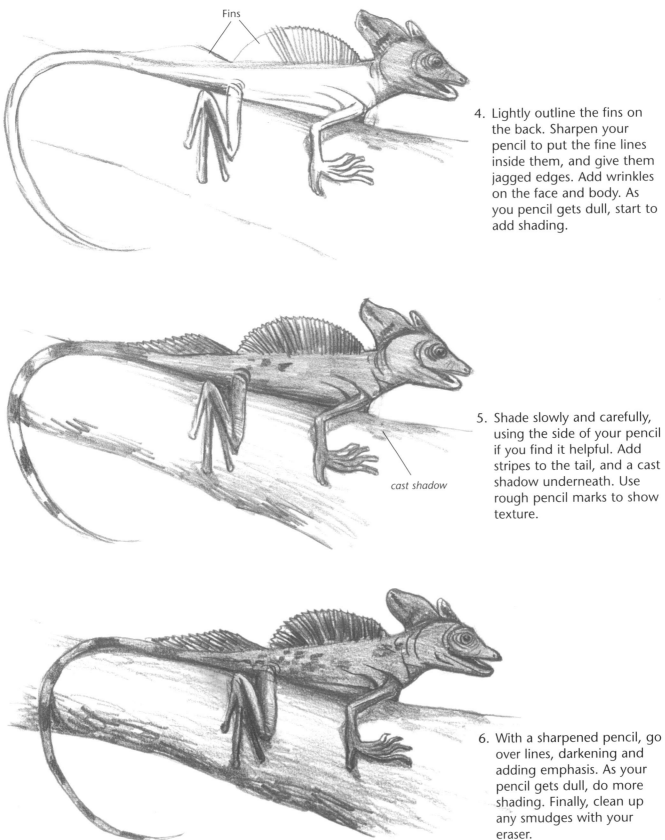

Fins

4. Lightly outline the fins on the back. Sharpen your pencil to put the fine lines inside them, and give them jagged edges. Add wrinkles on the face and body. As you pencil gets dull, start to add shading.

5. Shade slowly and carefully, using the side of your pencil if you find it helpful. Add stripes to the tail, and a cast shadow underneath. Use rough pencil marks to show texture.

cast shadow

6. With a sharpened pencil, go over lines, darkening and adding emphasis. As your pencil gets dull, do more shading. Finally, clean up any smudges with your eraser.

Chimpanzee

Pan troglodytes: Africa. Intelligent and expressive animals, chimpanzees spend most of their time on the ground, walking on all fours and occasionally standing erect. They are good climbers. They eat plant materials, plus insects and eggs – they even use tools like twigs to extract ants or termites!

1. In this drawing, the face is important, so take time to get it right! Draw two light circles, with a tall oval touching the bottom of both.

2. Near the bottom of the lower oval, draw a line for the mouth. At the top of the oval, draw two nostrils with heart-shaped outline. Add curved lines for eyes.

3. Draw the lower lip. what other details do you see? Add them!

4. Add radiating lines to complete the head. Add ears.

5. Lightly draw two overlapping ovals for the body. Which is higher? Which is bigger? Which is flatter?

6. Look at the back legs. Which lines go straight up and down (vertical)? Where does each leg start? Which direction does it go? Now draw them – very lightly until you've got them just right.

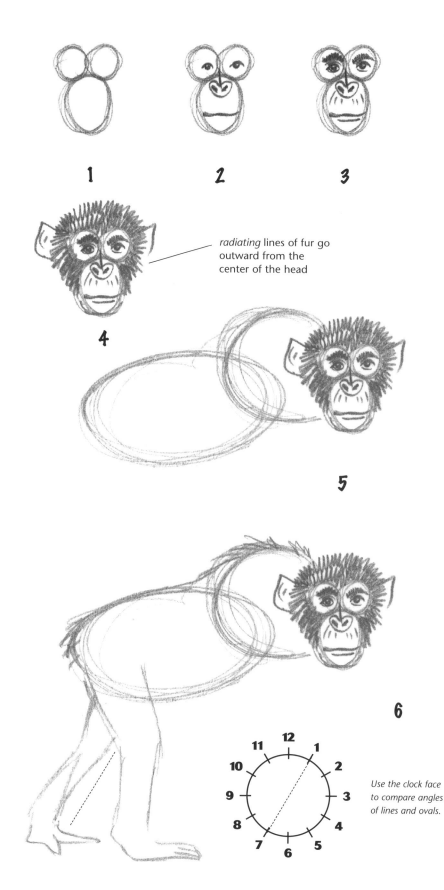

radiating lines of fur go outward from the center of the head

Use the clock face to compare angles of lines and ovals.

7. Lightly draw the arms. (If it helps you, add a line for the ground.) Look carefully at the shape of the arms and hands.

   Make short pencil guide lines showing the direction of the fur.

8. Following those guide lines, add fur to the body. Look how the ovals disappear – no need to erase! Add a slight cast shadow on the ground.

 Turn your drawing as you draw to avoid smudging it with your hand.

Sit back, take a deep breath and really look at your drawing (perhaps in a mirror). Does it need darker fur? Sharper details on the face or hands? If so, do them now.

Clean up any smudges with your eraser.

cast shadow

Pssssst...if nobody's listening, make some chimp sounds....

Emerald Tree Boa

Boa caninus: South America
Size: 1.2 m (4 ft). Brilliant green
snake with prehensile tail spends its
life in trees, where it lies in wait for
prey, often birds and bats. Fast, and
a good swimmer.

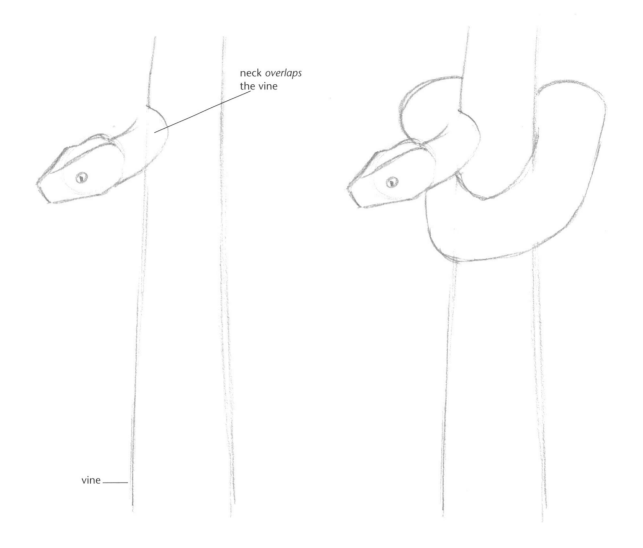

neck *overlaps*
the vine

vine

*Be creative! Draw this snake in different positions. You
don't have to follow my drawing exactly!*

1. Start with two light *vertical* lines for the vine. Draw
   the head with eye, and the first section of the
   body, *overlapping* part of the vine.

   Make the front of the head blunt. Each eyebrow
   bulges slightly.

2. Add the next section of the body, forming a rough
   U shape.

Turn your drawing as you draw to avoid smudging it with your hand.

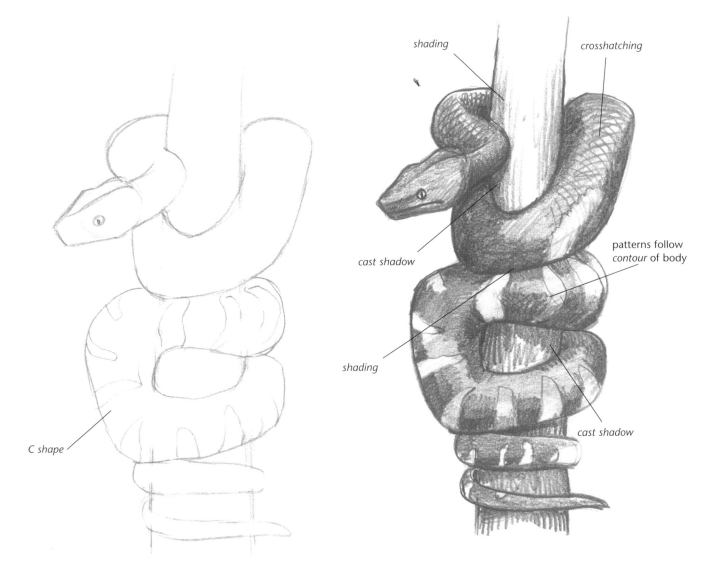

shading *crosshatching*

cast shadow

shading

patterns follow *contour* of body

cast shadow

C shape

3. Below the U shape, make another section of the body, this time a fat C shape. Add a couple more sections, getting smaller and smaller….

Notice that the snake doesn't wrap around the vine in one continuous spiral. The tail wraps all the way around, but the larger parts of the body reverse direction to form 'clamps' to hold to the vine.

4. Now try to make the snake and vine look round.

Look carefully for:
• the pattern of curving white spots,
• crosshatching to suggest scales,
• shading on the snake and the vine, and
• cast shadows on the vine and snake.

You're on your own! Keep shading until it looks like it's ready to jump off the page!

Good looking boa!

Flying Squirrel

Anomalurus beecrofti (Beecroft's flying squirrel): West and central Africa. Size: 53-84 cm (20-33 inches) overall length. Lives in trees. Feeds mostly on berries, seeds and fruit. Glides up to 90 m (300 ft) from tree to tree.

Always draw lightly at first!

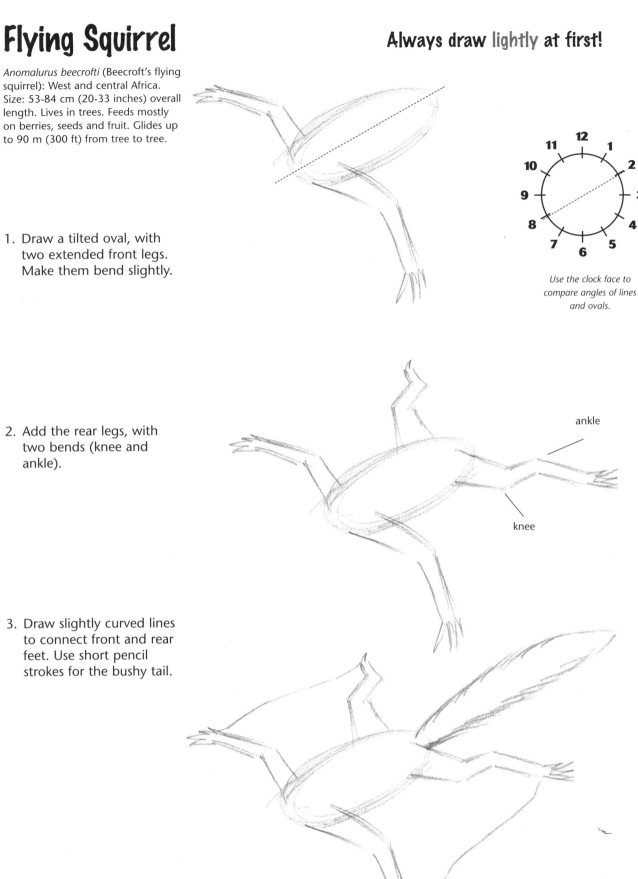

Use the clock face to compare angles of lines and ovals.

1. Draw a tilted oval, with two extended front legs. Make them bend slightly.

2. Add the rear legs, with two bends (knee and ankle).

ankle

knee

3. Draw slightly curved lines to connect front and rear feet. Use short pencil strokes for the bushy tail.

4. Draw an oval for the head, slightly pointed at the nose. Add the eye and ears.

5. Draw the fur, using short pencil strokes. Leave some areas white. Add detail to the eye. Draw whiskers. Sharpen details. Clean up any smudges with your eraser.

Idea: add some leaves behind the squirrel. Draw the branch the squirrel just launched from.

Frog 1 (Arrow Poison)

Dendrobates auratus: Central and South America. Size: 4 cm (1.5 inches). Bright red coloring warns predators that this frog is poisonous! Local tribesman know how to extract the poison, which they use on the tips of hunting arrows.

1. Draw two overlapping ovals. Draw them very lightly! You'll see why in a moment.

2. Add a bump for the hip, a bump at the top of the head, a bump for the nose, and one more for the throat. Erase the ovals where they overlap. Draw a circle for the eye – leave a small white spot when you darken it. Add the curving lines for the top and bottom of the eye.

3. Add the legs. Look where and how each leg attaches to the body, and the angles of each segment of the legs. Erase the oval where the leg overlaps it.

4. As your pencil gets dull, add shading. Leave part of the back very light to help make it look shiny. When you sharpen your pencil, go over details and outlines to make them sharper.

    Add the cast shadow under the frog. Clean up any smudges with your eraser.

    If you want to use color, make the frog bright orange with black spots.

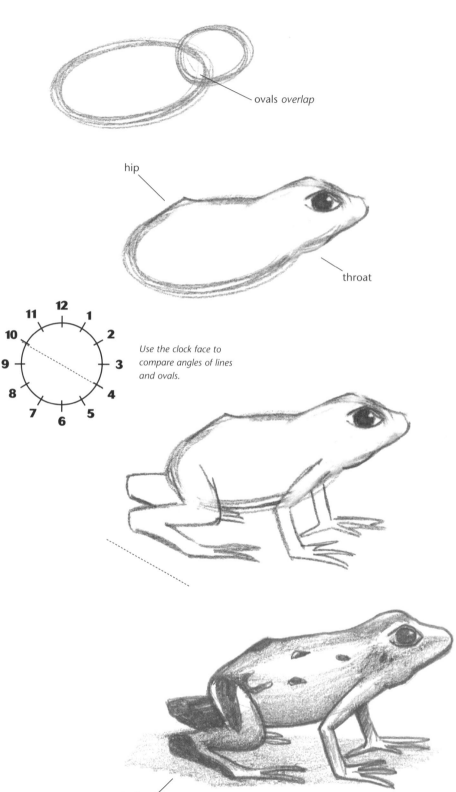

ovals *overlap*

hip

throat

Use the clock face to compare angles of lines and ovals.

cast shadow

Frog 2 (Flying)

Rhacophorus nigropalmatus (Wallace's flying frog): Southeast Asia. This 10-cm (4-inch) long frog glides from tree to tree. The webs and skin flaps act like a parachute.

1. Draw a tall, narrow triangle for the body. Add two L-shaped arms to it.

2. Add bumps on the triangle for the nose and eyes. Draw four fingers to each arm. Connect the ends of the fingers to make the webs. Draw Z-shaped legs.

3. Add toes and webbing to the legs. Draw curves in the arms and legs.

4. Shade the dark, webbed parts of the feet. Add shading to the rest of the frog.

   Clean up any smudges with your eraser.

Idea: you're looking down on a frog gliding high above the ground. What would it see below it? Can you draw that?

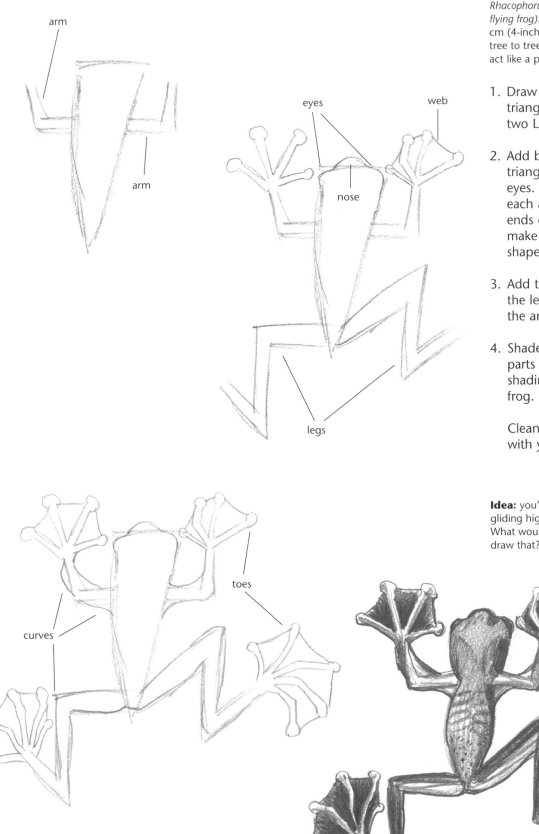

arm

arm

eyes

web

nose

legs

curves

toes

Frog 3 (Tree)

Phyllomedusa appendiculata (Lutz's Phyllomedusa): Southeast Brazil. Size: 4 cm (1.5 inches). Lives in trees, feeds on insects. Lays eggs in a protective leaf over water. When the tadpoles hatch, they fall into the water.

Use the clock face to compare angles of lines and ovals.

12 11 1 10 2 9 3 8 4 7 6 5

In this view, you don't see the whole frog. Look at the final drawing. See how many parts of the body *overlap*.

1. Start with 2 upside-down V shapes for the front leg.

2. Add three fingers. Draw a curving line for the bottom part of the body, then a straight line for the mouth.

3. Add two sideways V shapes for the other front leg. Draw the rear toes.

4. Draw toes for the other front leg, then carefully draw curving lines for the branch.

   With so many toes overlapping the branch, it's easier to draw them first, then add the branch behind.

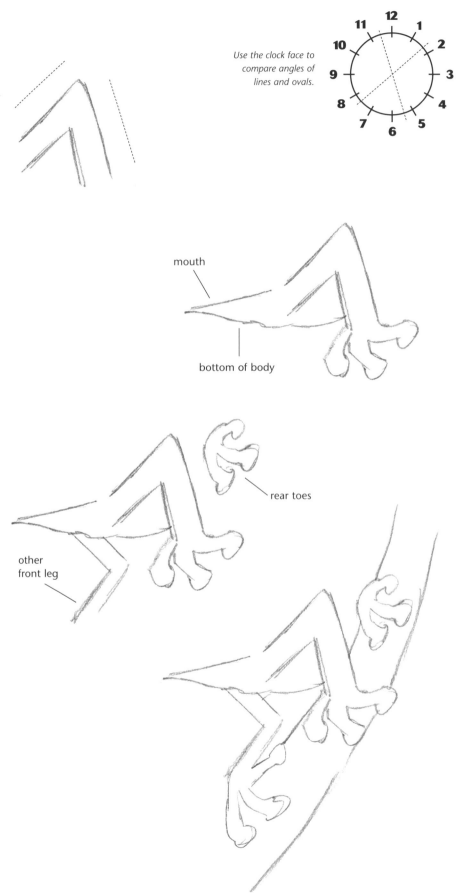

mouth

bottom of body

rear toes

other front leg

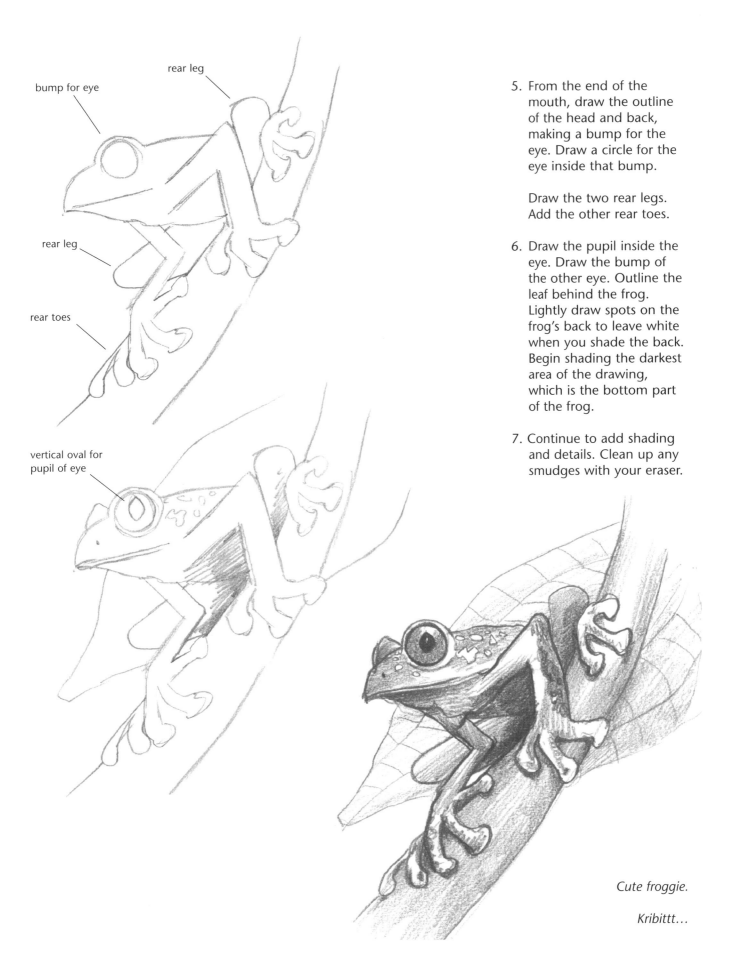

bump for eye

rear leg

rear leg

rear toes

vertical oval for pupil of eye

5. From the end of the mouth, draw the outline of the head and back, making a bump for the eye. Draw a circle for the eye inside that bump.

   Draw the two rear legs. Add the other rear toes.

6. Draw the pupil inside the eye. Draw the bump of the other eye. Outline the leaf behind the frog. Lightly draw spots on the frog's back to leave white when you shade the back. Begin shading the darkest area of the drawing, which is the bottom part of the frog.

7. Continue to add shading and details. Clean up any smudges with your eraser.

Cute froggie.

Kribittt…

Gorilla

Gorilla gorilla: Africa, in rain forests to fairly high elevations. Size: male height 1.7-1.8 m (5.5-6 ft); female height 1.4-1.5 m (4.5-5 ft). Largest of the primates, gorillas are gentle animals unless threatened. They eat mainly plants. They live in small groups. *Easy scientific name!*

1. Draw two small circles on top of a larger oval. Make a line across them to help emphasize the strong brow of the gorilla.

2. Draw a line for the mouth. Add eyes, with lines under them. Draw slanting nostrils.

3. From the edge of the eyebrow, draw a line up to a point and back down – like a pyramid on the gorilla's head. This part of the head is almost as high as the face! Add the ear, and short pencil lines on the chin, face and forehead.

4. From the back of the head, make a long swooping line for the back, joined by another swooping line for the back of the leg.

5. Lightly draw the leg and arm, with toes and fingers. Notice the shape of the arm. Look how close the shoulder comes to the face.

another curve

another leg

guide lines

another arm

6. Add the other leg and arm. Before you add fur, make light *guide lines* to remind you which direction the shading needs to go.

7. Cover the whole body with short pencil strokes. Be sure to follow the direction of your *guide lines.*

Pay attention to areas that are lighter and darker. Go over lines that need to be darker or sharper, and refine details of the face if you need to.

Add a cast shadow underneath.

Which areas are lightest? Which areas are darkest?

Bright idea: if a gorilla charges you in the wild, *stand your ground.* If you run, you'll be in big trouble.

cast shadow

Draw Rainforest Animals   **19**

Hoatzin

Opisthocomus hoazin: South America. Size: 61 cm (24 inches). Bizarre bird lives in trees, and doesn't fly well. Eats fruit and leaves. Young can swim, and have claws on the hook of each wing to help them climb trees…nests are built over water so they can drop to safety if a snake approaches!

1. Draw a tilted oval. At the top, add a curve like an upside-down smile. This will become the top of the head.

2. From the top of the head, draw the neck and breast. Add the mouth, and the eye.

   Lightly draw curved lines to show where the first three layers of wing feathers end. The longest feathers extend beyond the oval. Draw the outline of the wing, then add light lines for the feathers.

3. Draw the wild feathers sticking out the top of the head. Outline the eye and beak and light feathers running down the neck. Darken the top of the head. 'Ruffle' the breast feathers with short pencil strokes.

   Add feathers on the back. Outline a small space at the end of each layer of feathers on the wing – leave this area white. Add points on the end of the longest feathers.

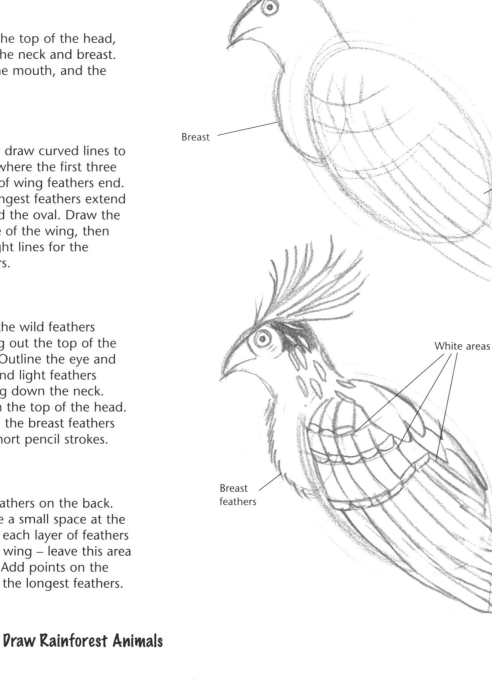

Breast

Wing

White areas

Breast feathers

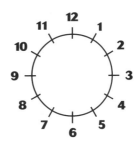

Use the clock face to compare angles of lines and ovals.

Tail feathers

4. Add a tree branch, with the bird's claws. Lightly draw the tail feathers.

5. Take a moment to look at the final drawing, noticing white and dark areas. Add shading. Finish the tail feathers, leaving the ends white.

 Turn your drawing as you draw to avoid smudging it with your hand.

Handsome hoatzin!

Draw Rainforest Animals

Howler Monkey

Alouatta seniculus (red howler monkey): northern South America, mainly Colombia. Size: 160-180 cm (63-71 inches). Lives in trees, eats leaves and some fruit. Sturdily built, with prehensile tail. They're loud! Male howler monkeys shout to let other monkeys know their territory.

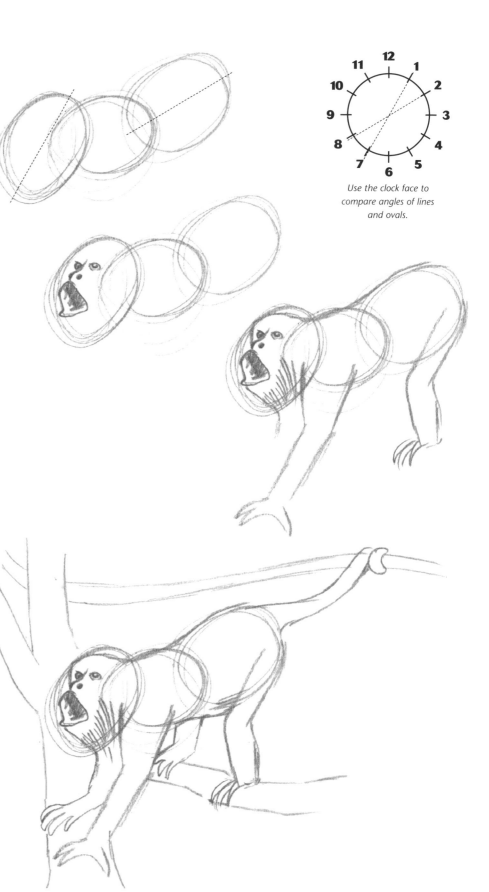

Use the clock face to compare angles of lines and ovals.

1. Start by drawing three overlapping ovals. Notice how each tilts at a different angle.

2. Draw the face, one feature at a time, starting with the mouth.

3. Add the outline of the head, and join the ovals to make the curved back. Draw the arm and leg on the side closest to you – pay attention to the way they bend. Add fur to the chin.

4. Draw the remaining arm and leg, and the tail. As you draw them, add branches. Notice how the tail curls around one branch.

5. Use your eraser to clean up lines you won't need in the finished drawing. Starting with the darkest areas, make short pencil lines for fur.

6. Look carefully at which parts of the monkey are darkest, and which are lightest. Continue adding fur. Draw shading on the branches.

While your pencil is sharp, go over fine details. As it gets duller, add shading.

 Turn your drawing as you draw to avoid smudging it with your hand.

Clean up any smudges with your eraser.

Iguana

Iguana iguana (common iguana):
Central and South America.
Size: 1-2 m (3.5-6.5 ft). Iguanas live
in trees, but lay eggs in holes they
dig in the ground. They feed on
plants, but can defend themselves
from other animals with sharp teeth
and claws. They drop from trees into
water to escape – they're great
swimmers! *Easy scientific name!*

Always draw lightly at first!

*Use the clock face to
compare angles of
lines and ovals.*

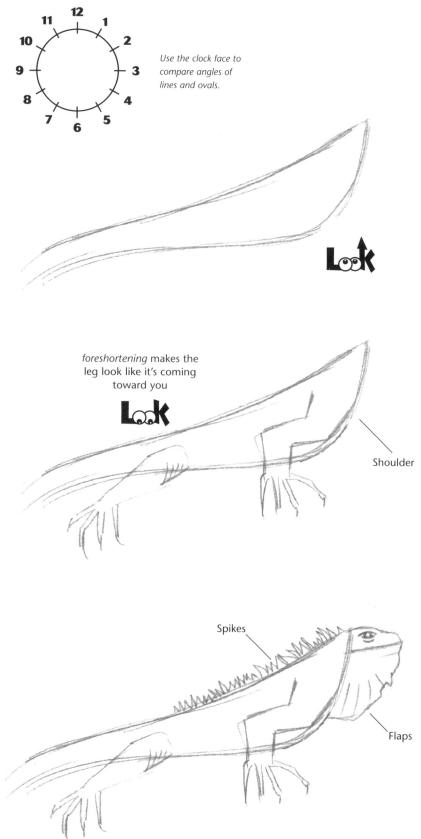

1. Begin with the swooping
   shape for the body. Notice
   how the bottom line
   becomes almost vertical at
   the head. Don't join the
   lines at the tail yet – it
   gets a lot longer!

foreshortening makes the
leg look like it's coming
toward you

2. Look at the legs. The front
   leg starts at the shoulder,
   goes down, back, then
   down again. The back leg
   is foreshortened. This
   means that part of it (the
   part connecting to the
   body) comes straight
   towards you. Now draw
   the legs, and add toes and
   claws.

Shoulder

3. Add the top of the head,
   and eye. Draw a line for
   the mouth, then add the
   flaps of skin beneath the
   mouth. Add the distinct,
   jagged row of spikes along
   the iguana's back. They
   don't need to be even.

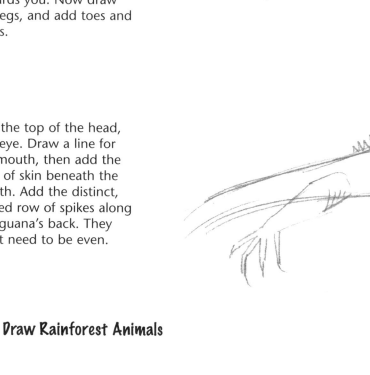

Spikes

Flaps

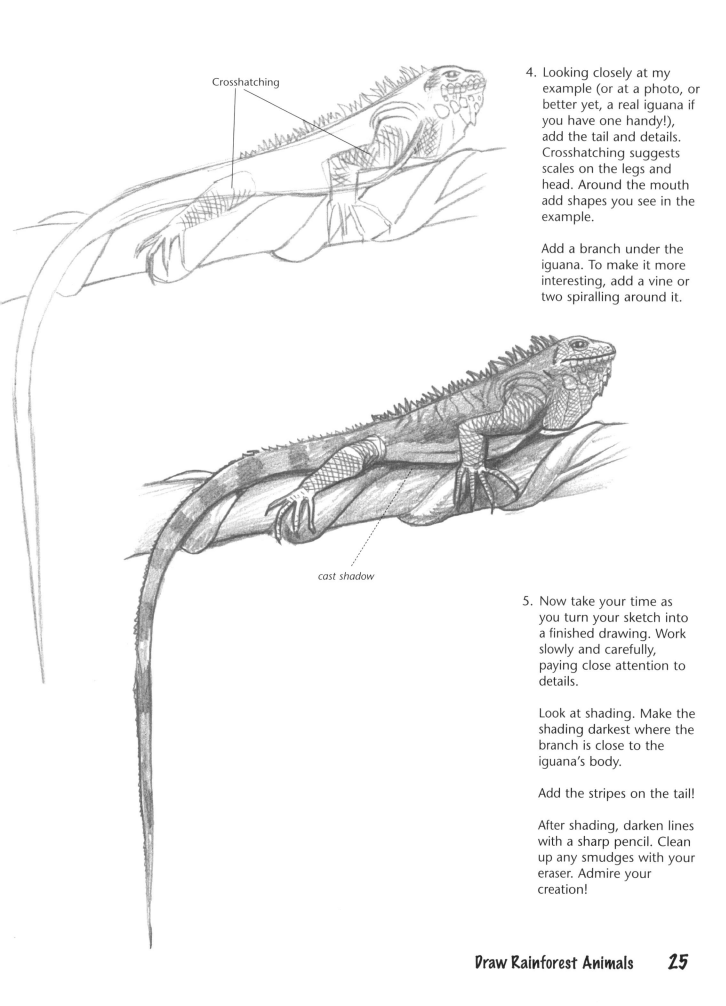

Crosshatching

4. Looking closely at my example (or at a photo, or better yet, a real iguana if you have one handy!), add the tail and details. Crosshatching suggests scales on the legs and head. Around the mouth add shapes you see in the example.

Add a branch under the iguana. To make it more interesting, add a vine or two spiralling around it.

cast shadow

5. Now take your time as you turn your sketch into a finished drawing. Work slowly and carefully, paying close attention to details.

Look at shading. Make the shading darkest where the branch is close to the iguana's body.

Add the stripes on the tail!

After shading, darken lines with a sharp pencil. Clean up any smudges with your eraser. Admire your creation!

Jaguar

Panthera onca: Central and South America. Size: 1.5-1.8 m ((5-6 ft). Climbs trees to lie in wait for prey. Feeds on a variety of animals, even fish. Powerful animal with deep chest and strong limbs.

1. Start by drawing two light, *overlapping* circles.

2. Add the two sides of the mouth slanting downward, with the small vertical line in the center.

3. Add a flat triangle for the nose.

4. Directly above the outside of the nose, draw two upside-down L shapes.

5. Make eyes by drawing curves down from the outside of the L shapes. Add ears.

6. Make a circle for the center of the eye – leave a small highlight in it.

7. Darken the rest of each eye. Add rows of dots on the muzzle and whiskers.

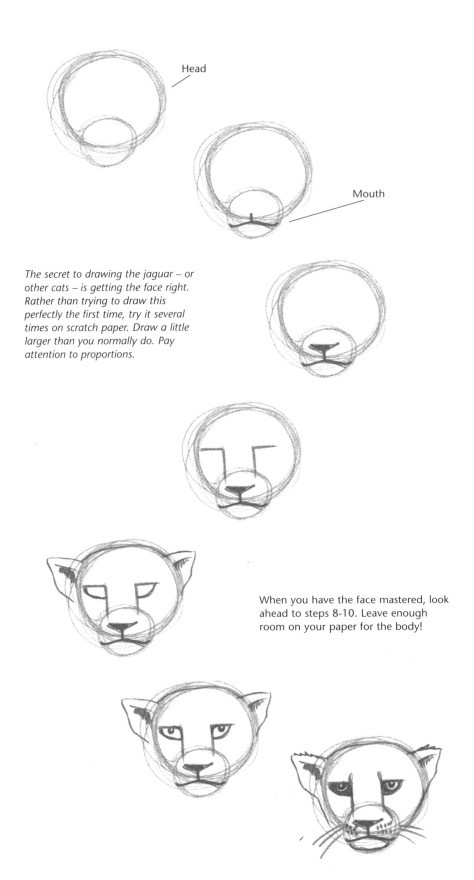

The secret to drawing the jaguar – or other cats – is getting the face right. Rather than trying to draw this perfectly the first time, try it several times on scratch paper. Draw a little larger than you normally do. Pay attention to proportions.

When you have the face mastered, look ahead to steps 8-10. Leave enough room on your paper for the body!

(1)   (2)   (3)

8. Measure three heads back for the length of the body. Make the back level with the bottom of the eyes, with a little curve at the neck. Make the front of the body slant slightly.

9. Add the legs and paws. *Draw lightly at first.* Look at your jaguar. Is everything the way you want it?

   If something looks wrong, try looking at your picture in a mirror, or hold it up to a light and look through the back.

10. Next add spots to the jaguar – dark patches, with one or more darker spots inside. These large spots become smaller spots and stripes on the legs and tail.

   Lightly lay out the pattern, then carefully add shading. It takes a while, but it's worth it!

   While your pencil is sharp, go over fine details. As it gets duller, add shading.

    Turn your drawing as you draw to avoid smudging it with your hand.

Clean up any smudges with your eraser.

Here, kitty…nice kitty…

Kinkajou

Potos flavus: Central and South America. Size: 81-113 cm (32-45 inches). Kinkajous live in trees, feeding at night on fruit and insects. Agile climbers, they use their prehensile tail to hold onto branches, leaving their hands free for gathering food.

1. Start by drawing downward-curving lines for the branch, and a titled oval. The angle of the branch helps emphasize the kinkajou's prehensile tail in this drawing.

Head

2. Lightly draw an oval for the upper body and a small circle for the head.

overlapping

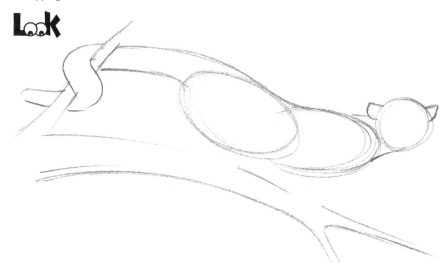

3. Add another small branch behind the animal, and draw the tail curling around it (look closely at my example to see how to do this!). Add ears and the outline of the back and neck.

4. Sketch in the legs, one at a time. You can't see all of each leg, so this takes careful observation. Draw very lightly at first!

eyes in *middle* of the head

Look!

5. When you get the legs just right, draw the face. Place the eyes in the middle of the circle, then add nose, mouth and whiskers below them.

Carefully erase lines you no longer need. Begin drawing the fur on what will be the darkest parts of the body. Use loose, short pencil marks to capture the texture and direction of the fur.

6. Keep drawing fur until the whole body is covered. Add leaves to the branches. Look at your drawing in a mirror (or through the back of the paper) to spot any areas you can make better. Go over parts that you didn't get dark enough the first time.

Finally, clean up any smudges with your eraser.

Ruffed Lemur

Varecia variegata: Madagascar. Size: 120 cm (47 inches) including tail. This agile climber rarely comes to the ground. It eats fruit, leaves and bark, and is most active at dusk and the early part of the night.

1. Start with the eyes: small circles with a spot inside them, surrounded by wider, darker circles.

2. Draw the outline of the head, a rectangle above the eyes and a rounded triangle below the eyes.

3. Add the nose and mouth.

4. From the top sides of the head, lightly draw lines going out and up. Then draw the outline of the curving ruff, or collar, or beard, or whatever you want to call it.

   Draw lightly at first!

   Once you have the light outline in place, add radiating lines for the fur.

— Ruff

5. Draw a light curving line for the back. Continue adding lines for fur around the face.

radiating lines go out from the center

6. Draw the curve of the leg. *What number does this look like?* Add five radiating curved lines for the toes.

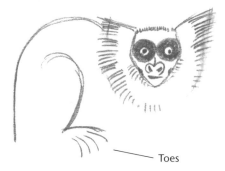

— Toes

belly curves upward

7. Complete the rear foot. Draw the front arm and hand, with all five fingers. Draw the lines of the branch, adding a tiny bit of the thumb of the other hand.

8. Add a small upward curve for the lemur's belly, and the dark fur of the other arm. With short pencil strokes radiating from the shoulder, draw more fur. Add jagged lines along the back for texture, and a few fur lines on the face and body.

   What's missing?

9. A fat, long tail! Try drawing it using only short lines for the fur.

   While your pencil is sharp, go over fine details. As it gets duller, add shading.

    Turn your drawing as you draw to avoid smudging it with your hand.

   Clean up any smudges with your eraser.

   Idea: add leaves and other branches in the background. Draw a dark background to make a night setting for this nocturnal animal.

Macaw

Ara macao (Scarlet macaw): Mexico to northern South America. Size: 85 cm (33.5 inches). Most familiar of South American parrots. Threatened by destruction of rain forest and people stealing baby birds to sell as pets. Don't buy them!

1. Lightly draw the top part of the beak, then the bottom.

2. Add a roughly triangular shape for the macaw's face. At the top of it, draw the eye. Add the pattern of spots on the cheek, and a few curved lines to suggest the texture of the beak.

3. From the top of the beak, draw the outline of the macaw's head. From the bottom of the beak, draw the throat. Connect front and back with a shoulder line.

4. LIghtly draw an oval for the bird's body. Draw two claws grasping a branch.

5. Sketch in the tail feathers. Notice that they stick out a bit, rather than pointing straight down.

Top of beak

Bottom of beak

Use the clock face to compare angles of lines and ovals.

Head

Shoulder

shoulder line

Claws

Tail feathers

32   Draw Rainforest Animals

Layers

6. Add lines to these wing feathers, then draw the tail feathers, pointing downward underneath the wing feathers. Add three layers of feathers on the wing.

7. Carefully shade the feathers. While your pencil is sharp, go over fine details. As it gets duller, add shading.

 Turn your drawing as you draw to avoid smudging it with your hand.

Look at your drawing in a mirror (or through the back of the paper) to spot any areas you can make better.

Clean up any smudges with your eraser.

Red

Yellow

Green tips

Blue

Blue

Red

Idea: draw it in color!

Margay

Felis Wiedii: Central and South America. Size: 1.1-1.7 m (43-67 inches), including tail. Margays usually hunt at night for small mammals, birds and snakes. They're good at not being seen, either by their prey or by people. During the day, they sleep on a branch or in vegetation.

Use the clock face to compare angles of lines and ovals.

1. Begin by lightly drawing a tilted oval. Add a triangle for one eye, and an oval shape with circle inside for the other.

2. Draw a triangle for the nose. Add the mouth, and facial markings. Spend some time with the face to get it right.

3. Add ears and more facial markings. Lightly draw the front leg, and a horizontal line for the chest.

4. Lightly sketch the other front leg and paw. Look carefully at the angles!

paws

5. From the ear, draw the curving back, and the line on the bottom, curving into the rear leg.

   Now add the rear leg. Where do the lines connect to the body?

Back

LOOK

Turn your drawing as you draw to avoid smudging it with your hand.

6. Look how far back the other rear leg goes! Draw it. Add the tail – where does it connect? Draw whiskers, and a branch for the margay to stand on.

Last chance to fix the basic shapes of your cat! Look at it carefully – is everything OK?

Look at your drawing in a mirror (or through the back of the paper) to spot any areas you can make better.

7. Before drawing spots, look closely at this drawing. Notice how some spots curve to show the contour of the body. Which parts of the drawing are dark, and which are light? Is the tail as dark as the ears? What's the darkest part of the drawing?

Be patient as you finish the drawing. Work slowly and carefully as you add the spots.

Clean up any smudges with your eraser.

Magnificent Margay!

Draw Rainforest Animals 35

Okapi

Okapia johnstoni: Zaire.
Size: 1.5-2.3 m (5-7.5 ft).Lives alone except in breeding season. Long tongue – an okapi can clean its own eyes and eyelids with its tongue! Feeds on leaves, shoots, grass and fruit.

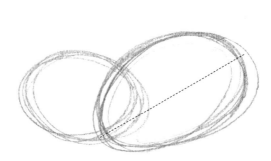

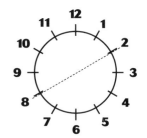

Use the clock face to compare angles of lines and ovals.

1. Start by drawing two light ovals for the body.

   Notice that
   • they overlap,
   • they're tilted and
   • they're different sizes.

2. Add the lines to join the two ovals top and bottom. Draw the neck, then very lightly add an oval for the main part of the head. Add the front of the head, with the mouth and eye.

3. Add the ear and small horns at the top of the head. Draw the rear leg and the front leg, looking closely at the angles in the drawing. Add the tail.

4. Carefully erase the the body ovals where they *overlap.* (You did draw them *lightly,* didn't you?) Lightly outline the distinctive stripes on the upper legs. Add the dark part on the lower legs. Draw some jagged lines for grass.

5. To complete your drawing, shade the body with pencil strokes showing the direction of the fur. Carefully erase the head oval, then add details and shade the head.

Take a good look at your drawing. Are there areas that need to be darker? Darken them. Are details getting fuzzy?

While your pencil is sharp, go over fine details. As it gets duller, add shading.

 Turn your drawing as you draw to avoid smudging it with your hand.

Clean up any smudges with your eraser.

Idea: the okapi looks like it's stretching to reach food. Add a branch with leaves on it. Draw the okapi's long tongue grabbing a leaf.

Orangutan

Pongo pygmaeus: Sumatra, Borneo. Size: 1.2-1.5 m (4-5 ft). The orangutan's arms are larger and stronger than its legs, and it is an agile climber. All adults have fatty throat pouches; only mature males have the distinctive cheek flaps surrounding the face. The shaggy fur is reddish-brown.

1. Draw the outline of the face, a tilted rectangle with a rounded bottom. Draw two lines near the middle of the rectangle for the mouth.

2. At the top of the rectangle, draw a series of curved lines to make the eyes. Draw two nostrils, and two lines to define the outside of the nose. Add radiating pencil strokes to make the 'beard.'

   Add hair at the top of the head. Lightly sketch the cheek flaps that surround the face. It may take you a try or two to get them just right.

3. Add the throat pouches, which look like a collar. Add shading to the face, cheek flaps and throat pouches.

4. Here's a big jump! *Draw lightly at first*, and redraw any parts that don't look right the first time. Draw an oval for the body. Add the legs, looking carefully at the position and the way the lines run. Add the outstretched arms, then draw the branch and vine for the orangutan to swing on.

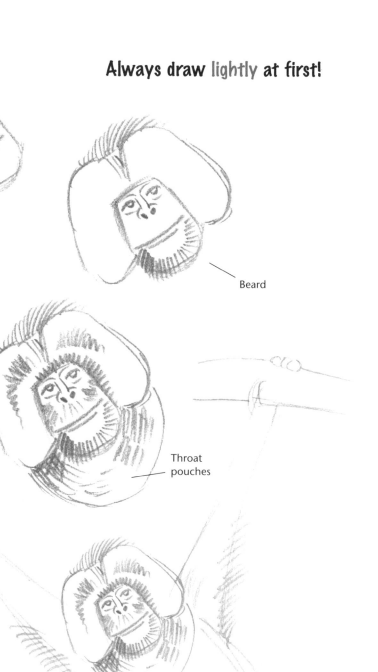

Beard

Throat pouches

5. Add another branch or two. Using short pencil strokes, draw the hair on the body. Pay close attention to the direction of the hair. Draw hair on arms and legs, pointing outward from the body. Add shading and texture to the branch and vine.

Notice areas that are darker and areas that are lighter. Go over any lines that need darkening.

While your pencil is sharp, go over fine details. As it gets duller, add shading.

Turn your drawing as you draw to avoid smudging it with your hand.

Clean up any smudges with your eraser.

Idea: turn to pages 60-61, and fill the space around the orangutan with leaves, trees, and vines.

Ouakari

Cacajao calvus (bald ouakari): West Brazil. Size: 66-73 cm (26-29 inches) including tail. Lives in treetops. Bald head, red face and a beard! Walks on all fours; has a short tail and doesn't leap much. Eats mainly fruit. Active in the daytime.

1. Look carefully at the shapes in this drawing before you draw. Start with the branch, then add the banana-like oval of the body.

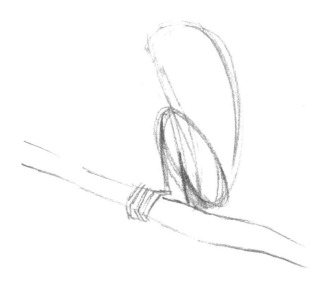

2. Add *(lightly!)* a second *overlapping* .oval for the top of the leg. Draw the bottom part of the leg, with toes curling around the branch.

3. Erase the first oval where the leg *overlaps* it. Draw the arm, with fingers.

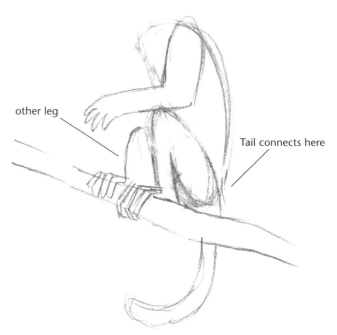

other leg

Tail connects here

4. Draw a small curved line for the other leg. Add toes. Draw the tail, starting from the base of the back.

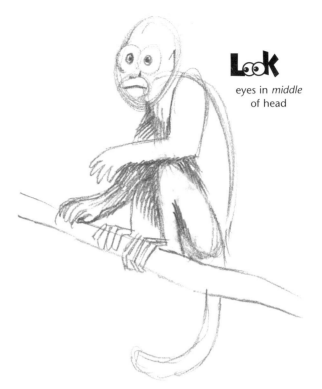

eyes in *middle* of head

4. Add the second arm. Darken it with short pencil strokes for hair. Notice the direction of the hair.

5. Draw an oval for the head. In the middle, add two circles for the eyes, and an oval beneath them, with a line through the middle, for the mouth.

6. Carefully Shade the face and add long hair. Shade lightly at first! You can always make it darker.

6. Add lots and lots of hair! Make some areas darker. Use short pencil lines to make the back and tail look shaggy.

Draw Rainforest Animals **41**

Pangolin

Manis tricuspis (tree pangolin): Central Africa. Size: 84-105 cm (33-41 inches, including tail). Good climber with distinctive pointed scales. Feeds at night on ant and termite nests in trees, which it tears open with its sharp claws. Sleeps during the day in a tree, or in a hole it digs in the ground.

Always draw lightly at first!

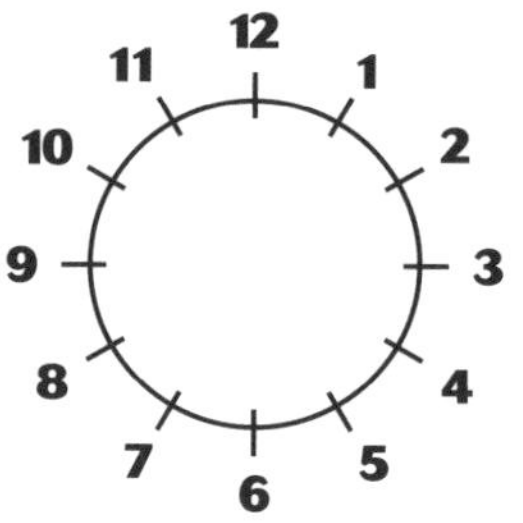

Use the clock face to compare angles of lines and ovals.

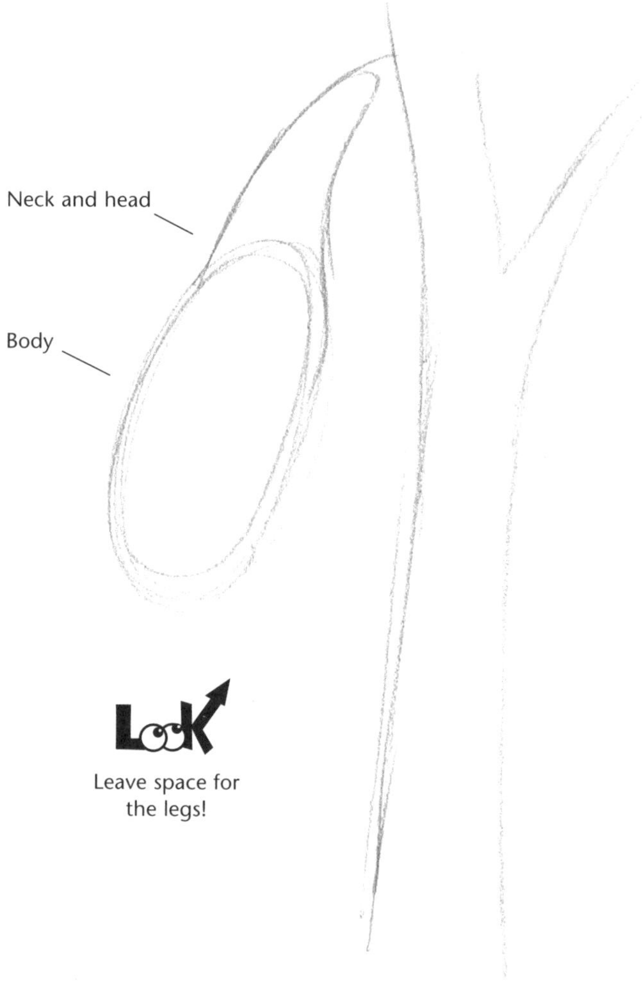

Neck and head

Body

L👀K

Leave space for the legs!

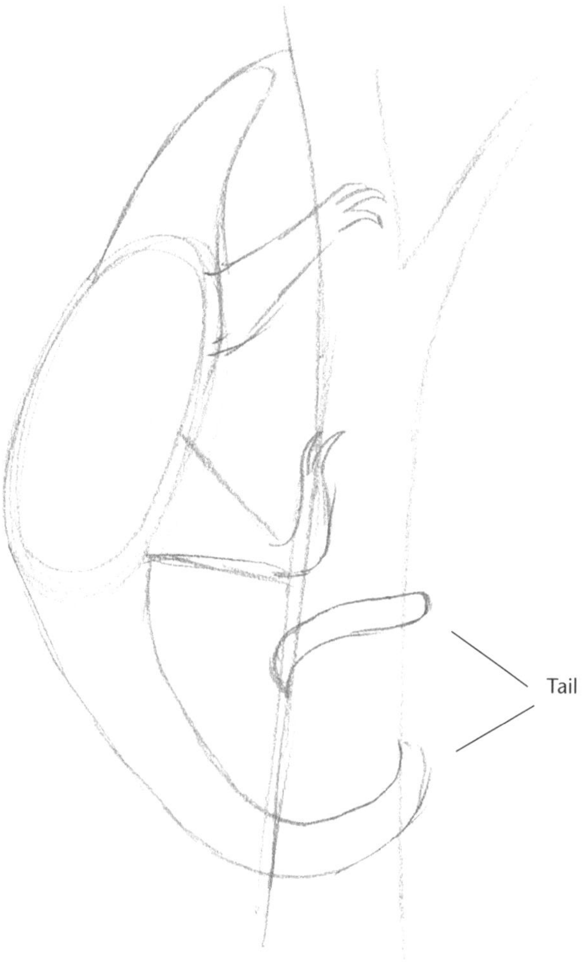

Tail

1. Lightly sketch the tree. Leaving room for the legs, draw a vertical, slightly tilted oval for the body. Draw a long curving shape for the neck and head.

2. Add the front leg, with its sharp claws. Draw the L-shaped rear leg. Extend the lower end of the oval to make the tail, curling around the tree.

Turn your drawing as you draw to avoid smudging it with your hand.

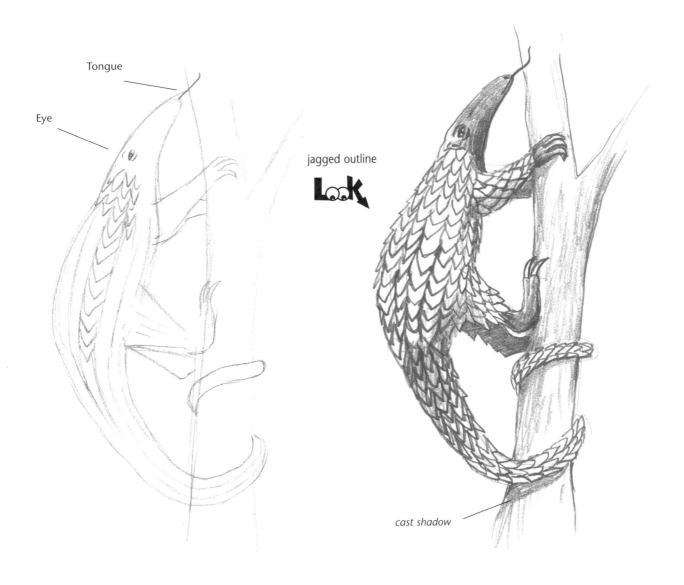

Tongue

Eye

jagged outline

L👀K

cast shadow

3. Add the little bit you can see of the other two legs. Draw the long tongue (termites – yum!). Add the eye. Now you have the basic body parts in place. Next draw the scales. Start with light guide lines, like stripes, and draw little V shapes inside them.

4. Cover all but the face and feet with scales. Shade the head and feet, making the legs farthest away darker. Add some texture to the tree with light pencil strokes. Draw a little bit of *cast shadow* on the tree from the tail and legs.

Idea: add some termites on the tree for the pangolin to eat!

Quetzal

Pharomachrus mocinno: Mexico, Central America. Size: 30 cm (12 inches); tail feathers 61 cm (24 inches). Lives in lower layers of rainforest trees. Feeds on fruit and small animals like lizards and frogs. Long tail feathers, shed every year, were prized by the Maya, to whom the bird was sacred.

1. Start by drawing a light circle for the head. Add the eye and beak.

Use the clock face to compare angles of lines and ovals.

2. Make two short lines for the neck and back of the head, then draw a line for the front edge of each wing. Notice the direction each line points; think of a clock face.

3. Continue the lines of the head to form the body. Add curved lines for the inside part of each wing. Make light marks for spacing before drawing the feathers.

4. Draw the feathers.

5. Add feet and the main tail feathers. Draw short, radiating lines for feathers on the head. Darken the eye, leaving a white spot in it. Add more lines, in the center of each feather. Use short dark pencil strokes for feathers on the head, neck and breast.

Look!

feathers *radiate* outward

Tail feathers

Feet

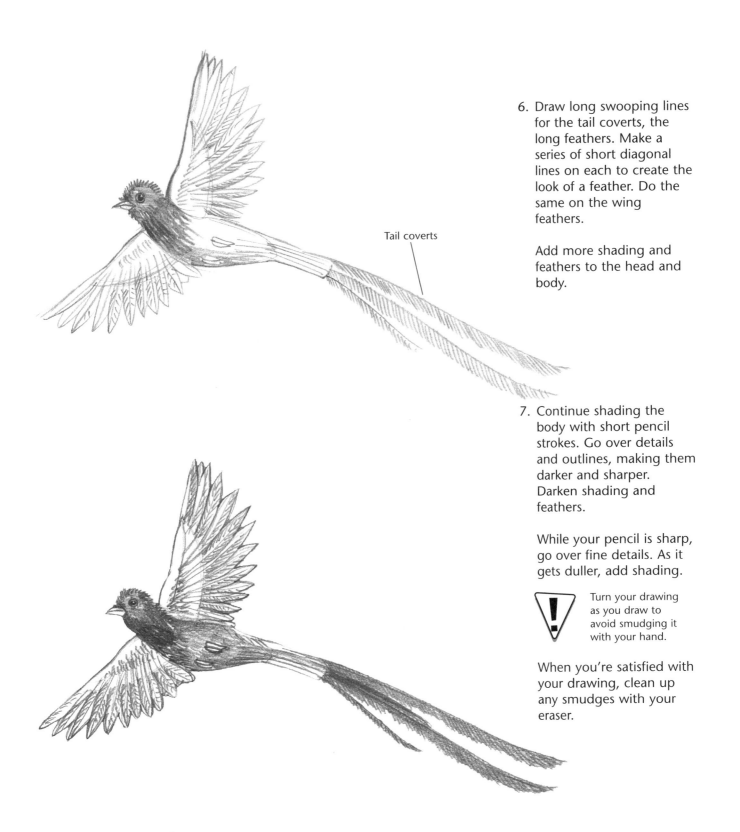

6. Draw long swooping lines for the tail coverts, the long feathers. Make a series of short diagonal lines on each to create the look of a feather. Do the same on the wing feathers.

Add more shading and feathers to the head and body.

Tail coverts

7. Continue shading the body with short pencil strokes. Go over details and outlines, making them darker and sharper. Darken shading and feathers.

While your pencil is sharp, go over fine details. As it gets duller, add shading.

Turn your drawing as you draw to avoid smudging it with your hand.

When you're satisfied with your drawing, clean up any smudges with your eraser.

Quite the quetzal!

Slender Loris

Loris tardigradus: Sri Lanka, southern India. Size: 18-25 cm (7-10 inches). Lives in trees, grasping carefully with its hands. Feeds at night; sleeps during the day in a tree, rolled up in a ball. To eat, it grabs insects (grasshoppers are a favorite), lizards, and small birds with its hands.

Always draw lightly at first!

Look!

leave space for legs!

1. Draw two lines for a branch. Make it interesting by adding a curve or two. Above the branch, lightly draw a rectangle.

Use the clock face to compare angles of lines and ovals.

2. Draw the front legs. The one closest to you has two parts. You only see part of the other leg.

Look

one leg *overlaps* the other

3. Add the rear legs. Notice that they bend opposite to the front legs. Lightly draw the foot.

Foot

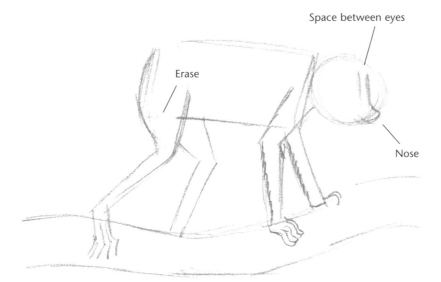

Space between eyes

Erase

Nose

4. Erase the rectangle where the rear leg *overlaps* it. Add the front feet. Lightly draw an oval for the head. Draw two lines to make the white space between the eyes. Add a bump for the nose.

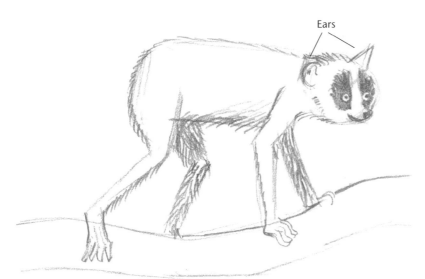

Ears

5. Darken the tip of the nose. Add mouth and eyes. Add dark areas around each eye. Draw the ears – one a triangle and one rounded. Add short pencil strokes for fur. Start with the darkest areas.

! Turn your drawing as you draw to avoid smudging it with your hand.

6. Add fur to cover the whole body. Add texture and shading to the branch. Sharpen details such as the feet.

Clean up your drawing by erasing any smudges.

Idea: add epiphytes (see page 61) and other vegetation.

Sloth

Bradypus tridactylus: Central and South America. Size: 56-67 cm (20-26 in). Ve-ee-ee-ry slo-o-ow mo-oo-ving animal. Spends most of its life hanging upside down in trees. Eats leaves and tender buds.

Always draw lightly at first!

1. Draw two lines for the tree branch. Make it interesting by adding curves. Below the branch, draw an oval for the sloth's body

Leave space for the legs!

2. Draw straight lines upward for the legs, at angles. Notice how one leg *overlaps* part of the one behind it. Draw just part of one front leg, to save space for the head.

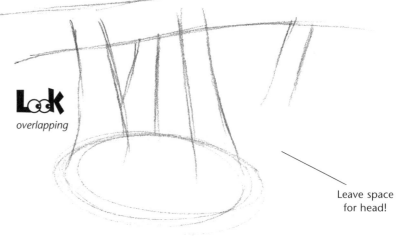

overlapping

Leave space for head!

3. Lightly draw a circle for the head. Where is it in relation to the body?

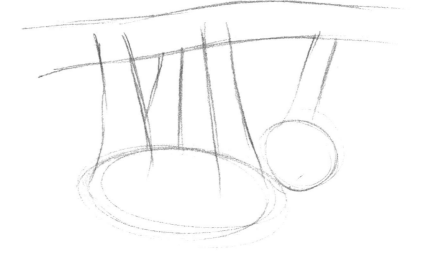

4. Add claws curving around the branch. Begin to add fur with short, downward strokes. The fur on a sloth grows this way because the sloth spends most of its life upside down!

5. Draw the face by starting with a small line for the mouth, at an angle, in the *center* of the circle. Add the nose, and the eyes just to the side of the nose. Draw dark fur areas extending from the eyes.

Add short pencil strokes for the fur on the arms and legs, and on the back and neck.

6. Keep drawing short pencil lines to add fur to the rest of the body. Notice the areas that are darker, and the direction of the lines. Shade the tree branch. Fix any details you might have missed. Finally, clean up any smudges with your eraser.

Idea: add epiphytes (see p. 61) and other vegetation for this slo-o-ow sloth to hang out with.

Spider Monkey

Always draw lightly at first!

Ateles paniscus (black spider monkey): Northern South America. Size: 1-1.4 m (39-55 inches). Tree dweller. Very agile, with a long reach and strong prehensile tail. Spider monkeys eat mostly fruit and nuts, and live in groups of 15-30.

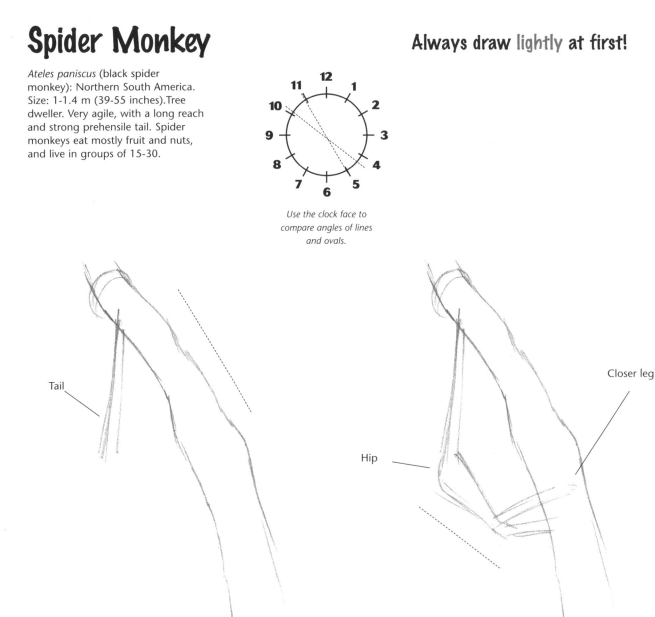

Use the clock face to compare angles of lines and ovals.

1. Draw the tree trunk, lightly. Make the lines interesting, not just straight!

   Draw two lines straight up for the tail. Then make the tail curling around the tree.

2. Add the hip and rear legs. The leg closer to you *overlaps* part of the one behind.

50   *Draw Rainforest Animals*

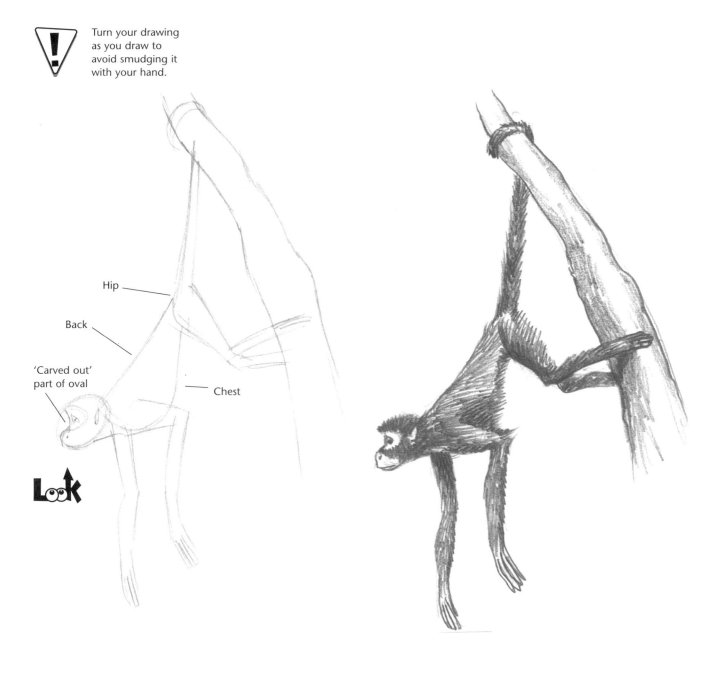

Hip

Back

'Carved out' part of oval

Chest

L👀k

3. From the hip, draw a straight line for the back, and a swooping curve for the chest.

Next, add long, spindly arms.

Lightly draw an oval for the head, then 'carve out' part of it to make the space above the nose. Draw the ear, eye, and nose. Draw a line to connect the head with the body.

4. With many short pencil strokes, add the fur. Notice the direction of the fur on different parts of the body. Also, notice that it's darker in some places.

Look for any lines that might need to be darkened. Add some shadows to the tree trunk. Clean up any smudges with your eraser.

Idea: this monkey looks like it's ready to reach for something, perhaps a vine or a branch…add vegetation to your drawing, including whatever the spider monkey is about to reach for.

Tamandua

Tamandua mexicana: Southern Mexico to South America. Size: 1.1 m (43 in) including tail. Tree-dwelling anteater with prehensile tail. Tears open nests with its strong claws, grabs ants and termites with its long, sticky tongue.

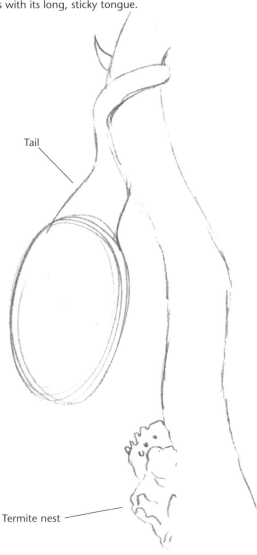

Tail

Termite nest

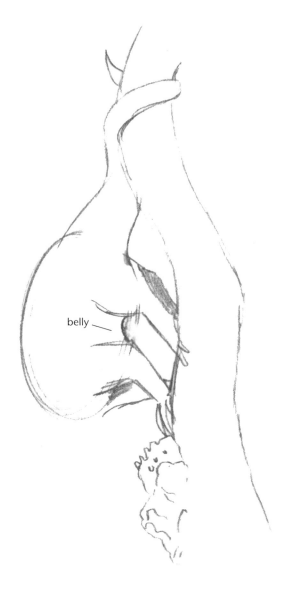

belly

1. Start by drawing an interesting tree trunk, which curves back and forth a little. At the bottom, draw a termite nest – it doesn't have to be fancy.

    Now draw an oval for the tamandua's body – *Draw lightly at first!* – and add the tail, curling up and around the tree.

2. Add the legs. Watch where they *overlap* each other. Draw lightly: remember, you can always make lines darker. Draw the sharp claws that the tamandua uses to tear open termite nests.

    Lightly erase parts of the oval where it *overlaps* the legs and tail. Make the belly curve inward between the front and rear legs.

Turn your drawing as you draw to avoid smudging it with your hand.

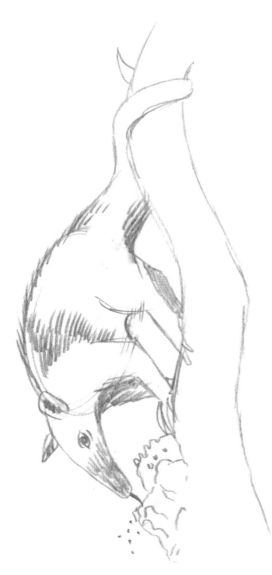

3. Draw the head, two curved lines with a rounded end where the tongue sticks out, scooping up termites (yum!).

Add the almond-shaped eye and the ears.

Look at the final drawing, noticing light and dark areas. Draw the dark fur with short pencil strokes.

4. Add more dark fur on the body. Leave the legs light. Draw shapes on the tree trunk to suggest peeling bark. Shade the tree trunk.

With a sharp pencil, sharpen any details that might be fuzzy – for example, the face or feet.

Use your eraser to clean up any smudges.

Extra bright idea: when you're finished, put your drawing on the wall where you can admire it the next time you and your friends are snacking on termites.

Tapir

Tapirus terrestris (Brazilian tapir): South America. Size: 2m (6.5 ft). Covered with short, bristly hair. Found near water (good swimmer). Feeds at night on leaves, buds, shoots, and small branches.

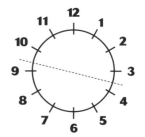

Use the clock face to compare angles of lines and ovals.

1. Drawing a tapir is quite easy. Start with a line for the ground, and above it, draw a slightly tilted oval.

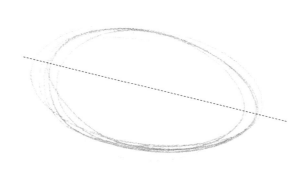

2. From the right side of the oval, draw the front leg with a bend in the middle, where it crosses the bottom of the oval. Erase the oval where the leg *overlaps* it. Draw the other front leg.

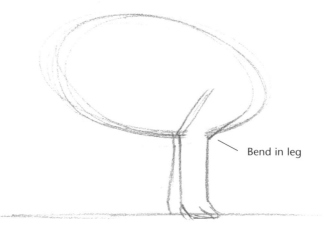

Bend in leg

3. Draw the short tail, and the back legs. Notice how and where these legs bend – well below the oval.

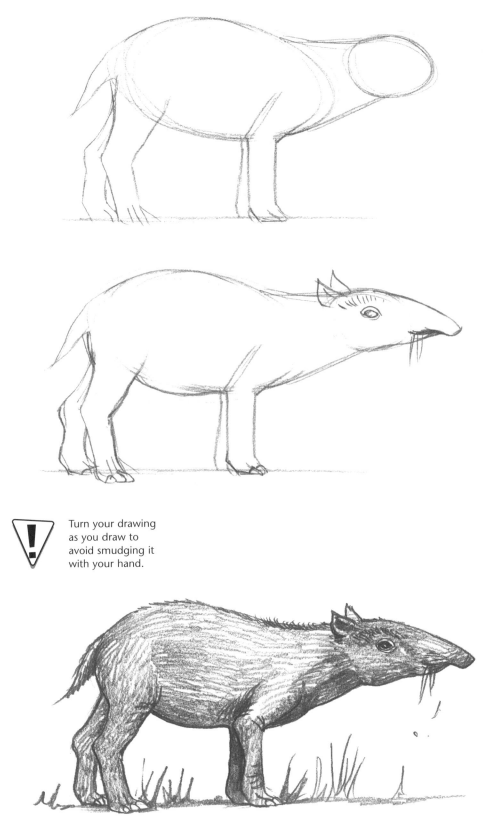

3. Lightly draw another oval for the head. Connect it to the body with two lines for the neck.

5. In the middle of the oval, draw an almond shape for the eye. Extend the top of the head to make the nose. From the nose, draw the mouth and the neck. Carefully erase what's left of the head oval.

Draw some leaves in the tapir's mouth. Add the short fur strokes above the eye. Draw the ears.

What a pretty face!

Turn your drawing as you draw to avoid smudging it with your hand.

6. To finish your drawing, make many short pencil lines for the fur. Notice which places are dark, and which are light. Darken outlines in shadow areas, such as underneath the body. Add bristly marks on the outline of the back.

Add grass on the ground, and a bit of *cast shadow*, then clean up any smudges with your eraser and you're done!

Idea: add bushes and trees in the background.

Toucan

Ramphastos toco (Toco toucan): South America, mainly Amazon basin. Size: 61 cm (24 inches). Toucans eat a variety of fruits and large insects. Strong claws help them hang onto tree branches. Toucans grab food with their beak, then toss their head backwards to get it into their mouth.

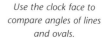
Always draw lightly at first!

Use the clock face to compare angles of lines and ovals.

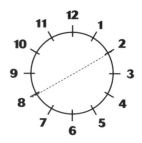

1. Draw the horizontal branch.

   Above it, at an angle, draw a titled oval, not quite touching the branch.

   Add vertical lines for the legs, with claws wrapping around the branch.

Shoulder

2. Add the wing, with a slight bulge at the shoulder.

   Draw lines on the wing to suggest feathers.

3. Extend the bottom of the oval for the tail. Draw the end of the tail behind and below the branch, with lines for feathers. Add small curved lines on the claws. Shade the leg.

Vertical!

Throat

White area

Beak

Tongue

Yellow-orange

Red

4. Draw a line from the shoulder for the top of the head. Make the front of the head vertical where the beak attaches. Draw the throat. Add the eye, and the triangle around it. Outline the white area on the front of the body.

5. Now draw the beak – but first, look carefully at its curves. Make the top part of the beak wider than the bottom. Add the dark spot at the tip. Draw the tongue.

6. Look at the final drawing. Shade the dark areas of the bird. Add the pattern to the beak. Darken lines that seem important. Add shading to the branch.

While your pencil is sharp, go over fine details. As it gets duller, add shading.

⚠ Turn your drawing as you draw to avoid smudging it with your hand.

Look at your drawing in a mirror (or through the back of the paper) to spot any areas you can make better.

Clean up any smudges with your eraser.

Idea: draw a berry in the toucan's beak. Add color to your drawing…

Draw Rainforest Animals   57

Vine Snake

Oxybelis fulgidus: Central America and part of South America. Size: 1.5-2 m (5-6.5 feet). Slow-moving predator barely a half inch (1.25 cm) wide. Hard to see because it looks like a vine. Eats lizards and steals young birds from nests.

1. Start by drawing a thin branch with a few leaves. Your drawing doesn't have to look exactly like mine!

   Draw lightly at first!

2. Lightly sketch the outline of the snake. Make it curve this way and that. Position the snake's body so that it *overlaps* branches and leaves in several places. This drawing works best when the snake looks like it's slithering behind and in front of the branches.

Notice the extra lines where the snake's body comes toward you.

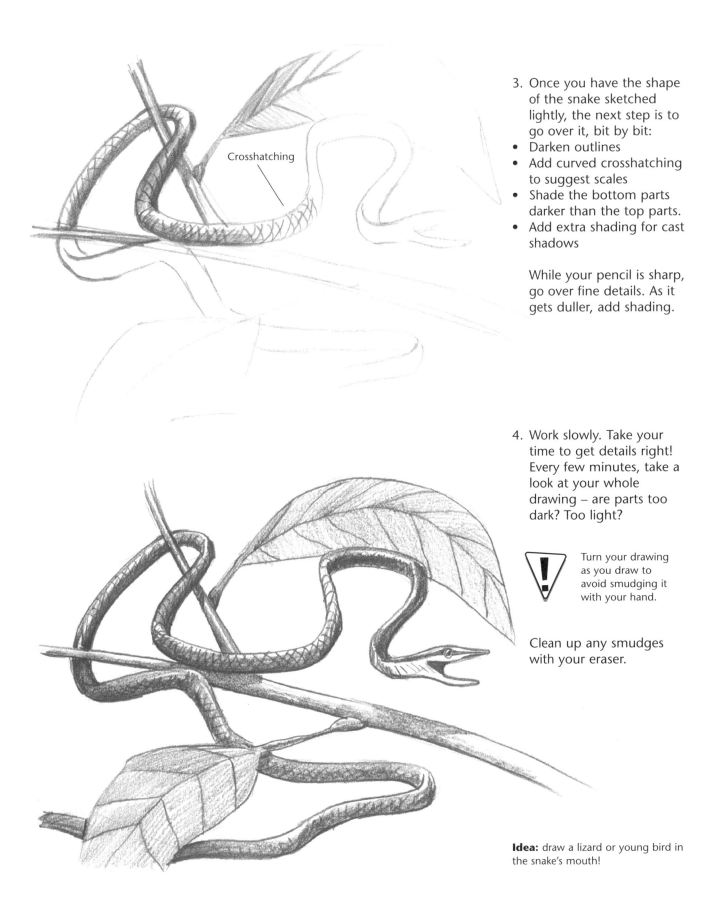

3. Once you have the shape of the snake sketched lightly, the next step is to go over it, bit by bit:
- Darken outlines
- Add curved crosshatching to suggest scales
- Shade the bottom parts darker than the top parts.
- Add extra shading for cast shadows

While your pencil is sharp, go over fine details. As it gets duller, add shading.

Crosshatching

4. Work slowly. Take your time to get details right! Every few minutes, take a look at your whole drawing – are parts too dark? Too light?

Turn your drawing as you draw to avoid smudging it with your hand.

Clean up any smudges with your eraser.

Idea: draw a lizard or young bird in the snake's mouth!

Other ideas

When animals appear in the rainforest, chances are you won't see the whole animal because of the huge amount of vegetation all around them. To make your drawing more interesting, add foliage.

You'll find that it helps to draw the whole animal lightly, then draw the foreground elements, whether trees or leaves. Try not to cover up the most important parts of the drawing – for example, in the picture of the jaguar (right), I wouldn't want a leaf covering its face!

These two drawings are quick sketches – just a way of playing with ideas, to see what looks good and what doesn't. If I wanted to do a finished drawing of the howler monkey (below, right), I might do another sketch first, moving the leaves around to find a better arrangement.

The straight lines on the outside "crop" the drawing, to give a better idea how the finished drawing might appear.

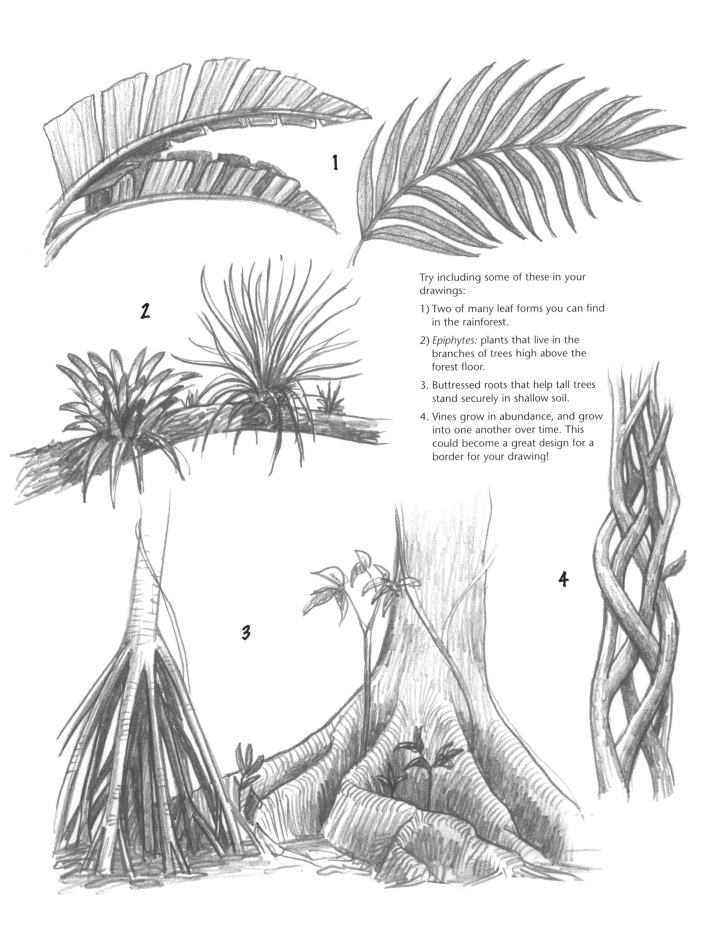

Try including some of these in your drawings:

1) Two of many leaf forms you can find in the rainforest.

2) *Epiphytes:* plants that live in the branches of trees high above the forest floor.

3. Buttressed roots that help tall trees stand securely in shallow soil.

4. Vines grow in abundance, and grow into one another over time. This could become a great design for a border for your drawing!

Save your work!

Whenever you do a drawing – or even a sketch – put your initials (or autograph!) and date on it. And save it. You don't have to save it until it turns yellow and crumbles to dust, but do keep your drawings, at least for several months. Sometimes, hiding in your portfolio, they will mysteriously improve! I've seen it happen often with my own drawings, especially the ones I knew were no good at all, but kept anyway….

Do-it-yourself portfolio

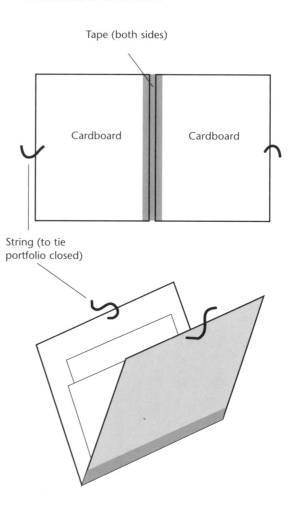

Tape (both sides)

Cardboard   Cardboard

String (to tie portfolio closed)

Index

Arrow Poison Frog 14

Basilisk Lizard...6

Boa, Emerald Tree 10

Chimpanzee 8

Emerald Tree Boa.................................10

Flying Frog 15

Flying Squirrel 12

Frog, Arrow Poison 14

Frog, Flying 15

Frog, Tree 16

Gorilla 18

Hoatzin..20

Howler Monkey 22

Iguana...24

Jaguar...26

Kinkajou 28

Lemur (Ruffed) 30

Lizard, Basilisk...6

Loris 46

Macaw 32

Margay..34

Monkey, Howler 22

Okapi 36

Orangutan..38

Ouakari...40

Pangolin 42

Quetzal..44

Ruffed Lemur...30

Scarlet Macaw 32

Slender Loris..46

Sloth...48

Snake, Emerald Tree Boa......................10

Snake, Vine..58

Spider Monkey 50

Squirrel, Flying 12

Tamandua 52

Tapir...54

Toucan 56

Tree Frog 16

Vine Snake...58

Learn about other books in
this series online at
www.drawbooks.com!

DRAW
INSECTS

by Doug DuBosque

 **PEEL** productions, inc.

Supplies...

Find a **comfortable place to draw** – with decent light, so you can see what you're doing.

As you start to learn about insect anatomy, shapes and proportions, don't worry too much about materials.

Use a **pencil that's longer than your finger.** Also, think about using colored pencils.

Sharpen your pencil when it gets dull!

Get a **separate eraser.** My favorite is a *kneaded* type, available in art supply and craft stores (the eraser on your pencil will disappear quickly).

For practice drawings, use **recycled paper** – for example, draw on the back of old photocopies or computer printouts.

Always **draw lightly at first**, so you can erase problems as you need to.

Save your drawings and learn from them.

Enjoy drawing cool insects!

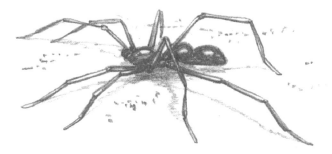

Published by Peel Productions, Inc.

Manufactured in China

Contents

Drawing Tips 2

Insects, A to Z 4

Our planet harbors about a million (who's counting?) species of insects. Rather than 20,000 insects on each page—or even 20—I've drawn insects I find interesting, fun, or representative, each with its own page. Hope you like my choices.

Insect Relatives 53

*Not all creepy-crawlies are insects. (For example, your neighbor's yappy little foo-foo dog, or your younger brother, are **not** insects: they may **act** like insects at times, but that doesn't make them insects.) Here you'll find a few favorite creepy-crawlies, and see why they're not insects, either.*

Index 64

And now, a brief and learned discourse on insects:

The world of insects includes amazing diversity—and insects are *everywhere*, from frozen snow fields to inside other animals' bodies. Some feed on plants, some suck blood from mammals, and plenty of them eat other insects, spiders, and other creepy-crawlies.

So what is an insect?

Insects are those critters belonging to the class *Insecta,* in the phylum *Arthropoda* (arthropods). They live in all habitats. Arthropods have hard exoskeletons and jointed limbs–lobsters and crabs are arthropods, but they're not insects.

Insects have
- *six legs*
- *two antennae*
- *three body parts*
- *wings? Four, or two, or none at all.*

So think **6 legs.** And look for the other stuff as well.

OK, class dismissed!

You may now draw…

*P.S. The **darkened images** on each page show you the actual size of what you're drawing.*

Ant

Order Hymenoptera
Family Formicidae

If you want to study insects, none are easier to find than ants! Their societies generally consist of wingless workers and winged reproducers. They live in underground nests or in dead wood. Most can 'bite' people if disturbed. Most ants scavenge, but some harvest seeds, cut leaves and farm fungus underground, or herd aphids to feed on their honeydew.

STUDY the final drawing *before you start!*

Do you see
- *three body parts?*
- *six legs?*
- *two antennae?*
- *wings?*
- *eyes?*

1. Draw the oval shape of the *head,* the peanut shape of the *thorax,* and the pointy oval shape of the *abdomen.*

2. Add the rear leg. *How many sections do you see?*

3. Draw the middle leg, and the front leg. Notice how the sections of the middle leg *overlap* to create depth.

4. Add *antennae, eye,* and *mouth.* Add the small visible bits of the other legs.

5. Add shading and texture. Draw a little tidbit and a cast shadow beneath the ant. Clean up any smudges with your eraser.

Great ant! To make your drawing more realistic, draw about a zillion of them, crawling all over the place....

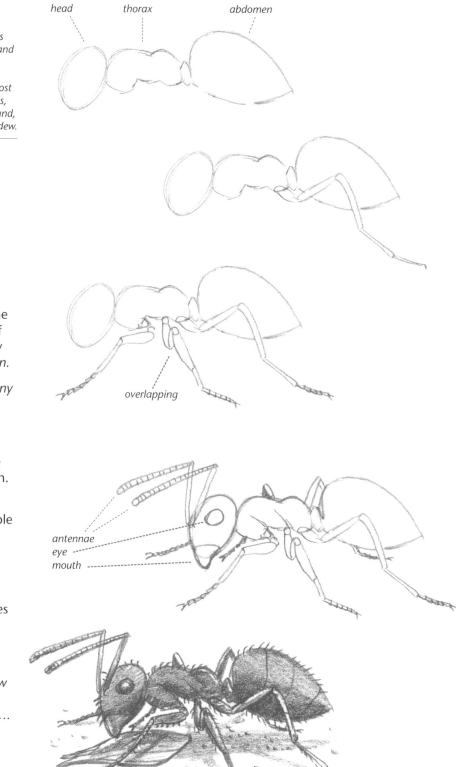

head   thorax   abdomen

overlapping

antennae
eye
mouth

Aphid

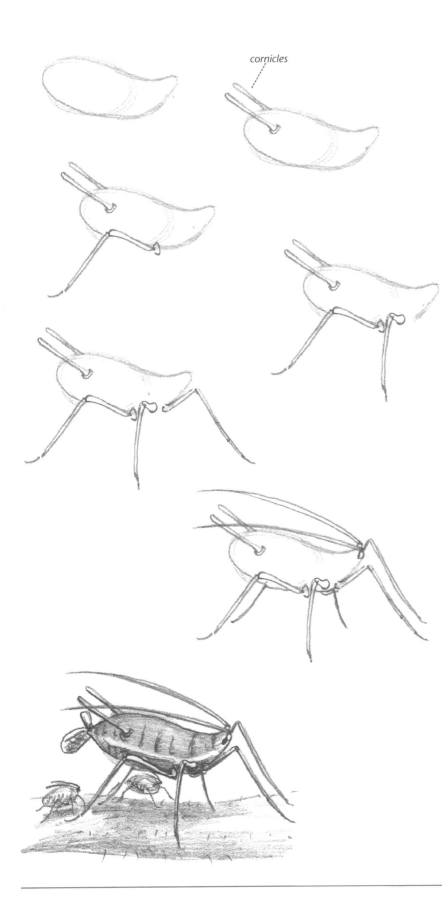

cornicles

Order Homoptera
Family Aphididae

Ask any gardener about aphids! These little plant-suckers appear in large numbers on leaves and stems of plants, leaving them wilted and curled. They can also spread plant diseases. Aphids give birth to young during spring and summer, and lay eggs to last through the winter. Ants help the process by gathering the eggs, storing them during the winter, then transporting the aphids from one food plant to another during the spring. Why? Because aphids also secrete something called honeydew, which the ants eat.

STUDY the final drawing *before you start!*

Do you see
- *distinct body parts?*
- *six legs?*
- *two antennae?*
- *wings?*
- *eyes?*

1. Draw the body, almost pear-shaped.

2. Add the distinctive *cornicles* at the rear end of the aphid.

3. Draw the rear leg,…

4. …the middle leg,…

5. …and the front leg.

6. Add the antennae and eye.

7. Finish your drawing by shading and going over fine lines with a sharp pencil. Add a little plant stem and shadows.

Now add a little flap in the back and more baby aphids popping out, eager to devour your house plants….

Assassin Bug

Order Hemiptera (true bugs)
Family Reduviidae

Assassin bugs have very strong front legs, which they use to grab and hold prey. They attack their victim with their short, sharp beaks and suck the body fluids out of them.

STUDY the final drawing *before you start!*

Do you see
- *three body parts?*
- *six legs?*
- *two antennae?*
- *wings?*
- *eyes?*

Does the insect look
- *shiny? smooth? fuzzy?*
- *hard? soft?*

1. Lightly draw the center line, and the six-sided *thorax.* Add the *head.*

2. Draw the *wings.*

3. Add the antennae, and the pointy shape of the *abdomen.*

4. Draw the first section of each leg. Which legs are the thickest and most powerful?

5. Carefully complete the legs. Draw veins in the wings. Add shading, texture, and details.

Idea! Draw another insect being attacked by the assassin bug....

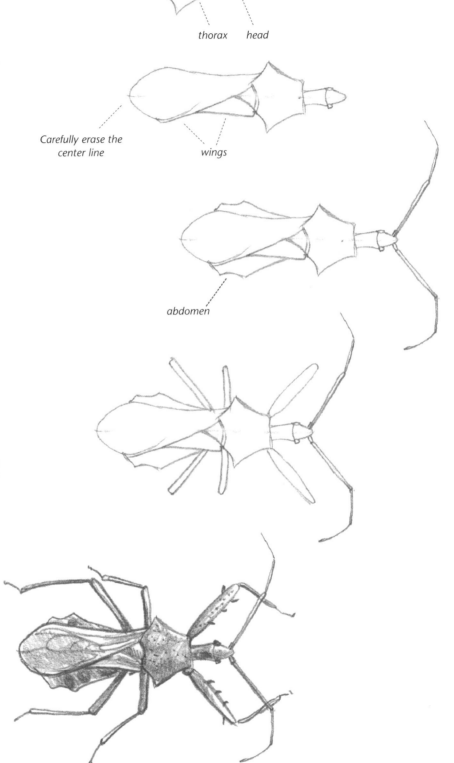

thorax   head

Carefully erase the center line

wings

abdomen

eye

proboscis

Back Swimmer

Order Hemiptera (true bugs)
Family Notonectidae

Back swimmers use their legs to paddle on the surface of water. They also dive, and can stay under water up to six hours. They catch tadpoles, small aquatic insects, and insects that get caught in the water. Swimming on their backs, they have protective coloring similar to many fish: dark on the top side and light on the bottom.

STUDY the final drawing *before you start!*

Do you see
- *three body parts?*
- *six legs?*
- *two antennae?*
- *wings?*
- *eyes?*

Does the insect look
- *shiny? smooth? fuzzy?*
- *hard? soft?*

1. Lightly draw the centre line, then *eyes* and *proboscis,* and the rounded sides of the body.

2. Draw the first section of each leg.

3. Add remaining, feather-like sections to the back legs.

4. Draw remaining sections to front legs, and give your back swimmer a little snack to munch on.

5. Add shading, and a few little ripples to suggest water.

Floating in your pool, munching on a snack… what a life!

Bon appetit!

Bed Bug

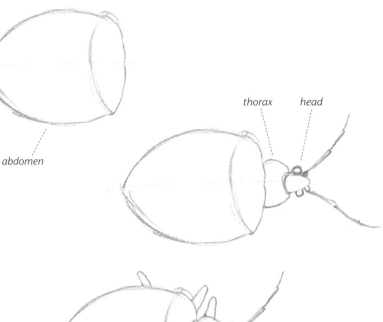

Order Hemiptera (true bugs)
Family Cimicidae

These flat, reddish-brown pests can really ruin a good night's sleep! They run surprisingly fast, and hunt for sleeping animals and birds at night when they can't find you. If they don't find anything, well, that's OK: adults have been known to live for a year without food.

abdomen

thorax   *head*

STUDY the final drawing *before you start!*

Do you see
- *three body parts?*
- *six legs?*
- *two antennae?*
- *wings?*
- *eyes?*

Does the insect look
- *shiny? smooth? fuzzy?*
- *hard? soft?*

1. Draw the acorn-shaped *abdomen.*

2. Add the *thorax* and *head,* with beady little eyes looking for the best place to attack you in your sleep. Add antennae.

3. Draw the first segment of all six legs.

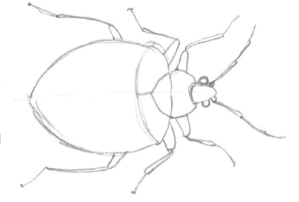

4. Add the remaining segments to each leg.

5. Add shading, texture, and stubbly little hairs, and a *cast shadow.*

   Sleep tight!

   Don't let the bedbugs bite!

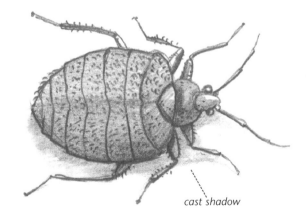

cast shadow

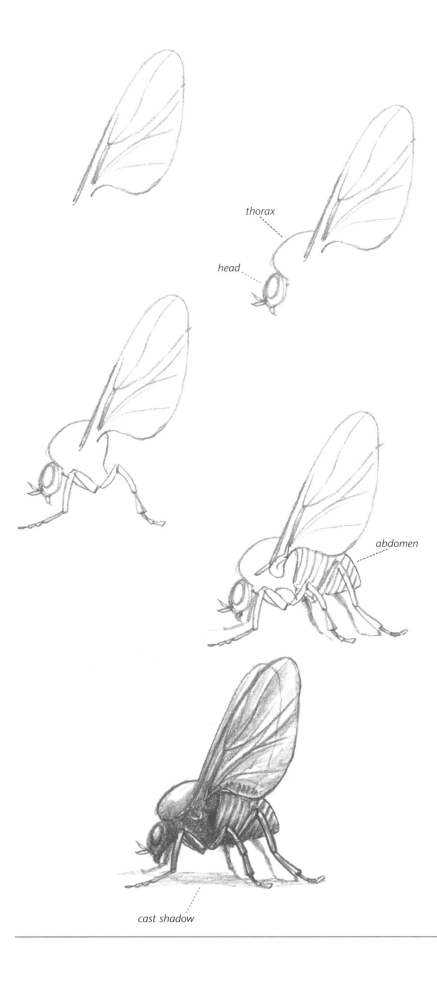

Black Fly

Order Diptera
Family Simuliidae

Black flies lay their eggs in streams and rivers. The larvae pupate in cocoons attached to rocks in the water. The adults burst out, rise on a bubble of air, and go forth to drive people crazy with their bites, in late spring or early summer. Some species transmit a type of malaria that kills ducks, geese, swans and turkeys.

STUDY the final drawing *before you start!*

Do you see
- *three body parts?*
- *six legs?*
- *two antennae?*
- *wings (how many)?*
- *eyes?*

Does the insect look
- *shiny? smooth? fuzzy?*
- *hard? soft?*

1. Start by drawing the slightly tilted wing. Look carefully at the example and draw the outline, almost straight on one side and more curved on the other. Add veins.

2. Draw the curved top of the *thorax, head,* eye and smaller details on the head.

3. Add two legs.

4. Draw the rear leg. Now add the segmented abdomen. Next, draw the legs on the far side of the fly.

5. Add shading and a bit of *cast shadow.* Shade the body and eye, leaving light areas to show the round forms. Lightly draw the outline of the other wing, and add shading and a *cast shadow.*

thorax

head

abdomen

cast shadow

Bumble Bee

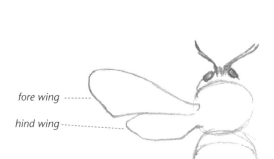

Order Hymenoptera
Family Apidae

Bumblebees usually live in cooler areas, where their thick hair protects them from the cold. Usually they build nests underground. Their very long proboscises can reach into the deepest flowers, and some depend almost completely on bumblebees for fertilization. When the English brought clover to New Zealand, for example, it didn't grow well until they imported bumblebees. The English biologist Charles Darwin made the suggestion.

STUDY the final drawing *before you start!*

Do you see
- *three body parts?*
- *six legs?*
- *two antennae?*
- *wings (how many)?*
- *eyes?*

Does the insect look
- *shiny? smooth? fuzzy?*
- *hard? soft?*

1. Draw the circle of the *thorax,* leaving white spaces on either side where the wings attach. Add the flattened oval of the *abdomen,* with lines showing segments.

2. Add head, eyes, and antennae.

3. Carefully outline one *fore wing* and *hind wing.*

4. Repeat on the other side, and add veins to the wings.

5. Now draw the six legs.

6. Add shading, shadow, and texture. Notice which parts of the body are darker, and which are lighter.

thorax

abdomen

fore wing

hind wing

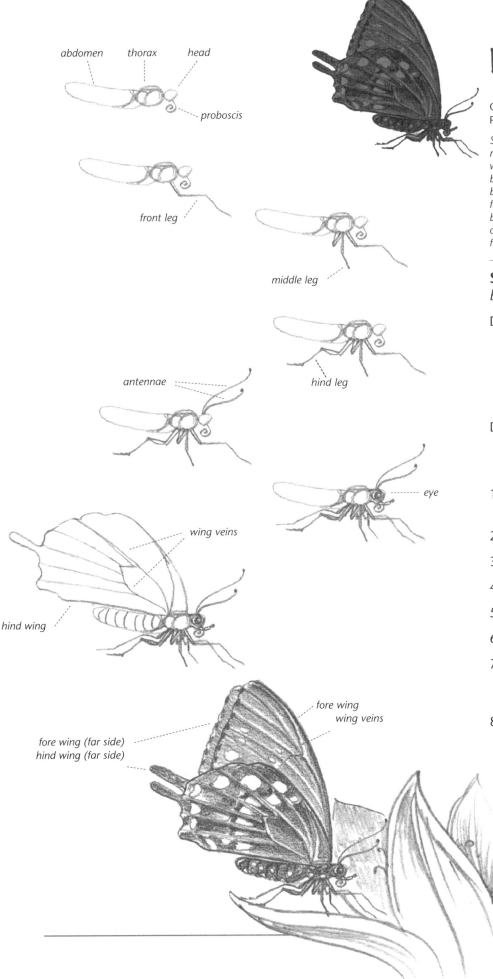

abdomen   thorax   head

proboscis

front leg

middle leg

antennae

hind leg

eye

wing veins

hind wing

fore wing (far side)
hind wing (far side)

fore wing
wing veins

Butterfly

Order Lepidoptera
Family Papilionidae

Swallowtail butterflies are easily recognized by the long tails on the hind wings. Their wings have patterns of black, yellow, or white, and can have blue or red spots. Papillon, *a word taken from this family of butterflies, means butterfly in French. (The German word, on the other hand, is* Schmetterling. *Go figure.)*

STUDY the final drawing *before you start!*

Do you see
- *three body parts?*
- *six legs?*
- *two antennae?*
- *wings (how many)?*
- *eyes?*

Does the insect look
- *shiny? smooth? fuzzy?*
- *hard? soft?*

1. Draw the *thorax, head* and *proboscis.*

2. Add the *front leg…*

3. …*middle leg…*

4. …and *hind leg.*

5. Draw the two *antennae.*

6. Add the *eye.*

7. Carefully outline the *hind wing* and its *veins.* Add lines for abdominal segments.

8. Draw the *fore wing.* Add the small visible portion of the fore wing and hind wing on the far side of the insect. Add shading. Go over lines with a sharpened pencil.

Caterpillar

Order Lepidoptera

Caterpillars are young butterflies or moths. They may have horns, spines, and bristles; they show distinct colors and patterns. All caterpillars have three pairs of legs in the thorax, and up to five pairs of abdominal "prolegs."

STUDY the final drawing *before you start!*

Do you see
- *three body parts?*
- *six legs?*
- *two antennae?*
- *wings?*
- *eyes?*

Does the insect look
- *shiny? smooth? fuzzy?*
- *hard? soft?*

1. Draw two tall, rounded rectangles with tiny projections for *legs.*

2. Add a triangle shape and another leg, and small bump with a dot for the head. Draw a little horn on top.

3. Draw two more rounded rectangles of the *abdomen.*

4. Add another, with a little bump for a *proleg…*

5. …and another…

6. …and two more…

7. …then three plain segments and a last segment with another proleg.

6. Now add pattern and shading, leaving a light area on each segment to make the caterpillar look shiny. And give it a little something to munch on!

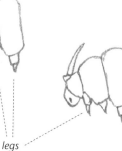

legs

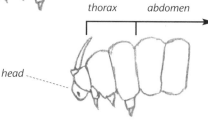

thorax   abdomen

head

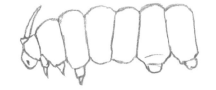

proleg

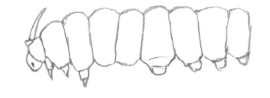

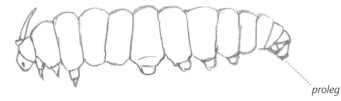

proleg

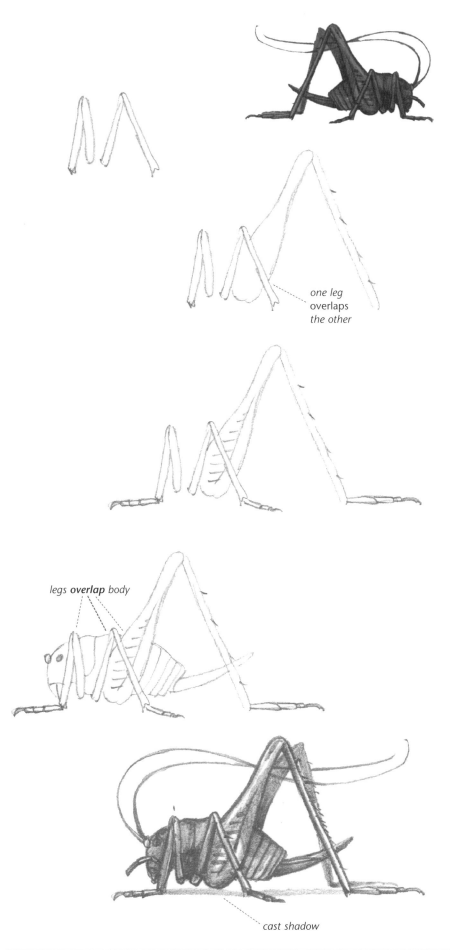

one leg
overlaps
the other

legs **overlap** body

cast shadow

Cave Cricket

Order Orthoptera
Family Gryllacrididae

Most crickets in this family have no wings. They live in caves and basements, or in dark places under logs, rocks, or bark. Some types make a scratchy sound, but most—unlike field crickets—make no sound at all. Their long antennae and leg bristles warn them of approaching predators, such as spiders or centipedes.

STUDY the final drawing *before you start!*

Do you see
- *three body parts?*
- *six legs?*
- *two antennae?*
- *wings?*
- *eyes?*

Does the insect look
- *shiny? smooth? fuzzy?*
- *hard? soft?*

1. Start with two bending legs forming an M shape.

2. Draw the powerful rear jumping leg behind.

3. Add additional segments to each leg, and the pattern on the largest leg.

4. Now draw the body behind the legs. Look carefully, and draw one part at a time.

   Because you drew the legs first, it's easy to show them overlapping *the body, adding depth to your drawing.*

5. Add shading, very long antennae, the other rear leg (shaded solid gray), and a slight *cast shadow*.

   Pretty cool looking critter!

Cicada

Order Homoptera
Family Cicadidae

Cicadas live in trees and make loud, pulsating buzzing sounds. They lay eggs on twigs, which usually die and fall to the ground. The nymph cicadas then feast on roots before crawling up a tree. Certain cicadas repeat this cycle only once every 13 or 17 years.

STUDY the final drawing *before you start!*

Do you see
- *three body parts?*
- *six legs?*
- *two antennae?*
- *wings (how many)?*
- *eyes?*

Does the insect look
- *shiny? smooth? fuzzy?*
- *hard? soft?*

1. Draw a rounded triangle with a little circle on the bottom and one side.

2. Add the peanut shape of the body on the other side of the triangle.

3. Outline the *fore wings.* Notice how one points down on the page, while the other points up at an angle.

4. Add the *hind wings.*

5. Carefully outline the veins in one wing. Take your time! Look carefully!

6. Complete your drawing by carefully adding veins to the other wings. Draw legs and segments of the body. Then add shading, and go over any fuzzy lines with a sharp pencil to make them look cleaner.

fore wings

hind wing

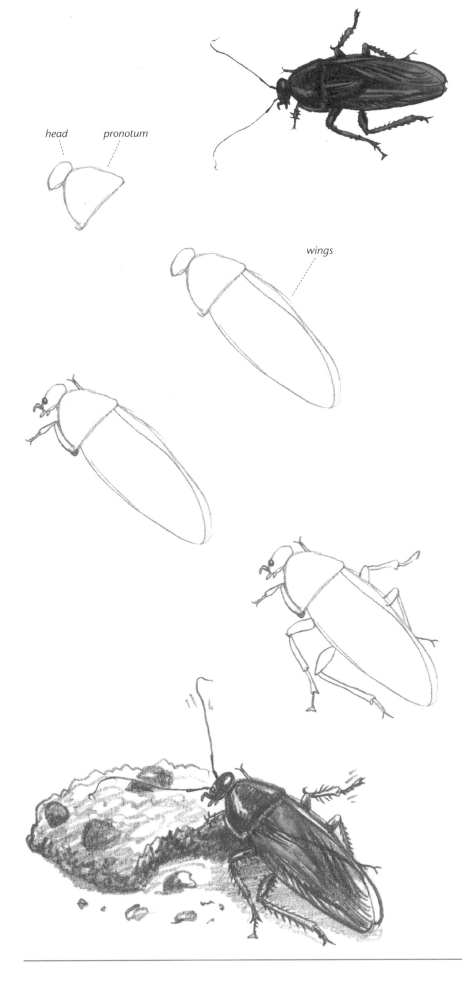

head   pronotum

wings

Cockroach

Order Blattodea
Family Blattidae

Cockroaches do not transmit human disease, but…they infest buildings, contaminate food, and have an unpleasant smell. They are active and fast runners at night; during the day they hide in cracks. They almost never fly, though they are among the oldest winged insects (350 million years). Some have become almost immune to pesticides after numerous attempts to eradicate them. And don't bother trying to starve them to death: some have lived for months on little more than dust!

STUDY the final drawing *before you start!*

Do you see
- *three body parts?*
- *six legs?*
- *two antennae?*
- *wings (how many)?*
- *eyes?*

Does the insect look
- *shiny? smooth? fuzzy?*
- *hard? soft?*

1. Draw a small flat oval for the *head* and a half-circle for the *pronotum.*

2. Add the long shape of the *wings.*

3. Draw details on the head, and add the visible bits of front legs.

4. Carefully add the remaining two pairs of legs.

5. Add antennae, bristly hairs on the legs, and shading.

For added realism, make your cockroach nibbling on a chocolate chip cookie!

Cow Killer

Order Hymenoptera
Family Mutillidae (Velvet-ants)

I had no idea this insect existed until I spotted one in the back yard while working on this book. It moved so fast I couldn't tell how many legs it had, and buzzed as it raced around. I'm glad I didn't try to pick it up: the sting from this wingless wasp is so painful that some people say it could kill a cow! Cow killers invade bumblebee nests and lay their eggs in them. They are bright red and black.

STUDY the final drawing *before you start!*

Do you see
- *three body parts?*
- *six legs?*
- *two antennae?*
- *wings?*
- *eyes?*

Does the insect look
- *shiny? smooth? fuzzy?*
- *hard? soft?*

1. Start with the oval shaped head, eye, and segmented antennae.

2. Draw two more oval shapes for the *thorax* and *abdomen.*

3. Add fuzzy hair covering the whole body. If you have colored pencils, make the light areas bright red, and the dark areas black.

4. Draw a long, bristly leg…

5. …and another…

6. …and another.

7. Finish your drawing by adding the other three legs, and some grains of sand or small pebbles, and a cast shadow beneath the body.

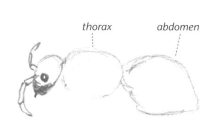

thorax   abdomen

Crane Fly

Order Diptera
Family Tipulidae

These flies seem to dance in midair. Larva feed on rotting vegetation and fungus, but adults don't eat at all! They live in humid areas, often near lakes or streams, and lay slender eggs in moist dirt.

STUDY the final drawing *before you start!*

Do you see
- *three body parts?*
- *six legs?*
- *two antennae?*
- *wings (how many)?*
- *eyes?*

Does the insect look
- *shiny? smooth? fuzzy?*
- *hard? soft?*

1. Draw the long, slender *abdomen* with lines dividing it into segments. Add the bulbous *thorax,* small pointy *head* and *eyes.*

2. Draw the two long wings, wing veins, and the tiny antennae.

3. Add the two very long rear legs.

4. Draw the middle legs, looking carefully at how they bend.

5. Add the front legs. Go over lines to darken them. Clean up any smudges with your eraser.

abdomen   thorax   eyes/head

Deer Fly

Order Diptera
Family Tabanidae

This pest looks like a jet airplane when it lands after circling above its prey – and it feels like one too when it bites! As with horse flies and mosquitoes, only female deer flies feed on blood; the males drink plant juices. The larva feed on small aquatic insects. Some deer flies transmit bacteria that can cause tularemia in rabbits and hares...and occasionally people.

STUDY the final drawing *before you start!*

Do you see
- *three body parts?*
- *six legs?*
- *two antennae?*
- *wings (how many)?*
- *eyes?*

Does the insect look
- *shiny? smooth? fuzzy?*
- *hard? soft?*

1. Starting with the *head* and two eyes, then add rounded rectangles of the *thorax* and *abdomen.*

2. Draw the wings, extending beyond the abdomen.

3. Add six legs, and antennae.

4. Look closely! Draw the markings on the back and the veins on the wings. Add markings on thorax and abdomen, and shade the eyes, leaving highlights.

5. Add shading to head, thorax, and abdomen. Shade the wings to make them look translucent: you can see shapes through them, but they're not completely clear.

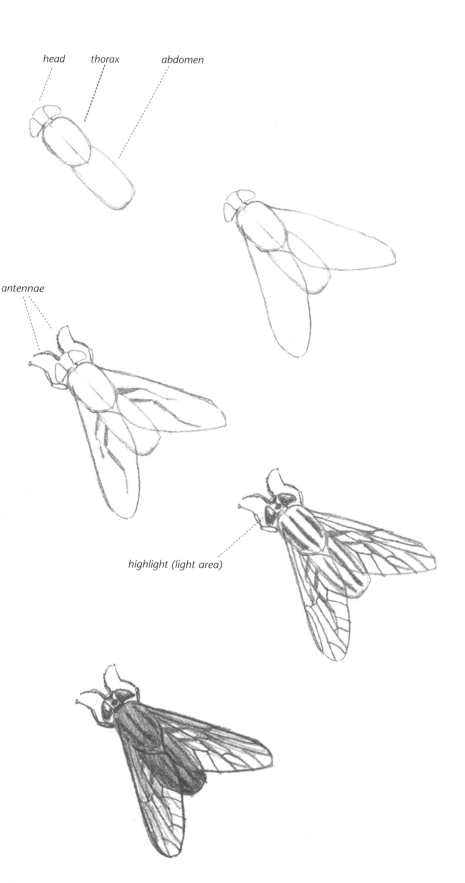

head   thorax   abdomen

antennae

highlight (light area)

Digger Wasp

Order Hymenoptera
Family Scoliidae (Scoliid Wasps)

Green June beetles have a good reason not to like digger wasps: the female wasps dig (possibly several feet) into the ground to find a beetle larva. Then she stings it, digs a little chamber around it and lays on egg on its back. When the egg hatches, the wasp larva eats the beetle larva.

STUDY the final drawing *before you start!*

Do you see
- *three body parts?*
- *six legs?*
- *two antennae?*
- *wings (how many)?*
- *eyes?*

1. Draw the long, tilted *abdomen* and rounder *thorax,* connected by the narrow *pedicel* (waist).

2. Add the head and neck, large eye with a highlight to make it look shiny. Draw mouth parts. Add antennae.

3. Carefully draw the legs, counting the sections of each. Notice how the middle leg *overlaps* the rear leg in flight.

4. Draw the wings (in this view, we see only the closer two). Make light guide lines to show the segments of the abdomen.

5. Add shading and texture.

Test question!
Why does a digger wasp dig?

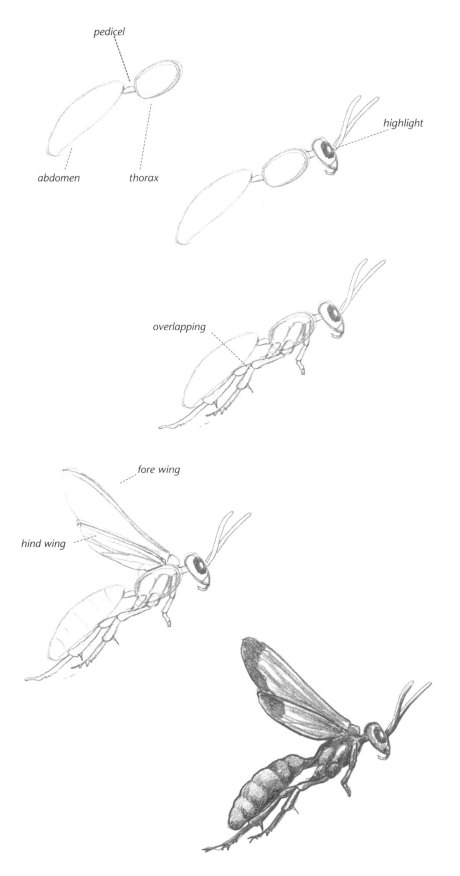

Dragonfly

Order Odonata
Suborder Anisoptera

Dragonfly nymphs live in ponds and streams, so you often see adult dragonflies around water, though they can range several miles. Often brightly colored, dragonflies fly well and often, catching mosquitoes and midges in flight. They're fast! No wonder they have such big eyes!

head

thorax

abdomen

hind wing

fore wing

STUDY the final drawing *before you start!*

Do you see
- *three body parts?*
- *six legs?*
- *two antennae?*
- *wings (how many)?*
- *eyes?*

Does the insect look
- *shiny? smooth? fuzzy?*
- *hard? soft?*

1. Start with two small circles for the *head* and *thorax,* and draw the long rectangle of the *abdomen.*

2. Draw one *hind wing.*

3. Add the *fore wing.*

4. Draw wings on the other side as well.

5. Add details on head, front legs, veins in wings, and lines on the abdomen.

6. Complete your drawing by adding more shading and about a zillion cells on each wing. Look closely at the example, and take your time drawing them!

    Dazzling dragonfly!

Earwig

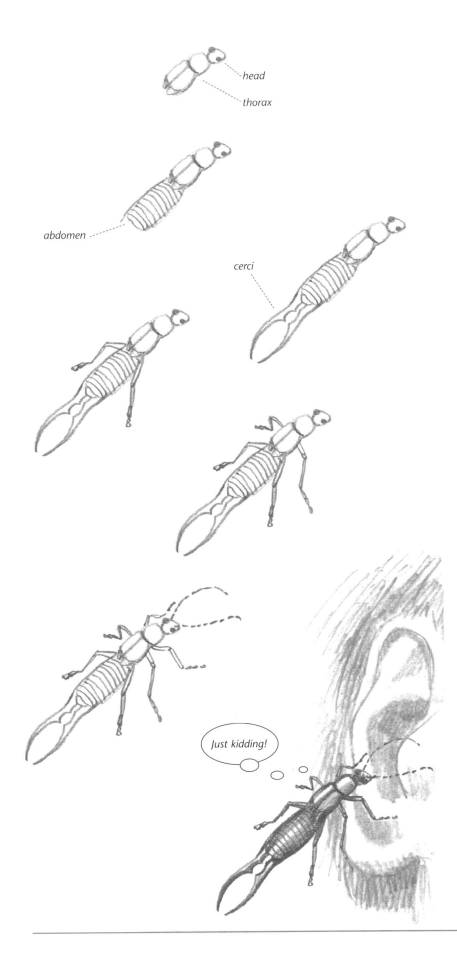

head

thorax

abdomen

cerci

Just kidding!

Order Dermaptera
Family Forficulidae

Their strange name comes from an old superstition that these insects got into people's ears (they don't...I don't think). They live and lay their eggs in plant debris, scavenging or feeding on plants at night. They use their pincerlike cerci in defense, and can pinch painfully. They also squirt a foul-smelling liquid if handled.

STUDY the final drawing *before you start!*

Do you see
- *three body parts?*
- *six legs?*
- *two antennae?*
- *wings (how many)?*
- *eyes?*

Does the insect look
- *shiny? smooth? fuzzy?*
- *hard? soft?*

1. Start by drawing the *head* and *thorax.*

2. Add the long *abdomen* with curving lines...

3. ...and add the nasty-looking *cerci* at the end.

4. Draw the rear legs...

5. ...the middle legs...

6. ...and then the front legs and segmented antennae.

7. Add shading, leaving light areas on the back to make the form look round.

I can understand the "ear" part, but where do you suppose the "wig" comes from?

Firefly (Lightning Bug)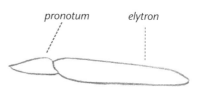

Order Coleoptera
Family Lampyridae

During spring and early summer, these beetles use their luminous abdominal sections to attract other fireflies for mating. Although other insects can glow, fireflies are unique in being able to flash, and the rhythms are distinct for each species. Active at night, they live under bark or in moist places under debris.

STUDY the final drawing *before you start!*

Do you see
- *three body parts?*
- *six legs?*
- *two antennae?*
- *wings (how many)?*
- *eyes?*

Does the insect look
- *shiny? smooth? fuzzy?*
- *hard? soft?*

1. Start by drawing the *pronotum* and *elytron* (one of two hard fore wings).

2. Draw the triangular head (almost completely covered by the *pronotum*) and the front leg.

3. Add the middle leg…

4. …and the rear leg.

5. Draw the body, and shade most of it dark. Leave the end of the abdomen light: this is the part that flashes. Make the eye dark, leaving a little reflective white spot.

6. Draw antennae, and the other three legs.

7. Carefully shade your drawing, leaving a light area at the top of the shiny protective shell. Draw a little branch for it to sit on.

pronotum   elytron

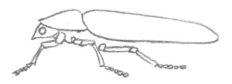

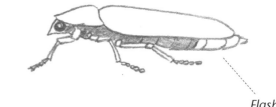

Flash!
Flash!
Flash!

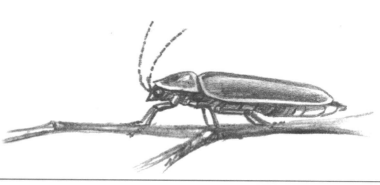

Flea

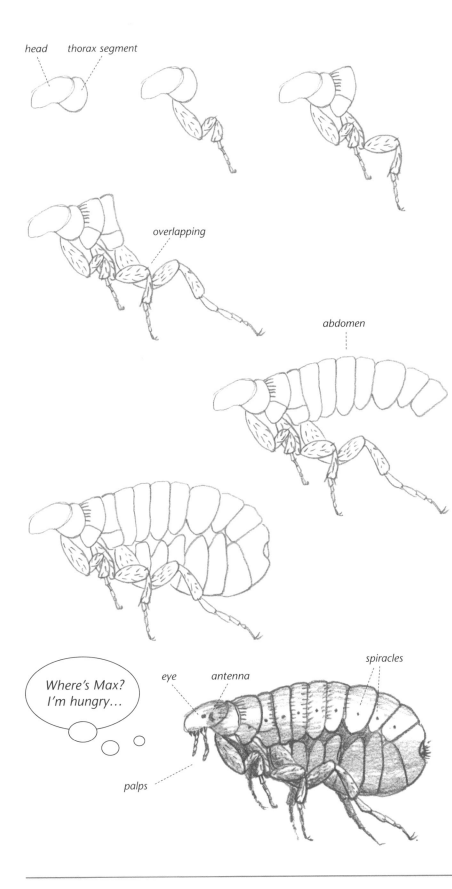

head   *thorax segment*

overlapping

abdomen

Where's Max?
I'm hungry...

eye   *antenna*

spiracles

palps

Order Siphonaptera
Family Pulicidae

Fleas are annoying parasites that live off the blood of their host; they lay eggs on their host or in its nest. Fleas help pets get tapeworm and can spread disease such as bubonic plague.

STUDY the final drawing *before you start!*

Do you see
- *three body parts?*
- *six legs?*
- *two antennae?*
- *wings?*
- *eye?*

1. Draw the head and first *thorax segment.*

2. Draw the front leg, attached to the first thorax segment. Count the sections of the leg, and look carefully at which direction each goes.

3. Draw the second thorax segment and middle leg, *behind* the front leg.

4. Draw the third thorax segment and powerful rear leg, *behind* the middle leg.

5. Add the top part of the abdomen...

6. ...and the bottom.

7. Add *eye, antenna, palps,* three more legs, and shading. Don't forget the breathing *spiracles!*

Giant Beetle

Order Coleoptera
Family Scarabaeidae

Why do you suppose this is called the Giant Beetle? Put you hand over it to get an idea how big it is. Despite its scary-looking horns, this beetle wouldn't hurt you…in fact, it might feel kind of cool walking across your hand and up your arm….

STUDY the final drawing *before you start!*

Do you see
- *three body parts?*
- *six legs?*
- *two antennae?*
- *wings (how many)?*
- *eyes?*

Does the insect look
- *shiny? smooth? fuzzy?*
- *hard? soft?*

1. Draw the front beetle wings *(elytra)* and *thorax.*

2. Add the *head* and ferocious-looking *horns.*

3. Draw the front legs.

4. Add the middle and hind legs.

5. Add the club-like antennae on either side of the center horn. Shade the beetle, leaving very light areas to make it look shiny. Go over lines with a sharp pencil. Use a dull pencil to add shading and a *cast shadow.*

Awesome!

elytron;
plural elytra

thorax

head

horns

cast shadow

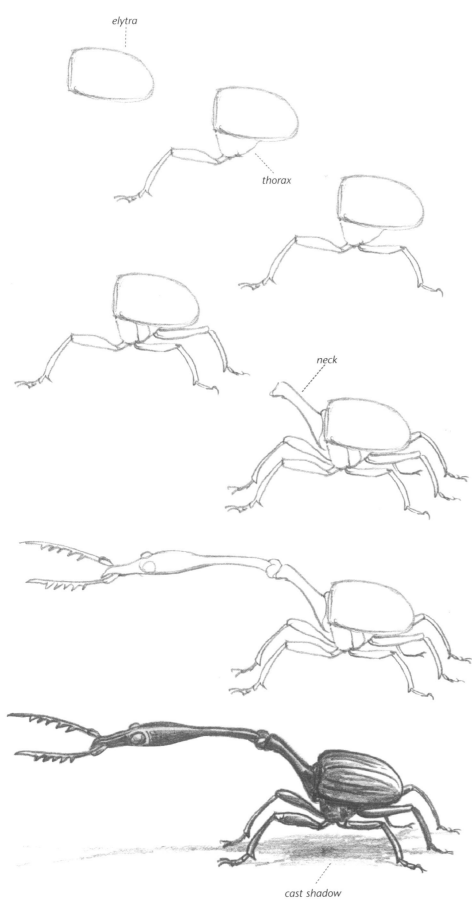

elytra

thorax

neck

cast shadow

Giraffe Beetle

Order Coleoptera
Family Curculionidae (snout beetles and weevils)
This little monster belongs to a group of hard-shelled beetles that chew holes in fruits, nuts, and other parts of plants. One member, the boll weevil, is well known for destroying cotton crops in the southern U.S. after accidental introduction from Mexico.

STUDY the final drawing *before you start!*

Do you see
* *three body parts?*
* *six legs?*
* *two antennae?*
* *wings?*
* *eyes?*

Does the insect look
* *shiny? smooth? fuzzy?*
* *hard? soft?*

1. Draw the flattened oval shape of the *elytra* (protective fore wings).

2. Draw the visible triangle of the *thorax.* Look carefully, then add the front leg,…

3. …the rear leg,…

4. …and the middle leg. Add lines to show the segments of the thorax.

5. Add visible parts of other legs, and the first section of the *neck.*

6. Now draw the rest of the neck and head.

7. Add shading, texture, and a *cast shadow* to complete your drawing.

   "Why is the neck on this beetle so long?" you ask. *Good question!*

Horse Fly

Order Diptera
Family Tabanidae

As with mosquitoes and deer flies, only female horse flies feed on blood, while the males eat pollen and nectar from flowers. Quieter than house flies, horse flies sneak up and give a nasty bite that continues to bleed because of an anticoagulant in the fly's saliva. A horse or cow can actually suffer serious blood loss if a number of horse flies attack it.

STUDY the final drawing *before you start!*

Do you see
- *three body parts?*
- *six legs?*
- *two antennae?*
- *wings (how many)?*
- *eyes?*

Does the insect look
- *shiny? smooth? fuzzy?*
- *hard? soft?*

1. Start with a light *guide line* for the center of the fly. Add *abdomen, thorax,* and those *big green eyes.*

2. Draw the wings.

3. Add the six legs and two antennae.

4. Draw lines for abdominal segments and veins in wings. Add shading and texture. Add enough shading on the wings to make them appear *translucent* – in other words, you can see the legs through them, but not real clearly.

abdomen   thorax   big green eyes

guide line

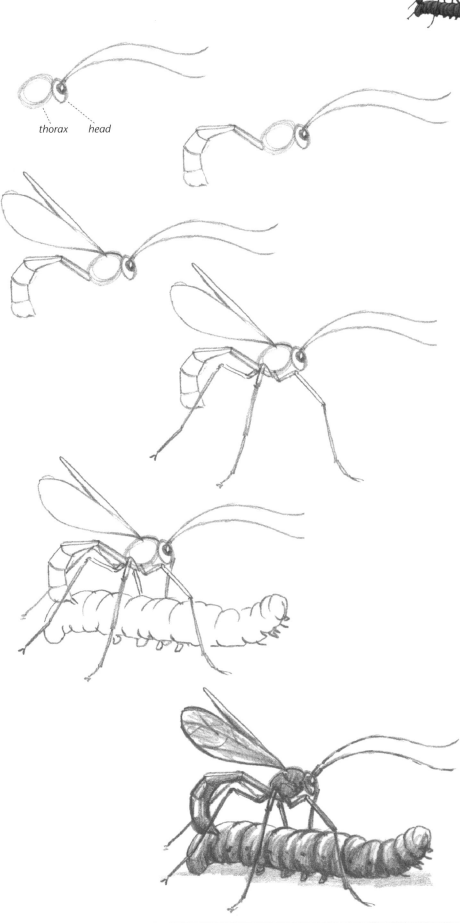

Ichneumon Fly

Order Hymenoptera
Family Ichneumonidae

Ichneumons (sometimes called ichneumonflies) are a large family of parasitic wasps. This ichneumon lays its egg on the back of an active caterpillar. The larva will burrow into the host, eventually killing it. Probably it won't kill the host until the caterpillar has made a cocoon: then the ichneumon larva will have a cozy little home in which to pupate as it feeds on the remains of its host.

STUDY the final drawing *before you start!*

Do you see
- *three body parts?*
- *six legs?*
- *two antennae?*
- *wings (how many)?*
- *eyes?*

Does the insect look
- *shiny? smooth? fuzzy?*
- *hard? soft?*

1. Draw ovals for the *thorax* and *head.* Add the shiny eye, and long, gracefully curving antennae.

2. Carefully draw the curving tail, one segment at a time.

3. Add the wings, one showing the curved shape, and the other just a sliver.

4. Draw the legs. Look closely

thorax   *head*

Japanese Beetle

Order Coleoptera
Family Scaribaeidae (scarab beetles)

The Japanese Beetle has been a familiar and widespread pest in the U.S. since its accidental introduction around 1916. Its body and legs are bright metallic green; the elytra (wing coverings) are brown or reddish orange. Larvae feed underground on roots; adults eat foliage, leaves, and fruits of more than 200 kinds of plants. Careful use of parasitic wasps has reduced its numbers in some areas.

STUDY the final drawing *before you start!*

Do you see
- *three body parts?*
- *six legs?*
- *two antennae?*
- *wings (how many)?*
- *eyes?*

Does the insect look
- *shiny? smooth? fuzzy?*
- *hard? soft?*

1. Start by drawing the *elytra* (hard fore wings) and *scutellum.*

2. Add the *pronotum, head,* and eyes.

3. Carefully draw the front legs…

4. …then the middle legs…

5. …and finally the rear legs. Add lines to the *elytra.*

6. Finish by adding shading, or, if you have colored pencils, by coloring the beetle dark green with shiny highlights, except for the *elytra,* which are reddish brown.

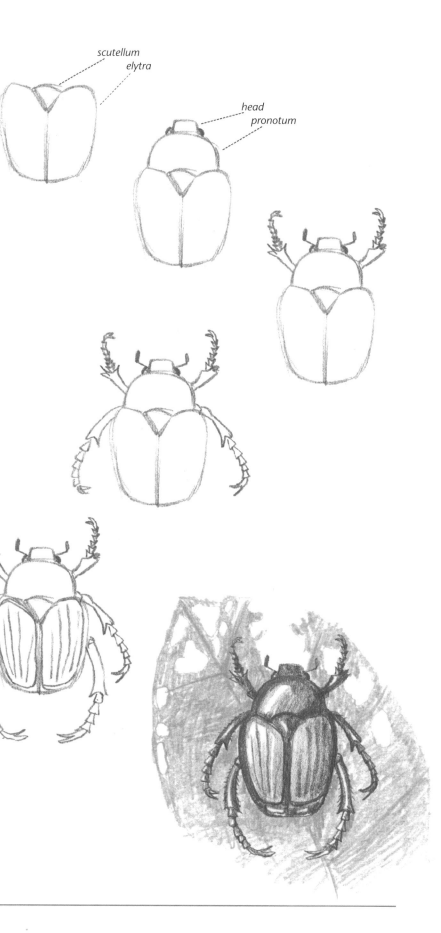

scutellum
elytra

head
pronotum

Lacewing

Order Neuroptera (net-veined insects)
Family Chrysopidae (Green Lacewings)

These common insects don't fly very well, but they're great at eating aphids, so they're welcome in the garden! They lay eggs at the end of tiny stalks, usually on foliage. They pupate in silken cocoons.

STUDY the final drawing *before you start!*

Do you see
- *three body parts?*
- *six legs?*
- *two antennae?*
- *wings (how many)?*
- *eyes?*

Does the insect look
- *shiny? smooth? fuzzy?*
- *hard? soft?*

1. Carefully draw the outline of the wing.

2. Add two main veins…

3. …and then create the pattern of cells inside of them.

4. Now add a row of veins and cells at the top of the wing,

5. and fill in the center section.

6. Draw one more row of cells on the bottom.

7. Add the body and head with its long antennae.

8. Draw the legs. Lightly shade a bit in the wings.

Lovely lacewing!

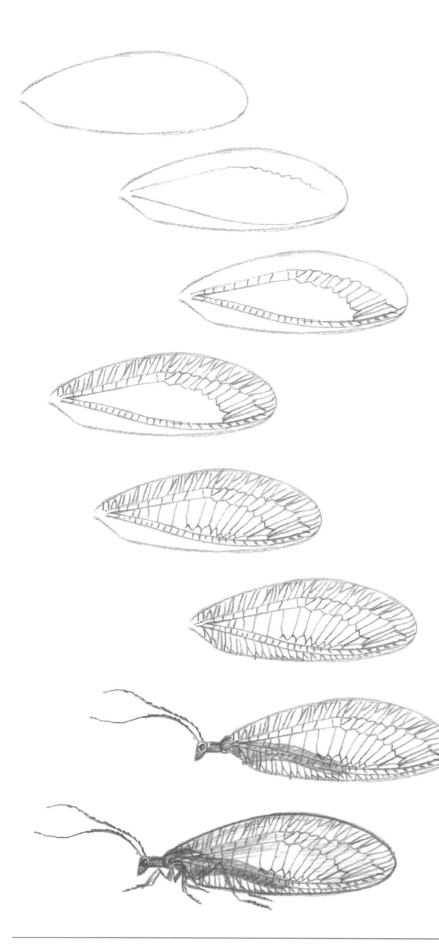

Ladybug Beetle

Order Coleoptera
Family Coccinellidae

Labybugs, also called Ladybirds, are welcome in the garden because they feed on aphids. They also eat scale insects and mites which otherwise damage plants

STUDY the final drawing *before you start!*

Do you see
- *distinct body parts?*
- *six legs?*
- *antenna?*
- *wing?*

Does the insect look
- *shiny? smooth? fuzzy?*
- *hard? soft?*

1. Draw the *fore wing* and the shape that looks like the head, but is actually the *pronotum,* which covers the head.

2. Add the front, middle, and rear leg.

3. Make a line for the edge of the stem, and draw the other three legs.

4. Add spots on the front wing and *pronotum.* Draw the *antenna (one of two; the other you can't see),* and the *beak.* Add shading and a *cast shadow.*

5. And now *(YES!!)* make the ladybug sucking the life out of an aphid.

   Guten appetit, ladybug!

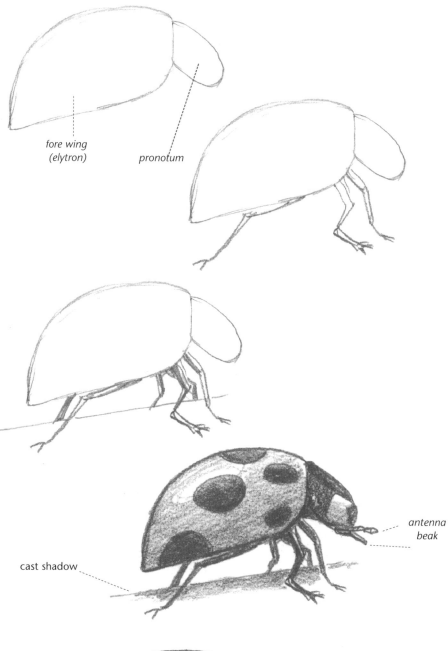

fore wing
(elytron)   pronotum

antenna
beak

cast shadow

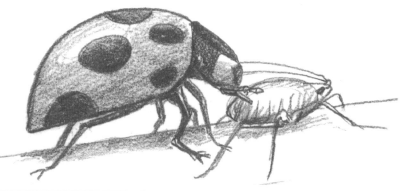

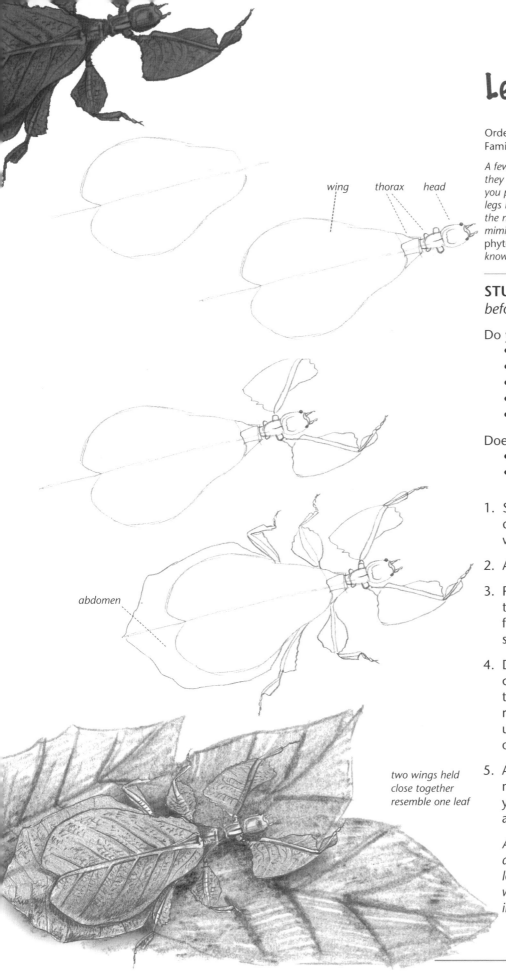

Leaf Insect

Order Phasmatodea
Family Phylliidae (leaf insects)

A few insects imitate plants so well that they won't move during the day, even if you pick them up! They can also drop legs if necessary, then grow them back the next time they molt. The ability to mimic plant structure is called phytomimesis *(thought you'd want to know).*

STUDY the final drawing *before you start!*

Do you see
- *three body parts?*
- *six legs?*
- *two antennae?*
- *wings (how many)?*
- *eyes?*

Does the insect look
- *shiny? smooth? fuzzy?*
- *hard? soft?*

1. Starting with a center line, draw the pear-shaped wings.

2. Add the *thorax* and *head.*

3. From the first segment of the thorax, draw two skinny front legs, then add the leaf shape to them.

4. Draw the middle legs connecting to the second thorax segment, and the rear legs sticking out from under the wings. Add the outline of the *abdomen.*

5. Add lines and shading to make it look like a leaf! Take your time, and look closely at the example for ideas.

   Add camouflage! Draw sticks and leaves, so that someone looking at your drawing won't even know there's an insect there....

wing   thorax   head

abdomen

two wings held
close together
resemble one leaf

Draw Insects   31

Locust

Order Orthoptera
Suborder Caelifera

Certain grasshoppers are called locusts, from the Latin word for grasshopper. Only nine of 5,000 species of the suborder Caelifera make mass migrations, but when they do, they eat all vegetation in their path. There's the Old Testament plague of locusts descending on Egypt; in modern times trains have been delayed during locust migrations because the tracks were "slimy" from dead insects. Grasshopper Glacier in Montana is full of dead locusts. In the US in the 1870s, a single swarm was estimated to contain 124 billion insects.

STUDY the final drawing *before you start!*

Do you see
- *three body parts?*
- *wings (how many)?*
- *six legs?*

1. Start with two small circles and a longer, rectangular shape for the *head, thorax,* and *abdomen.*

2. Draw the two front legs stretched out either side. Add details to the head, and antennae.

3. Add the second, short pair of legs pointing backwards, and the much longer rear legs. Draw short curved lines for the abdominal segments.

4. Carefully outline the wings.

5. Now add about a zillion little veins and cells. Take your time–it's worth it! Add shading and texture to the body.

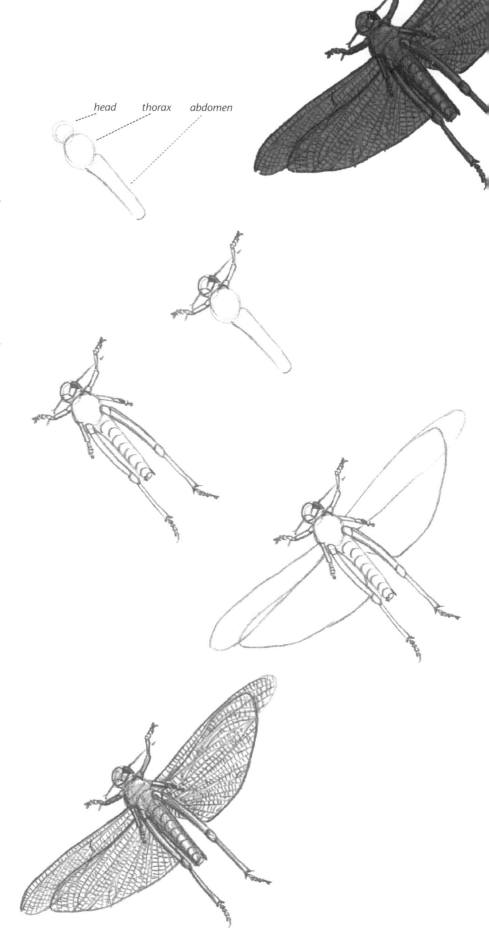

head   thorax   abdomen

Head Louse

Order Anoplura
Pediculidus humanus humanus

This louse glues little white eggs, called nits, to hair, usually on the back of the head. (Now you can figure out where the term "nit-picking" comes from.) Head lice can be easily transmitted from one person to another. Lice are sometimes called 'cooties.'

STUDY the final drawing *before you start!*

Do you see
- *three body parts?*
- *six legs?*
- *two antennae?*
- *wings?*
- *eyes?*

Does the insect look
- *shiny? smooth? fuzzy?*
- *hard? soft?*

1. Draw a small circle for the *head,* a larger oval for the *thorax,* and a much larger oval for the *abdomen.´*

2. Carefully divide the abdomen into segments, and add the little bits at the tail end.

3. Mark the thorax to show where three pairs of legs attach, and draw the rear legs…

4. …then the middle legs…

5. …and finally the front legs. Add more details to the head.

6. Finally, add shading, little bristly hairs and a few little human hairs to hold on ´to.

Cute cootie!

head

thorax

abdomen

Luna Moth

Order Lepidoptera
Family Saturniidae (giant silkworm
moths)

*This beautiful pale green moth is only
found in North America, and is
considered endangered. Many have been
killed by pesticides and pollutants.*

STUDY the final drawing
before you start!

Do you see
- *three body parts?*
- *six legs?*
- *two antennae?*
- *wings (how many)?*
- *eyes?*

Does the insect look
- *shiny? smooth? fuzzy?*
- *hard? soft?*

1. Draw a cocoon-shaped oval
   for the body, and add two
   feathery antennae.

2. Carefully (and lightly) draw
   one fore wing.

3. Carefully (and lightly) add
   the other fore wing.

4. Draw the hind wings, with
   their long tails. Go slowly;
   turn your paper if it helps
   you draw the curves.

5. Add wing veins, spots,
   shading and texture. (If you
   have colored pencils, shade
   it a light green color. The
   large *costal vein* is maroon.)

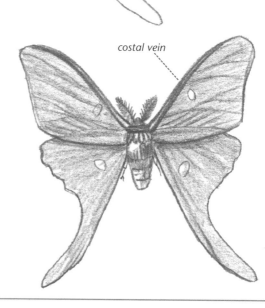

costal vein

Mosquito

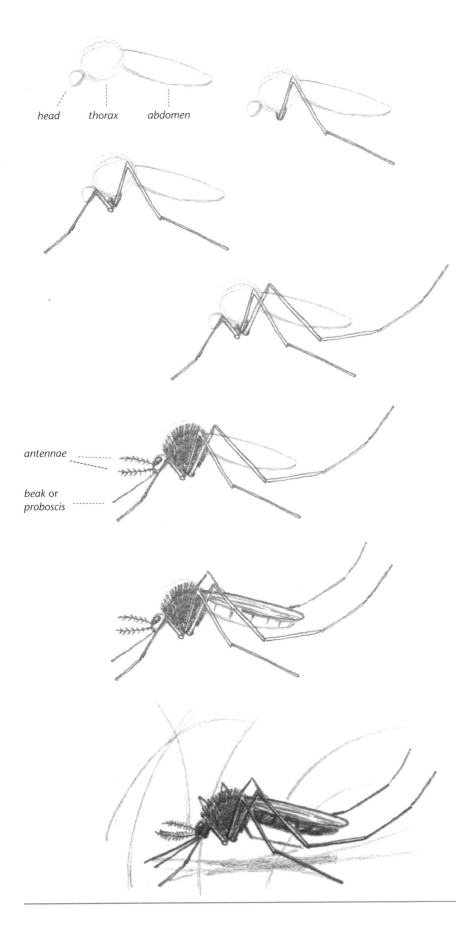

head   thorax   abdomen

antennae

beak or
proboscis

Order Diptera
Family Culicidae

You can tell this is a female mosquito because it has only a few hairs on the antennae (on males, they're more feathery), and lacks the male's two additional beak-like palps. Only the females bite. Mosquitoes can convey diseases such as malaria, generally only in tropical areas.

STUDY the final drawing *before you start!*

Do you see
- *three body parts?*
- *six legs?*
- *two antennae?*
- *wings (how many)?*
- *eyes?*

1. First, make some high-pitched, whining noises to get in the mood…. Now draw the *head, thorax,* and *abdomen.*

2. Add the middle leg…

3. …the front leg…

4. …and the hind legs, curving up into the air.

5. Draw the eye and *antennae,* and the *beak,* or *proboscis,* ready to do business. Add texture to the thorax.

6. Add the wing, covering part of the abdomen, and the lines for abdominal segments. Draw the other hind leg.

7. Add the other two legs, and shading, a bit of cast shadow and a few human hairs.

Moth in flight

Order Lepidoptera
Family Noctuidae (Noctuid moths)

Most moths are active at night, in contrast to butterflies, which fly only during the day. All but a very few moths suck nectar through their curved proboscis; one primitive group has jaws for eating pollen. Unlike butterflies, moths rest with their wings like a roof over their bodies, flat over their bodies, or flat against a support.

STUDY the final drawing *before you start!*

Do you see
- *three body parts?*
- *six legs?*
- *two antennae?*
- *wings (how many)?*
- *eyes?*

Does the insect look
- *shiny? smooth? fuzzy?*
- *hard? soft?*

1. Draw a small circle for the head, a smaller circle for the eye, and a larger oval for the *thorax.*

2. Add long antennae, and the front *leg.*

3. Draw middle and rear leg.

4. Add the *abdomen,* and the *hind wing,* showing the vein pattern in the wing.

5. Draw the *fore wing* and its main veins.

6. Carefully add shading to make the pattern in the wings. Now add shading, details and texture to the body.

Mahvellous moth!

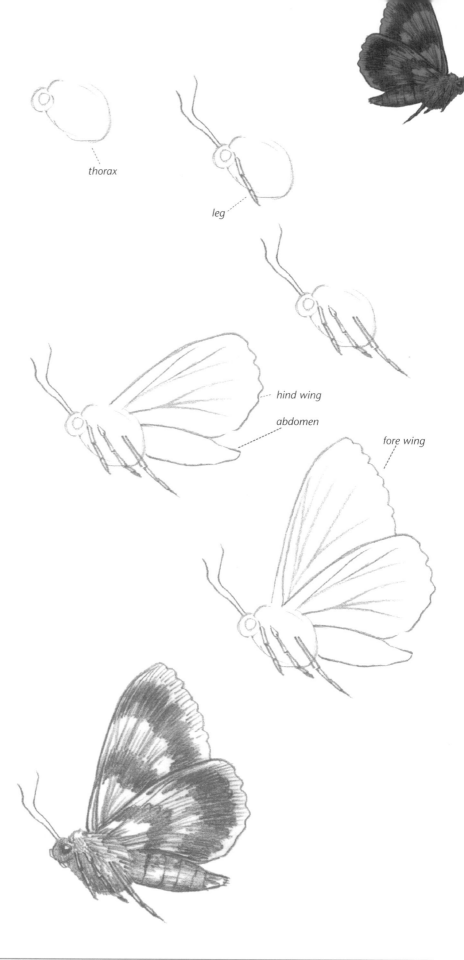

thorax

leg

hind wing

abdomen

fore wing

Mud Dauber

Order Hymenoptera
Family Sphecidae

Mud daubers are wasps that lay their eggs in tubular cells made from mud. The female paralyzes a spider with venom, stuffs it into a cell for food, lays an egg on top of it, and seals off the cell with mud.

head   thorax

pedicel   abdomen

fore wing   hind wing

STUDY the final drawing *before you start!*

Do you see
- *three body parts?*
- *six legs?*
- *two antennae?*
- *wings (how many)?*
- *eyes?*

Does the insect look
- *shiny? smooth? fuzzy?*
- *hard? soft?*

1. Start by drawing the *head,* antennae, short neck, and *thorax.*

2. Add the long, thin *pedicel* and the *abdomen.*

3. Draw the *fore wing* and *hind wing.*

4. Add the long rear leg.

5. Add two more legs. Darken the eye, leaving a white spot to make it look shiny.

6. Lightly draw the three legs on the far side of the body, and add a little bit of the other fore wing. Carefully draw veins in the wings, and add shading.

Looks kind of like a spaceship....

Potter Wasp

Order Hymenoptera
Family Vespidae (Vespid wasps)

Female potter wasps build small chambers that look like little jugs. Inside, they hang an egg from a string. They then sting weevil larvae to paralyze them, and drop them into the chamber for their own larva to eat. These solitary wasps are normally black and yellow.

STUDY the final drawing *before you start!*

Do you see
- *three body parts?*
- *six legs?*
- *two antennae?*
- *wings (how many)?*
- *eyes?*

Does the insect look
- *shiny? smooth? fuzzy?*
- *hard? soft?*

1. Draw the round head *overlapping* the oval-shaped thorax.

2. Add the *pedicel,* then the *abdomen,* a pointed oval.

3. Draw the slender wings.

4. Add jointed *antennae* and *front leg.*

5. Draw eyes and the other two legs, then add the wasp's clay "pot."

6. Add shading, texture, veins in wings and pattern on abdomen. Draw a few blades of grass…

   …and perhaps just the slightest glimpse of the weevil larva the wasp is dropping in to feed her own offspring *(yum!).*

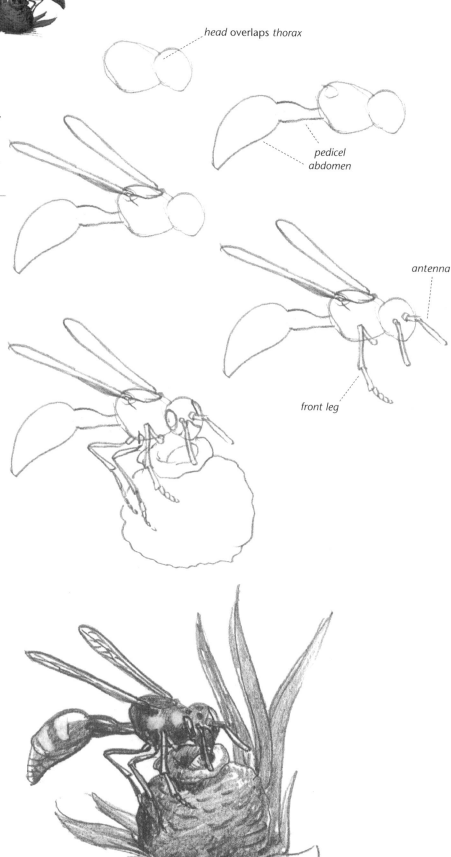

head overlaps *thorax*

pedicel
abdomen

antenna

front leg

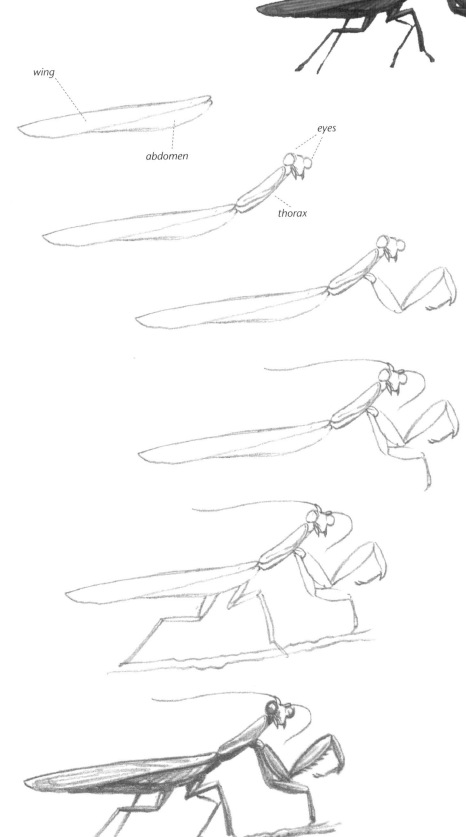

Praying Mantis

Order Mantodea
Family Mantidae

The praying mantis waits in ambush, suddenly moving its spiny fore legs to catch prey. With its strong mouthparts, it can cut through the heads of tough insects like wasps. Its flexible neck means the mantis can turn its head to look at you–a rather eerie feeling! Mantises are cannibalistic; the female often devours the male while mating.

STUDY the final drawing *before you start!*

Do you see
- *three body parts?*
- *six legs?*
- *two antennae?*
- *wings?*
- *eyes?*

Does the insect look
- *shiny? smooth? fuzzy?*
- *hard? soft?*

1. Draw the long *abdomen* and *wing.*

2. Add the *thorax* at a slight angle, then *eyes,* head, and mouthparts.

3. Draw the segments of the front leg, raised and ready to snare prey.

4. Add antennae and the other front leg.

5. Draw the two rear legs. Look carefully at the way each bends.

6. Now add the other two rear legs. Add shading, texture, and details.

And ask yourself, *"What is that insect thinking when it looks at me like that?"*

wing

abdomen

eyes

thorax

Pyrgotid Fly

Order Diptera
Family Pyrgotidae

This is not your normal insect attack! The Pyrgotid fly is actually laying its eggs in the back of the flying May beetle. When the eggs hatch, the larvae will feed on the beetle, killing it as they grow larger. Sounds like a science fiction film…

STUDY the final drawing *before you start!*

Do you see
- *three body parts?*
- *six legs?*
- *two antennae?*
- *wings (how many)?*
- *eyes?*

Does the insect look
- *shiny? smooth? fuzzy?*
- *hard? soft?*

1. Draw the *abdomen* and *hind wings* of the flying beetle.

2. Add six legs and the pattern on the abdomen.

3. Draw the *fore wings* or elytra (which, on beetles, don't move in flight). Leave space for the attacker.

4. Add the *head, thorax,* and *abdomen* of the attacker.

5. Draw the wings and antennae of the fly.

6. Add shading with a dull pencil, and go over lines with a sharp pencil, to finish your drawing.

Attack in midair!

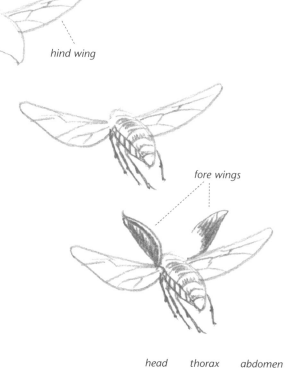

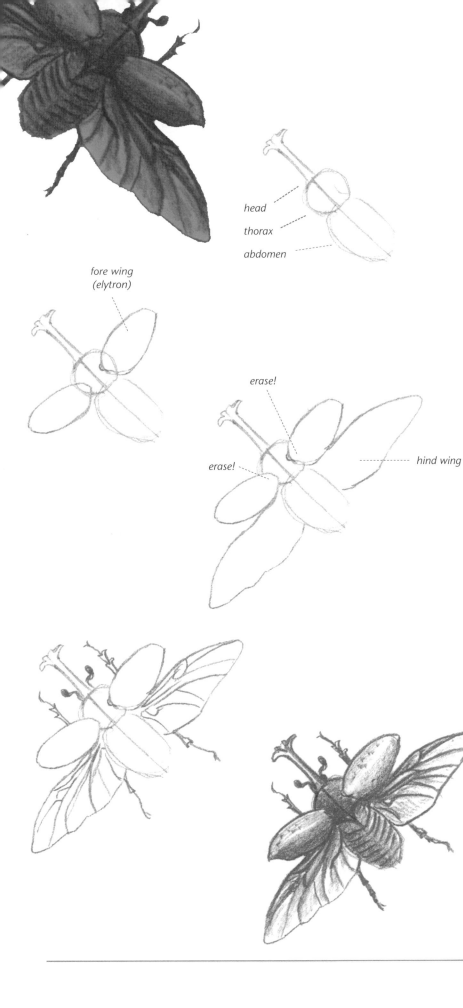

Scarab Beetle

Order Coleoptera
Family Scarabaeidae

This is one of about 20,000 kinds of scarab beetle! Some have fabulous metallic colors; others dramatic horns. All have distinctive, clubbed antennae. Ancient Egyptians put scarabs in much of their artwork, and their sun god had a beetle head, since they believed the sun was pushed through the sky the same way a dung beetle rolls a ball of dung along the ground.

STUDY the final drawing *before you start!*

Do you see
- *three body parts?*
- *six legs?*
- *two antennae?*
- *wings (how many)?*
- *eyes?*

Which parts look
- *shiny? smooth? fuzzy?*
- *hard? soft?*

1. Draw the *head* (with long horn), *thorax,* and *abdomen.*

2. Add the protective *fore wings (elytra).*

3. Erase the thorax outline where the front wings overlap it. Draw the *hind wings* (used for flying).

4. Carefully draw the veins in the wings, the front legs and hind legs, and the club-like antennae.

5. Add shading and details...

   ...cool beetle!

head

thorax

abdomen

fore wing
(elytron)

erase!

erase!

hind wing

Shieldbug

Order Hemiptera (true bugs)
Family Pentatomidae

Ladybugs can deliberately release a little of their own blood when attacked, in a process called reflex bleeding. When predators taste the extremely bitter, bright orange-yellow blood, they learn to associate the bright colors of the ladybug with an undesirable meal. Alas, not this shield bug, which is immune to the toxins in the ladybug's blood, and so reduces our little aphid-killing friend to a desiccated corpse.

STUDY the final drawing *before you start!*

Do you see
- *three body parts?*
- *six legs?*
- *two antennae?*
- *wings (how many)?*
- *eyes?*

Does the insect look
- *shiny? smooth? fuzzy?*
- *hard? soft?*

1. Lightly draw the *center line* and sides of the bug.

2. Divide *thorax* and *abdomen,* and draw the *scutellum.*

3. Add front wings (hiding the hind wings). The thickened base is called the *corium,* the thinner end the *membrane.*

4. Draw *head,* eyes, and checkered sides of the abdomen.

5. Add legs, beak and antennae.

6. Finish your drawing with shading, texture, and *(of course!)* the victim.

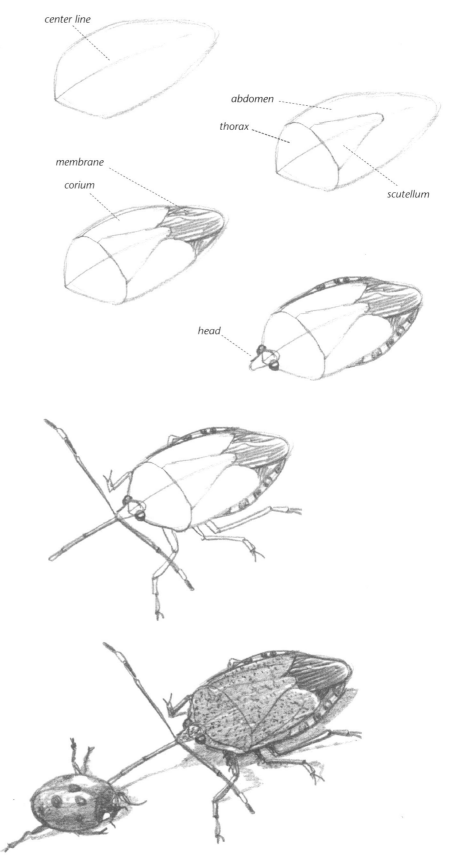

Silverfish

Order Thysanura (common bristletails)
Family Lepismatidae

The scaly covering of the silverfish makes it difficult for ants and spiders to grab it. It lives in warm, dry or damp places such as closets, and can be a pest: it eats starchy stuff, including flour, starch in clothing, and book bindings. It can survive without food for months.

STUDY the final drawing *before you start!*

Do you see
- *three body parts?*
- *six legs?*
- *two antennae?*
- *wings (how many)?*
- *eyes?*

Does the insect look
- *shiny? smooth? fuzzy?*
- *hard? soft?*

1. Start by lightly drawing the long, slightly curved, pointed oval of the body, and a much smaller oval for the *head.*

2. Draw the segments of the *thorax* and *abdomen.*

3. Add the distinctive, three-part bristly tail.

4. Make three little legs on one side.

5. Add three legs on the other side. Draw antennae and the small mouth parts *(maxillary palps).*

6. Add texture and shading, and a slight *cast shadow.*

Scintillating silverfish!

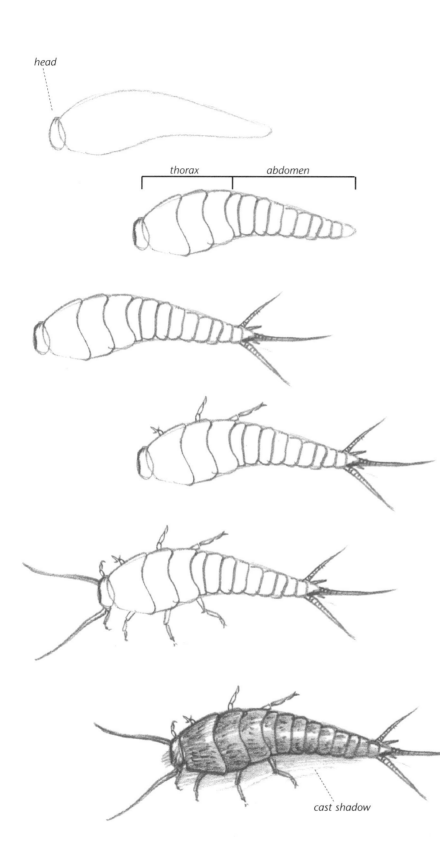

head

thorax   abdomen

cast shadow

Springtail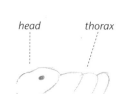

Order Collembola
Suborder Symphypleona

Tiny wingless springtails come in many varieties. Some types of springtail live on ice and snow! The furcula allows this type to jump several inches. Springtails may number several million per acre, scavenging and cleaning up. Usually they're not considered pests.

STUDY the final drawing *before you start!*

Do you see
- *six legs?*
- *two antennae?*
- *wings?*
- *eyes?*

Does the insect look
- *shiny? smooth? fuzzy?*
- *hard? soft?*

1. Draw the *head* with eye, and three *thorax* segments.

2. Add the jointed antenna and front leg.

3. Draw two more legs.

4. Add the *abdomen* and the *furcula.*

5. Draw segments of the abdomen. Add the other antenna and front leg.

6. Add shading and patterns. See if you can make the springtail look shiny by leaving small white spots on the top of the head, thorax, and abdomen.

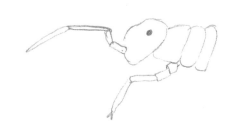

head   thorax

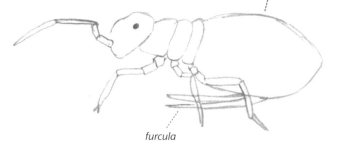

abdomen

furcula

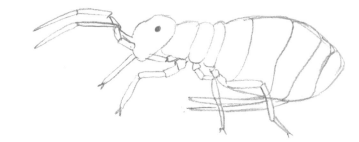

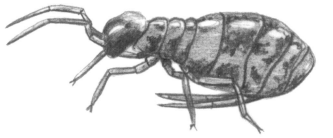

Stink Bug

Order Hemiptera (true bugs)
Family Pentatomidae

Stink bugs release foul-smelling fluid when disturbed. Some stink bugs eat caterpillars and larvae, while others live off plant sap.

STUDY the final drawing *before you start!*

Do you see
- *three body parts?*
- *six legs?*
- *two antennae?*
- *wings (how many)?*
- *eyes?*

Does the insect look
- *shiny? smooth? fuzzy?*
- *hard? soft?*

1. Lightly draw a *center line,* then the stinky *head* with its stinky little *eyes,* and the stinky *thorax.*

2. Add the triangular *scutellum,* and one wing (the *base of the wing* is solid; the *end* is translucent).

3. Draw the *other wing,* antennae, and the first section of each leg.

4. Complete the legs.

5. Finish your drawing by adding shading, details, and texture. With a dull pencil, make a *cast shadow.*

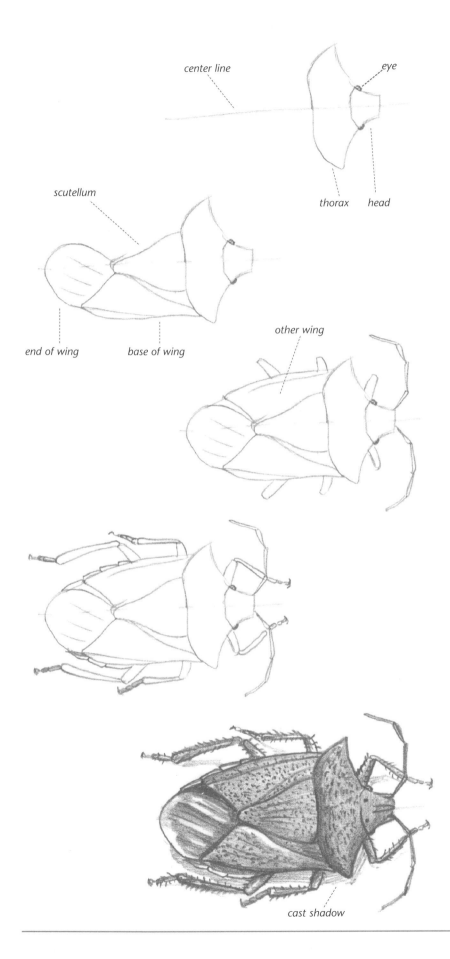

center line

eye

scutellum

thorax   head

end of wing   base of wing

other wing

cast shadow

Termite (worker)

Order Isoptera

Most termite species feed on wood, which they can digest because of special microorganisms in their intestines. Termites can be very destructive to buildings. Like ants, they have a highly evolved society, with workers, soldiers, and a reproductive caste which has wings. Some species even have a special caste with nozzles in their heads for secreting a fluid to build and repair nests. With this nozzle, they can spray repellent at invaders. Beware, ants!

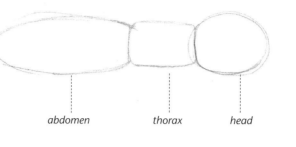

abdomen   thorax   head

STUDY the final drawing *before you start!*

Do you see
- *three body parts?*
- *six legs?*
- *two antennae?*
- *wings?*
- *eyes?*

Does the insect look
- *shiny? smooth? fuzzy?*
- *hard? soft?*

1. Draw the *abdomen, thorax,* and *head.*

2. Divide the thorax into three sections.

3. Carefully draw a pair of legs attached to each section.

4. Divide the abdomen into ten sections.

5. Draw antennae, *mandibles* and other details of the head. Add light shading and little hairs.

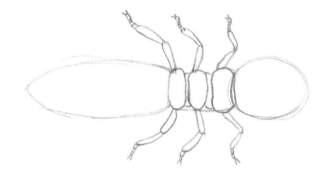

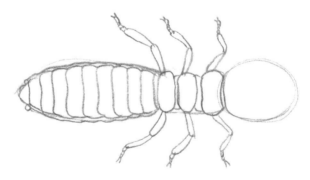

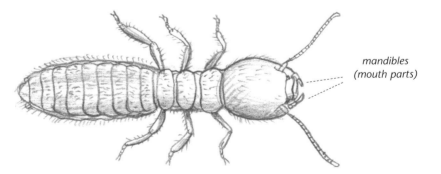

mandibles (mouth parts)

Tiger Beetle

Order Coleoptera
Family Cicindelidae

Tiger beetles are usually shiny metallic colors. You'll find them in bright sunlight in sandy areas. They run fast and fly fast, and are ferocious predators with their sharp mandibles (jaws). They're hard to catch, which is just as well: some of them have a painful bite.

STUDY the final drawing *before you start!*

Do you see
- *three body parts?*
- *six legs?*
- *two antennae?*
- *wings?*
- *eyes?*

Does the insect look
- *shiny? smooth? fuzzy?*
- *hard? soft?*

1. Start with two half circles for the eyes, tilting away from each other.

2. Add the outline of the head. Look carefully at the shape before you draw.

3. Darken the eyes, leaving a light spot in each. Draw the rounded shape of the *thorax*. Add the long, segmented antennae.

4. Draw the sickle-like mouth parts, and the front two legs on each side.

5. Add the *elytra* (fore wings) and the rear legs.

6. Finish your drawing with shading, patterns, and little bristly hairs.

Looks like something out of a science fiction movie!

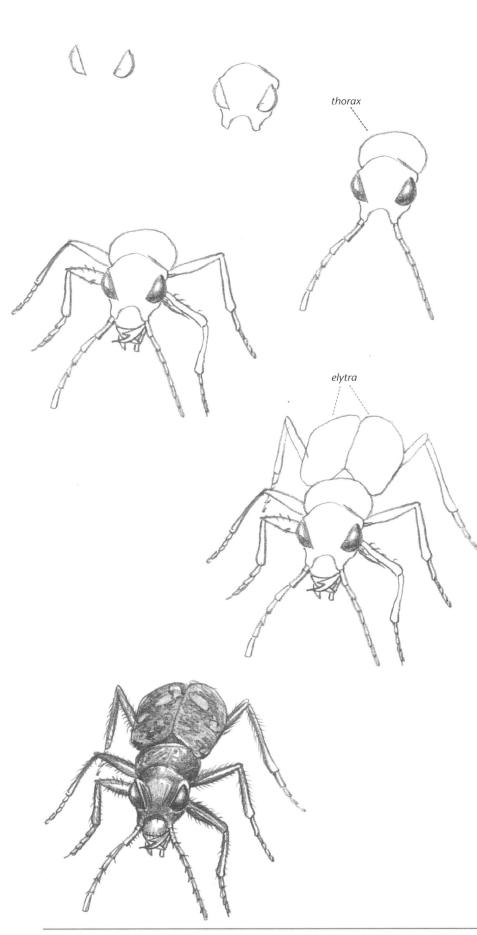

thorax

elytra

Tree Hopper

Order Homoptera
Family Membracidae

Treehoppers have an extended pronotum *(upper front section of thorax) that makes them look like a thorn. This protects them from predators. Treehoppers eat sap from plants. This species is bright green with red stripes.*

STUDY the final drawing *before you start!*

Do you see
- *three body parts?*
- *six legs?*
- *two antennae?*
- *wings (how many)?*
- *eyes?*

Does the insect look
- *shiny? smooth? fuzzy?*
- *hard? soft?*

1. Draw a horizontal line for the plant stem. Draw three segmented legs and the long wing.

2. Add the head and shiny eye.

3. Draw a long, curving line for the front of the *pronotum* (top front of thorax).

4. Add the rear curve of the *pronotum,* and lines which are part of its camouflage.

5. Add shading and texture, including veins in the wings. Draw a *real* thorn to give the treehopper something to blend in with, so it won't become a snack for some passing bird.

pronotum

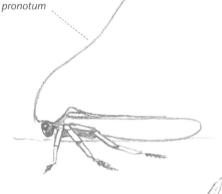

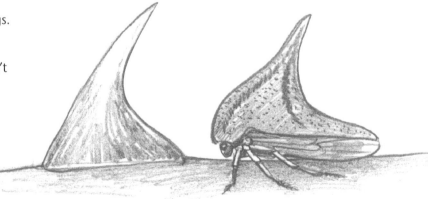

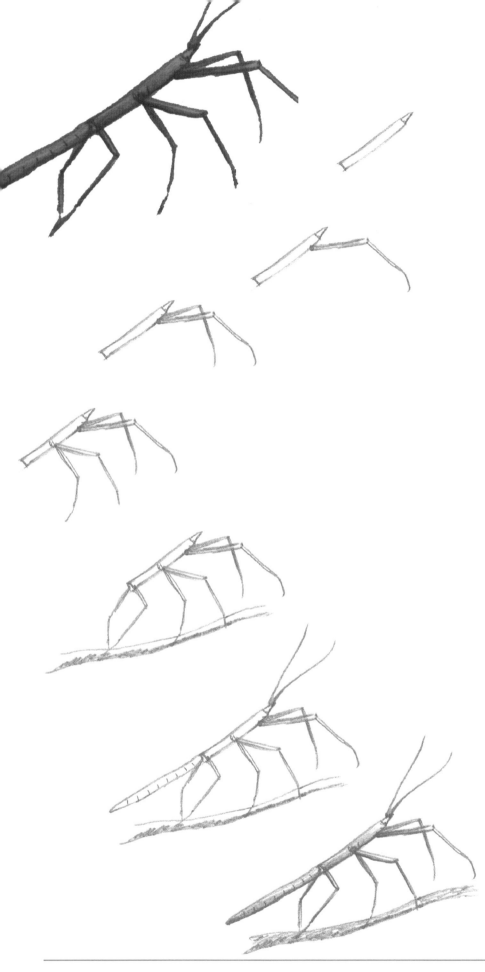

Walkingstick

Order Phasmatodea
Family Phasmidae

Walkingsticks stay still during the day, doing what they do best: looking like a twig so they won't get eaten. They're so good at imitating twigs that they won't defend themselves or try to flee if handled. They can regenerate lost legs. They feed on foliage. Females drop single eggs to the ground, where they hatch in the spring.

STUDY the final drawing *before you start!*

Do you see
- *three body parts?*
- *six legs?*
- *two antennae?*
- *wings (how many)?*
- *eyes?*

Does the insect look
- *shiny? smooth? fuzzy?*
- *hard? soft?*

1. Draw a little tilted pencil.

2. Add a long, slender leg…

3. …and another…

4. …and a couple more…

5. …and a couple more. Draw a twig underneath.

6. Draw antennae and abdominal segments.

7. Add a little shading, and *voila!*

Draw more twigs. See if you can make your walkingstick completely camouflaged!

Wart Biter

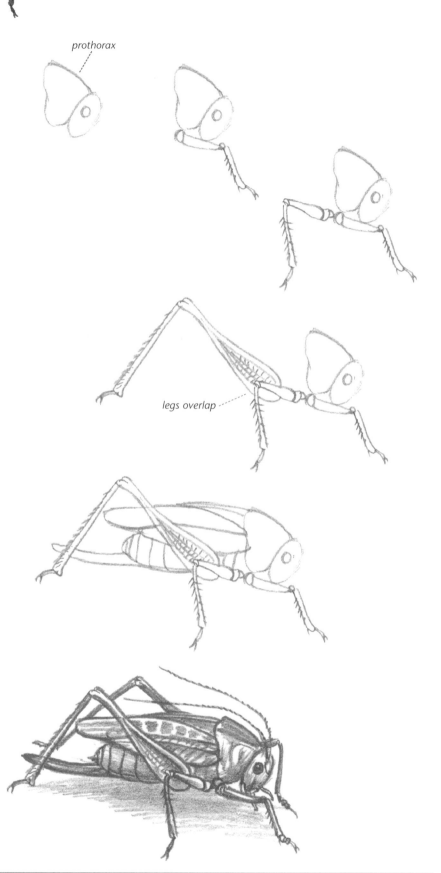

Order Orthoptera
Family Tettigoniidae

This European species may bite if you pick it up, at the same time vomiting brown stomach juices (cool trick!). Named in Sweden 200 years ago, it was believed that the bite-and-juice combo removed warts from skin. Apparently this folk remedy was still being used as recently as the late 1940s...with success...!

STUDY the final drawing *before you start!*

Do you see
- *three body parts?*
- *six legs?*
- *two antennae?*
- *wings (how many)?*
- *eyes?*

Does the insect look
- *shiny? smooth? fuzzy?*
- *hard? soft?*

1. Start with a tilted oval for the head, with a circle inside it for the eye. Add the irregular shape of the *prothorax* (the first thoracic segment).

2. Add the front leg...

3. ...then the middle leg...

4. ...and finally the large rear leg, partly overlapped by the middle leg.

5. Starting from the bottom or the top, draw the body parts and wings.

6. To finish, add shading, texture, and pattern.

"Take me to your wart!"

prothorax

legs overlap

Water Strider

Order Hemiptera (true bugs)
Family Gerridae

Water striders run around on the surface of salt and fresh water, feeding on what falls into the water or floats to the surface. Some varieties have wings and some don't.

STUDY the final drawing *before you start!*

Do you see
- *three body parts?*
- *six legs?*
- *two antennae?*
- *wings?*
- *eyes?*

Does the insect look
- *shiny? smooth? fuzzy?*
- *hard? soft?*

1. Draw the *body* and *wings* at a slight angle. Add eyes.

2. Draw antennae.

3. Add the Z-shaped front legs.

4. Draw the much longer middle legs, extending far forward. Remember there are at least three segments in each.

5. Draw the back legs.

6. Add shading and details (don't forget the veins in the wings!), and add little oval ripples and a bit of reflection.

What would it be like if you could walk on water?

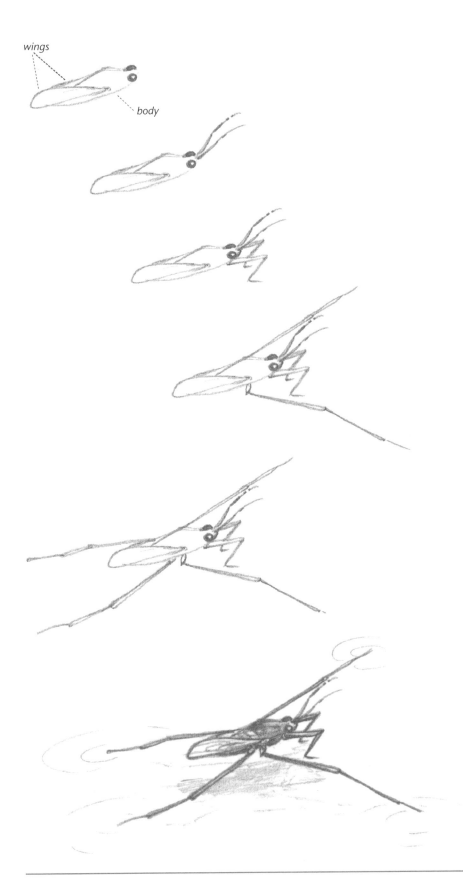

wings

body

Yellow Jacket

Order Hymenoptera
Family Vespidae

Yellow jackets are wasps that live underground, carry off food from picnics, and can sting repeatedly if you "bug" them at all. If you can find their nest, you can put a clear bowl over the opening and leave it there; they become confused, don't figure how to escape and starve to death. This sounds really cruel, unless you've been stung by a yellow jacket, or two, or three…or by one several times in a row….

STUDY the final drawing *before you start!*

Do you see
- *three body parts?*
- *six legs?*
- *two antennae?*
- *wings (how many)?*
- *eyes?*

Does the insect look
- *shiny? smooth? fuzzy?*
- *hard? soft?*

1. Draw a vertical oval for the head, with a pointed end facing down. Add two antennae.

2. Add *thorax* and *abdomen.*

3. Draw the wing and rear leg.

4. Add the middle and front legs. Include all the small segments!

5. Carefully sketch the pattern on the abdomen, and the lines of the *eye* and face.

6. Shade the patterned abdomen, fuzzy thorax and head. Shade the eye, leaving a light highlight to make it look shiny.

   Now tell this thing to get away from me!

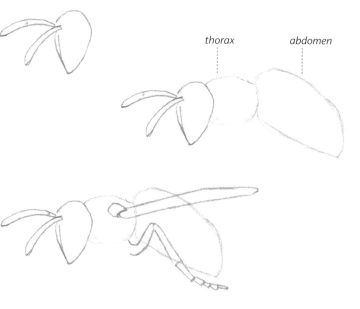

thorax   abdomen

eye

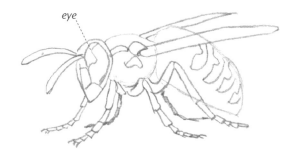

Insect Relatives

And now, a brief and learned discourse on creepy-crawlies:

As you'll recall from an earlier Brief and Learned Discourse, the primary distinguishing characteristic of members of the class *Insecta* in the phylum *Arthropoda* is the presence of six legs.

In other words, insects have **6 legs!! 6 legs!! 6 legs!!**

So, if a creepy-crawly **does not** have **6 legs**, what is it?

In the phylum *Arthropoda,* along with the class *Insecta,* you'll find a class *Arachnida* (arachnid: think spider), which includes eight-legged spiders, scorpions, mites, ticks, and daddy-long-legs (to name just a few).

Think of a school as a *phylum.* Inside the school there are classrooms, or *classes.* All the children with eight legs go to this *class,* all the children with six legs go to this (very big) *class,* and so on. And the difficult children with too many legs to count (especially because they *never sit still!!!*) go to another *class* called Myriapoda.

Obviously, I can't tell you everything there is to know about scientific classification.

Just remember this: they're all relatives.

Any one of them might show up at your birthday party.

OK, class dismissed!

You may now draw…

Wolf Spider

Order Araneae
Family Lycosidae (wolf spiders)

Wolf spiders usually live on the ground, either in a burrow, under a rock, or sometimes with no home at all. Females make a round egg sack which she drags around with her until the spiderlings hatch. Wolf spiders hunt at night. Their mottled colors make them hard to see among dead leaves and stones.

STUDY the final drawing *before you start!*

<u>Checklist:</u>

Do you see:
- *two body parts?*
- *eight legs?*
- *two pedipalps?*
- *eyes?*

Does it look
- *shiny? smooth? fuzzy?*
- *hard? soft?*

1. Draw a curve for the top of the head. Draw two big eyes, and six smaller eyes.

2. Add the *jaws (chelicerae)* and *pedipalps.*

3. To the sides of the body, draw three segments of the front legs.

4. Complete these legs.

5. Add the second set of legs, partly invisible where the front legs *overlap* them.

6. Draw two more pairs of legs, and the rounded *abdomen.*

7. Finish your drawing by carefully adding shading, texture, and a *cast shadow.*

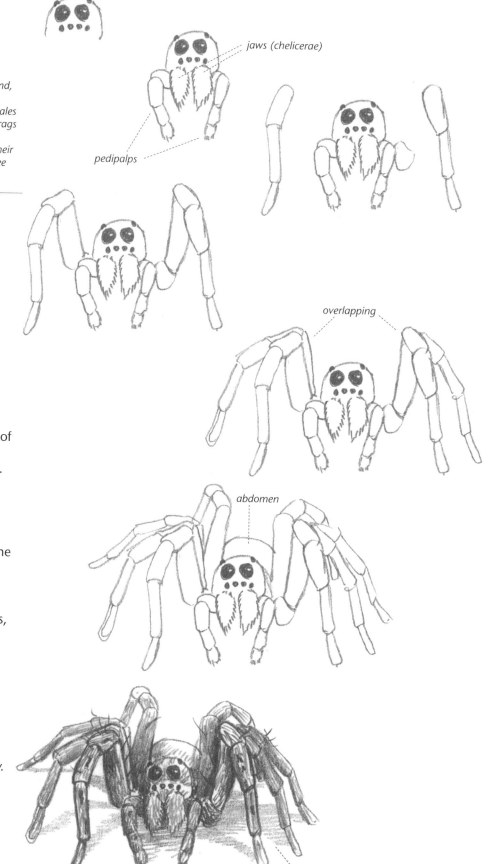

jaws (chelicerae)

pedipalps

overlapping

abdomen

cast shadow

Black Widow Spider

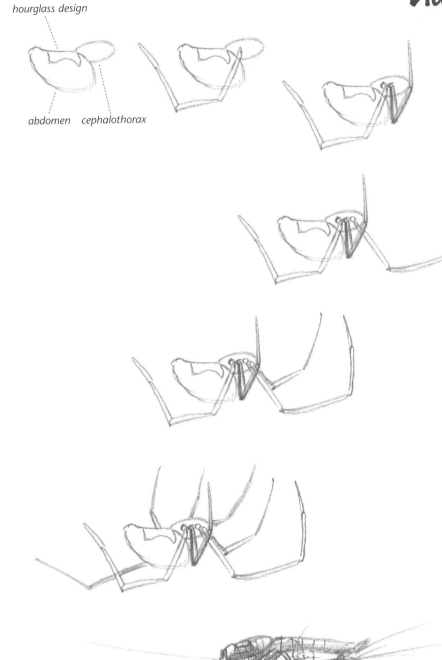

hourglass design

abdomen   *cephalothorax*

Order Araneae
Family Theridiidae (comb-footed spiders)

This feared spider with the red hourglass shape on its abdomen usually tries to flee rather than attack. Males don't bite. Females often eat males after mating, which is why they're called "widows."

STUDY the final drawing *before you start!*

Checklist:

Do you see:
- *two body parts?*
- *eight legs?*

Does it look
- *shiny? smooth? fuzzy?*
- *hard? soft?*

1. Draw the pointed oval of the *abdomen* with its distinctive *hourglass design,* then add the small, flat oval of the *cephalothorax.*

2. Draw one leg…

3. …and another…

4. …and another…

5. …and another.

6. Now add the visible portions of the other four legs.

7. Finish your drawing by shading the spider black. Add a few lines to suggest a web, and a dead grasshopper (or other insect of your choice) for the black widow's meal.

Scorpion

Order Scorpionida

Scorpions subdue or kill large insects, spiders, and sometimes lizards with a poisonous stinger. Most don't attack people, but their sting can produce painful swelling. Long ago, scorpion stings were feared as much as a lion's bite. Scorpions hunt at night, under a sky that has a constellation named for them.

STUDY the final drawing *before you start!*

Checklist:

Do you see:
  • *two body parts?*
  • *eight legs?*
  • *two pedipalps?*
  • *eyes?*

Does it look
  • *shiny? smooth? fuzzy?*
  • *hard? soft?*

1. Start by making the main body shapes.

2. Add lines on the *abdomen,* and carefully draw the sections of the tail, with the stinger at the end.

3. Draw a clawed *pedipalp…*

4. …and another.

5. Now add four walking legs, first on one side…

6. …then on the other.

7. Add shading and bristly hairs to complete your drawing.

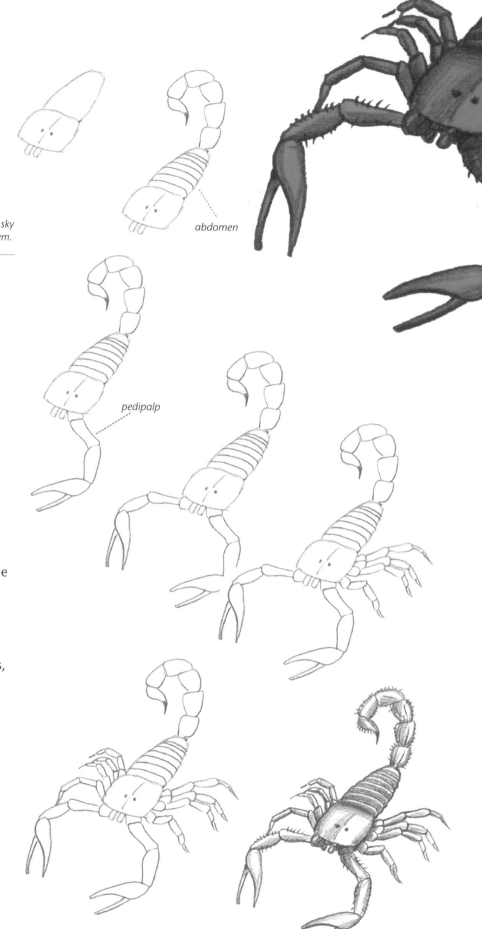

abdomen

pedipalp

Whipscorpion

Order Uropygi

Whipscorpions have a long tail instead of a stinger. They use it for spraying a liquid that attacks the victim's body covering. They hunt at night. Like scorpions, they carry their young on their back until the young have shed their first skin and can get around on their own.

STUDY the final drawing *before you start!*

Checklist:

Do you see:
- *two body parts?*
- *eight legs?*
- *two pedipalps?*
- *eyes?*

Does it look
- *shiny? smooth? fuzzy?*
- *hard? soft?*

1. Looking carefully at the shapes. draw the *cephalothorax* and segmented *abdomen.*

2. Add eyes, clawed *pedipalps,* and the long, whiplike tail.

3. Draw the first pair of legs…

4. …the second…

5 …the third…

6. …and the fourth.

7. Add shading and patterns to complete your drawing. Use a sharp pencil to make lines look crisper.

labels on diagram: pedipalps, cephalothorax, abdomen

Daddy-long-legs

Order Opiliones
Family Phalangiidae (Daddy-long-legs)

Daddy-long-legs feed on small insects and decaying organic matter. Their legs break off easily and don't grow back. Often a number of them gather together, standing with their legs interlaced. A more scientific name for them is phalangids. *The popular name for them in Germany is "tailors."*

STUDY the final drawing *before you start!*

Checklist:

Do you see:
- *two body parts?*
- *eight legs?*
- *two pedipalps?*
- *eyes?*

Does it look
- *shiny? smooth? fuzzy?*
- *hard? soft?*

1. Draw a flat oval to make the body, with tiny mouth parts pointing downward.

2. Add a long, wispy leg…

3. …and another…

4. …and another…

5. …and another…

6. …and…*hey, wait a minute! I've lost count!*

7. Count your legs. No, count the legs in your drawing. When you have eight, you're done. That's all there is to it!

   Unless, of course, you want to draw a gathering of daddy-long-legs, with their legs all interlaced…why not?

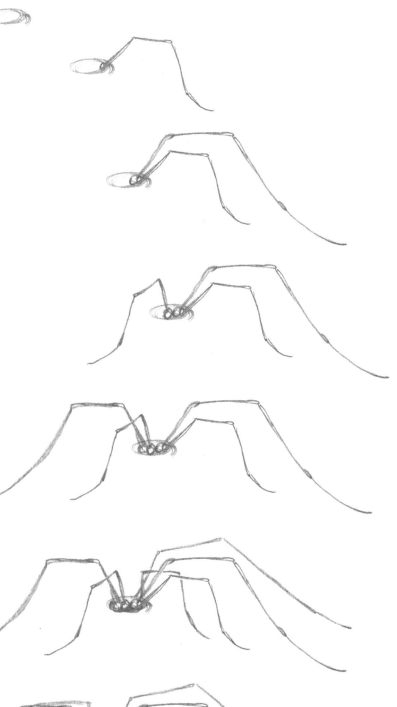

Ant-mimic Spider

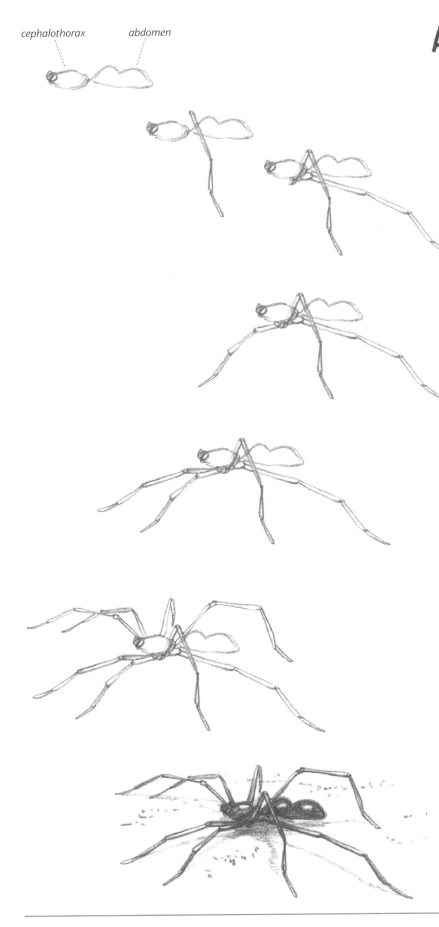

cephalothorax   abdomen

Order Araneae
Family Clubionidae (sac spiders)

These spiders look surprisingly like ants, and live near ant hills. Their appearance probably confuses predators. They feed on small insects. They are orange, brown, or black, and may have stripes or patterns. They spin tubular resting places inside a rolled leaf, or live under bark or a stone.

STUDY the final drawing *before you start!*

Checklist:

Do you see:
- *two body parts?*
- *eight legs?*
- *two pedipalps?*
- *eyes?*

Does it look
- *shiny? smooth? fuzzy?*
- *hard? soft?*

1. Draw the *cephalothorax* and *abdomen.* Notice how the abdomen is shaped so it looks like both the thorax and abdomen of an ant.

2. Draw the end of the closest leg…

3. …then connect it to the body. Draw the rear leg.

4. Add another leg…

5. …and another…

6. …and then all four legs on the other side of the spider.

7. Finish by shading, leaving parts of the body light to make it look shiny. Add a little shadow and a few spots to suggest dirt or sand.

   Nice ant…uh, spider!

Tick

Order Acarina

Family Ixodidae

Ticks feed on the blood of mammals, swelling to many times their size as they fill up. They then drop off to lay hundreds of eggs, and look for another host. They anchor themselves in the skin with a pointed probe with backwards-facing teeth. This is so strong that if you try to simply pull a tick off, you'll probably break off the head, which stays in the skin.

STUDY the final drawing *before you start!*

Checklist:

Do you see:
- *two body parts?*
- *eight legs?*
- *two pedipalps?*
- *eyes?*

Does it look
- *shiny? smooth? fuzzy?*
- *hard? soft?*

1. Start with a pair-shaped body, and little head and mouth parts.

2. Add a pair of segmented legs to help it hold on while it sinks its head into skin…

3. …and another two pairs…

4. …and yet another pair *(you know it's not an insect now, since it has too many legs).*

5. Finish your drawing by adding shading and texture.

    Or try drawing your tick as it looks after feeding on blood for a while…it will get bigger still before dropping to the ground.

    Yuck!

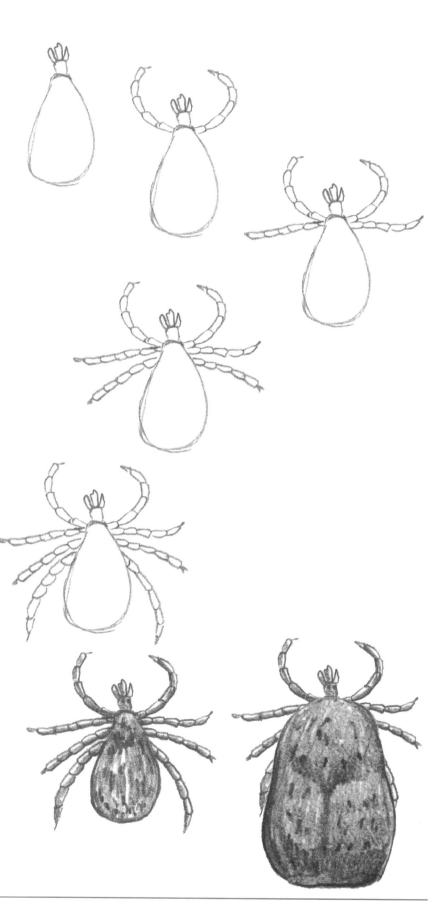

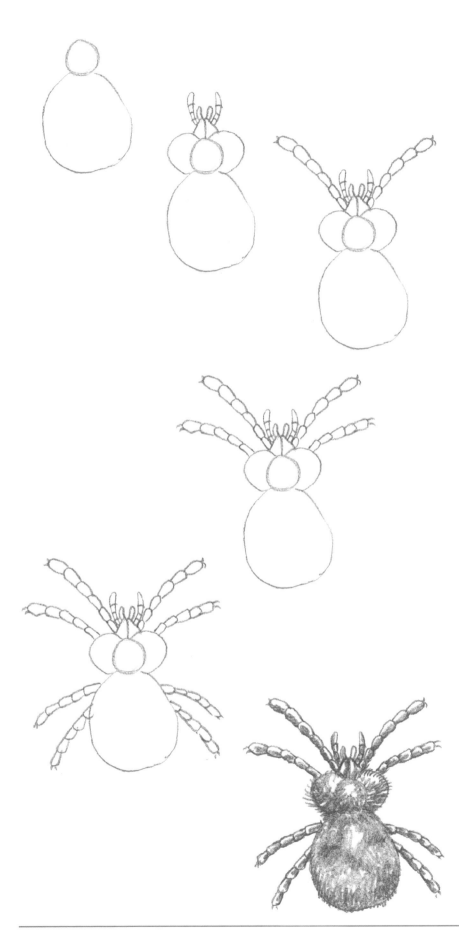

Mite

Order Acarina
Family Trombidiidae

There are perhaps 20,000 species of mites worldwide. Most are tiny, and they have a variety of shapes. Some are beneficial, feeding on aphid eggs; others feed on plants and weaken them. Velvet mites are bright red. Their parasitic larva attacks insects, spiders, daddy-long-legs, and scorpions.

STUDY the final drawing *before you start!*

Checklist:

Do you see:
- *two body parts?*
- *eight legs?*
- *two pedipalps?*
- *eyes?*

Does it look
- *shiny? smooth? fuzzy?*
- *hard? soft?*

1. Begin by drawing a small circle sitting on top of a much larger oval.

2. Add circular bulges either side of the little circle, triangles for the head, feelers and mouth parts.

3. Draw the first pair of segmented legs, up and out from the head.

4. Add the second pair, pointing more to the side.

5. Draw two more pairs.

6. Add shading and texture.

Idea! Create a cartoon character called

Mighty Mite!

Centipede

Order Scolopendromorpha

Centipedes run quickly with either 21 or 23 pairs of legs. They usually live under stones. The largest centipedes, like this one, live in tropical and subtropical areas. They are dangerous; their bite is very painful.

STUDY the final drawing *before you start!*

Checklist:

Do you see:
- *22body parts?*
- *42 legs?*
- *two pedipalps (feelers)?*
- *eyes?*

Does it look
- *shiny? smooth? fuzzy?*
- *hard? soft?*

1. Draw a long, curved worm.

2. Make a small oval area for the head, and draw its little segmented feelers. Then add 20 short, curving lines to make the body segments.

3. Draw the segmented antennae, and the last two legs sticking out the back end of the centipede. Then draw the first pair of legs, and the second…

4. …and on and on, until you have 21 pairs of legs! Add shading, leaving light areas along the top to make the body look shiny.

Sensational centipede! Do you think it would make a good pet?

Millipede

Class Myriapoda (air breathing arthropods)

Millipedes have been around for a very long time. This Giant Julid from Africa is part of a family that exists almost unchanged in Africa and South America, strong evidence that the two continents were once joined. Millipedes live in moist areas, and feed mostly on rotting vegetation. Their hard exoskeleton protects them, but most also have chemical defenses.

STUDY the final drawing *before you start!*

Checklist:

Do you see:
- *about a million body parts?*
- *about two million legs?*
- *two pedipalps?*
- *eyes?*

Does it look
- *shiny? smooth? fuzzy?*
- *hard? soft?*

1. Draw a fat, slightly curved worm.

2. Add little feelers, then draw small curved lines for the body segments. Draw them carefully, to make the body look round…

3. …and then add a ton more!

4. Now add little creepy-crawly legs, first a few…

5. …and then a ton more!

Finish your slithering little friend with shading, leaving the middle part of the body light to make it look round.

Magnificent millipede!

Index

ant .4
ant spider 59
aphid 5
assassin bug 6
backswimmer 7
bed bug 8
beetle, giant 24
beetle, giraffe 25
beetle, Japanese 28
beetle, ladybug 30
beetle, scarab 41
beetle, tiger 47
black fly 9
black widow 55
bug, assassin 6
bug, bed 8
bug, shield 42
bug, stink 45
bumblebee 10
butterfly 11
caterpillar 12
cave cricket 13
centipede 62
cicada 14
cockroach 15
cow killer 16
crane fly 17
cricket, cave 13
daddy-long-legs 58
deer fly 18
digger wasp 19
dragonfly 20
earwig 21
firefly 22
flea 23
fly, black 9
fly, crane 17
fly, deer 18
fly, horse 26
fly, ichneumon 27
fly, pyrgotid 40
giant beetle 24

giraffe beetle 25
horse fly 26
ichneumon fly 27
Japanese beetle 28
lacewing 29
ladybug 30
leaf insect 31
lightning bug 22
locust 32
louse .33
luna moth 34
mantis, praying 39
millipede 63
mite .61
mosquito 35
moth, luna 34
moth .36
mud dauber 37
potter wasp 38
praying mantis 39
pyrgotid fly 40
roach .15
scarab beetle 41
scorpion 56
shieldbug 42
silverfish 43
spider, black widow 55
spider, wolf 54
springtail 44
stink bug 45
termite 46
tick 60
tiger beetle 47
tree hopper 48
walkingstick 49
wart biter 50
wasp, potter 38
water strider 51
whipscorpion 57
wolf spider 54
yellow jacket 52

Learn about other books in
this series online at
www.drawbooks.com!